北京语言大学梧桐创新平台项目资助
（中央高校基本科研业务费专项资金）（项目批准号：19PT02）成果

翻译跨学科研究

第四卷

INTERDISCIPLINARY STUDIES ON
TRANSLATION AND INTERPRETING

主　　编：许　明

特邀顾问：李宇明
荣誉主编：李德凤
副 主 编：王建华　贺爱军
学术编辑：李秀英　刘　成　吴文梅

中国出版集团
中译出版社

图书在版编目（CIP）数据

翻译跨学科研究. 第四卷 : 汉文、英文 / 许明主编. -- 北京 : 中译出版社, 2025. 6. -- ISBN 978-7-5001-8314-3

I. H059-53

中国国家版本馆CIP数据核字第2025SC0196号

翻译跨学科研究（第四卷）
FANYI KUAXUEKE YANJIU (DI-SI JUAN)

出版发行	/ 中译出版社
地　　址	/ 北京市丰台区右外西路2号院中国国际出版交流中心
电　　话	/ (010) 68359827, 68359303（发行部）；68359725（编辑部）
邮　　编	/ 100069
传　　真	/ (010) 68357870
电子邮箱	/ book@ctph.com.cn
网　　址	/ http://www.ctph.com.cn

出 版 人	/ 刘永淳
出版统筹	/ 杨光捷
总 策 划	/ 范　伟
策划编辑	/ 刘瑞莲
责任编辑	/ 杨佳特

封面设计	/ 潘　峰
排　　版	/ 北京竹页文化传媒有限公司
印　　刷	/ 唐山玺诚印务有限公司
经　　销	/ 新华书店

规　　格	/ 787毫米×1092毫米　1/16
印　　张	/ 16.5
字　　数	/ 311千字
版　　次	/ 2025年6月第1版
印　　次	/ 2025年6月第1次

ISBN 978-7-5001-8314-3　　定价：62.00元

版权所有　侵权必究

中译出版社

编 委 会

特邀顾问：李宇明
荣誉主编：李德凤

主　　编：许　明
副 主 编：王建华　贺爱军

编　　委（按姓氏拼音排序）：

陈国华（北京外国语大学）　　　　　高明乐（北京语言大学）
黄忠廉（广东外语外贸大学）　　　　康志峰（复旦大学）
李正仁（上海外国语大学）　　　　　李正栓（河北师范大学）
刘和平（北京语言大学）　　　　　　覃江华（华中农业大学）
王斌华（英国利兹大学）　　　　　　王传英（南开大学）
王立非（北京语言大学）　　　　　　许明武（华中科技大学）
许文胜（同济大学）　　　　　　　　张法连（中国政法大学）
郑淑明（哈尔滨工业大学）　　　　　朱振武（上海师范大学）

学术编辑：

李秀英（大连理工大学）
刘　成（江西中医药大学）
吴文梅（厦门大学）

题　　字：李宇明

目 录

翻译跨学科研究

译作惯习的产生与诱发：《佐治刍言》译介与传播的社会
　　翻译学研究 ……………………………………………… 傅娜、刘晓峰 3
基于文献计量的中国典籍翻译研究概况及趋势（2011—2021）
　　可视化分析 ……………………………………………………… 谢文琦 20
《2024年政府工作报告》的文体特征和译文分析 ………………… 陈友勋 34
《丰乳肥臀》俄译本读者接受研究 …………………………………… 王小琳 47

翻译理论

军事典籍译者群体行为批评分析——以《孙子兵法》为例 ………… 王文慧、夏云 61
蓝诗玲《猴王：西游记》节译本的中国形象建构与阐释研究 ………… 张汨、阳思雨 76
中医术语英译的可行性研究 ……………………………………… 杨涵雅、刘锦 91
中医翻译过程中的不可译现象研究
　　——以"鬼门"一词为例 …………………… 胡亚柳、彭咏梅、王涵 104

翻译技术与本地化

《黄帝内经·素问》汉法平行语料库的构建路径与方法 …… 田知灵、许明、潘晓颖 113

i

医古文隐喻英译策略及隐喻效度研究
　　——以《黄帝内经·灵枢》三英译本为例 ················· 王子鹏、刘世英 124
人工智能辅助外宣翻译有效性研究
　　——以 ChatGPT 为例 ··· 沈伊晗 137

翻译教学与实践

技术赋能时代基于实践共同体的翻译教学探究 ··············· 白丽梅、胡文娟 151
齿轮类标准化文件翻译难点及应对方法 ·························· 郭情情、闫冰 163
中国高校校名中"科技"一词英译研究 ···························· 李鹏宇、孟宇 175

会议与述评

《字幕翻译：概念与实践》述评 ······································ 王芷珊、苏雯超 213
Chronological Development of Sense Ordering and Classication in
　The Oxford English Dictionary ····································· Akiko Matsukubo 219
Implicit Biases and English Textbooks ································ Masayuki Adachi 230
Acceptance and Background of Dutch Language Learning
　in the Mid-Edo Period ·· Koike Kazuo 239

Contents

Interdisciplinary Studies on Translation and Interpreting

The Emergence and Induction of Target-text Habitus: A Socio-Translation Study of
    Zuozhi chuyan's Translation and Dissemination ·············· *FU Na, LIU Xiaofeng* 19
Visual Analysis of the Overview and Trends of Research on Translation of Chinese
    Classics (2011—2021) Based on Bibliometrics ······························ *XIE Wenqi* 32
Stylistic Features and Translation Analysis of the "Report on the Work
    of the Government in 2024" ··· *Chen Youxun* 45
A Study of Readers' Acceptance of the Russian Translation of
    Big Breasts & Wide Hips ··· *WANG Xiaolin* 57

Translation Theories

Military Classics Translation Community Behavior Critique Analysis:
    A Case Study of "The Art of War" ························ *WANG Wenhui, XIA Yun* 75
Journey to the West and Image to the West: Image Construction and Explanation
    in *Monkey King* translated by Julia Lovell ···················· *ZHANG Mi, YANG Siyu* 89
A Feasibility Study on the Translation of TCM Terminology into English
    ·· *YANG Hanya, LIU Jin* 103
Discussion of Untranslatable Phenomena in TCM Translation
    —Taking "Ghost gate" as An Example ············ *HU Yaliu, PENG Yongmei, WANG Han* 110

Translation Technologies and Localization

Approach and Methods for Constructing Bilingual Parallel Corpus of *Neijing Suwen*
.... *TIAN Zhiling, XU Ming, PAN Xiaoying* 123

Chinese-English Translation Strategy and Metaphorical Force in Traditional Chinese Medicine Texts: A Case Study of the Three English Versions of "*Huangdi Neijing Ling Shu*" .... *WANG Zipeng, LIU Shiying* 135

Research on the Effectiveness of Artificial Intelligence Assisted Publicity-oriented Texts Translation – Taking ChatGPT as an example .... *SHEN Yihan* 147

Translation Teaching and Practice

Exploration of Translation Teaching in the Era of Technological Empowerment, Based on A Community of Practice .... *BAI Limei, HU Wenjuan* 161

Difficulties in the Translation of Gear Standardization Documents and Countermeasures .... *GUO Qingqing, YAN Bing* 174

A Study on English Translation of "*Ke Ji*" in Names of Chinese Colleges and Universities .... *LI Pengyu, MENG Yu* 188

Meeting and Review

A Book Review of *Subtitling: Concepts and Practices* .... *WANG Zhishan, SU Wenchao* 218

Chronological Development of Sense Ordering and Classification in *The Oxford English Dictionary* .... *Akiko Matsukubo* 219

Implicit Biases and English Textbooks .... *Masayuki Adachi* 230

Acceptance and Background of Dutch Language Learning in the Mid-Edo Period .... *Koike Kazuo* 239

翻译跨学科研究

INTERDISCIPLINARY
STUDIES ON TRANSLATION
AND INTERPRETING

译作惯习的产生与诱发:《佐治刍言》译介与传播的社会翻译学研究[①]

西安外国语大学　傅　娜[②]　刘晓峰[③]

【摘　要】傅兰雅和应祖锡合译的《佐治刍言》介绍了西方的政治、经济、教育和伦理等多方面的内容,对晚清社会发展影响深远。学术界对《佐治刍言》的译本和译介的思想有较大的关注,但鲜有翻译学和社会学的交叉性研究。本文以社会实践理论和行动者网络理论为指导,通过梳理《佐治刍言》的译介传播过程,追踪该书对推动晚清社会演变的积极作用。研究认为:《佐治刍言》作为非人行动者,也具备惯习特性,在被社会塑造的同时又建构社会。受迟滞效应影响,《佐治刍言》的译作惯习首先主要凭借译者的符号资本和自身的文化资本隐性存续,表现为书中资产阶级思想相关阐释反响平平,而后等场域发生变异,即甲午战争后才得以触发显现,和维新派产生思想共振,因而能在百日维新时期发挥重要作用。

【关键词】《佐治刍言》;译作惯习;迟滞与诱发;社会翻译学

一、引言

《佐治刍言》于 1885 年由洋务运动时期官督江南制造局翻译馆出版,译自英国

[①] 基金项目:本文为国家社会科学基金重大项目"中国翻译理论发展史研究"(项目编号:20&ZD312);西安外国语大学校级课题"译作惯习的产生与诱发:《佐治刍言》译介与传播的社会翻译学研究"(项目编号:2024SS015)成果之一。
[②] 傅娜(2000—　),西安外国语大学硕士研究生,研究方向为翻译理论与实践。邮箱:2602274809@qq.com。
[③] 刘晓峰(1971—　),博士,副教授,硕士研究生导师。研究方向:翻译理论与翻译教学,翻译史,社会翻译学等。邮箱:liuxiaofeng@xisu.edu.cn。

钱伯斯兄弟（The Chambers）出版的教育系列丛书中的 *Political Economy: For Use In Schools, And For Private Instruction*，但该书真正获得重视却在甲午中日战争之后。百日维新时期康有为、梁启超等人吸收了书中的精华，书中蕴含的资产阶级思想和"公天下"的社会改革理念启发了这些改革派，从而推动了中国社会的进步和转型。梁启超称之为"言政治最佳之书""论政治最通之书"（1897:10）。《佐治刍言》在百日维新时期产生的巨大功效，与该书诞生时期反响一般的境遇不相匹配，其中缘由关乎前后不同的社会历史语境和《佐治刍言》翻译与传播场域主导行动者的变化。因此，本文借助社会翻译学，考察《佐治刍言》译介和传播的过程，追踪该书作为非人行动者在晚清背景下的行动轨迹，考察其译作惯习的迟滞效应以及对晚清社会的建构作用，以推动晚清经济学译介与传播的社会翻译学研究。

二、研究现状与存在的问题

《佐治刍言》的讨论多散见于历史、经济、政治、法律和社会学等领域的著作中（王涛，1995；张登德，2009；方维规，2021 等），成果较为丰硕，呈现出一定的系统性。熊月之称《佐治刍言》"政法方面书籍影响最大""是戊戌以前介绍西方社会政治思想最为系统、篇幅最大的一部书，出版以后多次重版，对中国思想界影响很大。晚清思想界对它评价极高"（2010:408），突出了该书的社会影响力。孙青（2009）以《佐治刍言》为例，详细探讨了传教士译述在晚清时期对"西政"发展演变的形塑作用。张登德（2009）对比了《佐治刍言》《富国策》和《富国养民策》，强调了《佐治刍言》的政治治理价值。这类研究基本上都是文本翻译外围的研究。

期刊论文对《佐治刍言》的研究主要围绕历史学、经济学和翻译文体学等方面展开。韩国学者梁台根（2006）以《佐治刍言》为例，考证其底本 *Political Economy* 在东亚文化圈（日本—中国—韩国）中的译介传播路径，对于学界普遍认为的西学经由日本传往中国的观点提出疑问。王林（2008）对比了《佐治刍言》《富国养民策》和《富国策》，认为《佐治刍言》更有助于全面了解西方的政治经济思想，进而论述该书在晚清社会的接受程度和巨大影响。王洪焕（2014）认为晚清合译模式下的译作不可避免地会打上中国文法烙印，通过详尽的译例分析，发现译文符合传统论体文的三个特点，由此推测，《佐治刍言》是以论体文进行书写的。张德让团队成就最为瞩目。自 2012 至 2023 年，在知网和读秀等平台，以"《佐治刍言》""译"为主题词，共检索到 14 篇文章，大部分由张德让团队完成。

其中，张燕（2012）以纽马克的交际翻译理论为指导，认为《佐治刍言》"非忠实"的翻译策略源自其特殊的交际目的；周洁（2013）从改写理论视角讨论了《佐治刍言》通过对原文的增补、删减和改写形成了本土化特点，指出译文没有反映出原文的语言特色。

这两类研究虽有一定的基础，但从译文对原文的文本变形以及译本形成后随时代变化却有截然不同的社会建构功能入手，联系晚清特殊的社会历史语境对《佐治刍言》翻译传播和社会建构过程进行翻译与社会互动性的研究不足。基于此，本文基于社会实践理论和行动者网络理论，提出"译作惯习"概念，对《佐治刍言》中的文本变形追根溯源，考察译者惯习与译作惯习的形变与存续方式，采用文本－译者－社会三元结合研究模式，展现该书映现的译者惯习以及译作惯习对推动晚清社会演变的积极作用。

三、社会实践理论与行动者网络理论的弹性融合：译作惯习形成的理论基础

法国社会学家拉图尔（Bruno Latour）和卡龙（Michel Callon）提出的行动者网络理论（Actor Network Theory）以过程为导向，将社会活动中的参与者抽象为关键节点，从而研究行动者穿梭于各个节点之间形成的网状结构。拉图尔（1996：373）认为"任何发挥重要作用并确实改变了事态发展的人和物都是行动者"。文本、观念、知识、技术、生物、产品等非人类行动者享有和人类行动者同等的地位和能动性（2005）。行动者网络理论是"联结的社会学"，具有动态性特征，与翻译学译介与传播研究中的过程导向不谋而合。当前，社会翻译学蓬勃发展，行动者网络理论已经进入了社会翻译学的理论与应用层面，具备较强的合理性与解释力，并进入了理论反思与创新阶段，如王峰、乔冲（2023）深入挖掘了行动者网络理论对于翻译研究的方法论价值，指出当下存在的问题，总结未来的发展方向；汪宝荣（2022）以行动者网络理论为工具，梳理了中国文学译介与传播模式；骆雯雁（2022）探讨了行动者网络理论的命名与实质对于社会翻译学的意义。

布迪厄的社会实践理论是社会翻译学的另一主流理论来源，其中场域（Field）是指"行动者位置间客观关系的网络或构型"（Bourdieu, Wacquant, 1992: 97）。资本（Capital）是"一种以物化、具体化或肉身化形式显现出来的累积的劳动"（Bourdieu, 1986: 241），主要表现为四种类型：经济资本、文化资本、社会资本和象征资本。惯习（Habitus）是"持久稳定的性情倾向系统"（Bourdieu, Wacquant, 1992: 126），"是

被结构化了的结构"（同上：139）。

社会翻译学是借助于社会学结合翻译学等理论用来解决翻译问题的复杂的理论综合体，各理论元素在进行融合解决具体翻译问题时具有弹性和动态性特征；具体融合的元素、融合的方式和融合后解决问题的效用主要取决于融合的理论与研究问题的适配性（刘晓峰、惠玲玉，2023：17）。由于本研究最重要的抓手是《佐治刍言》译本，追问的是同一译本为何在不同时代具有不同的社会建构功能这样的问题，因此，我们认为，结合社会实践理论与行动者网络理论让译著《佐治刍言》获得行动者的身份，这样我们就会顺理成章地提出"译作惯习"和"译作资本"等概念，并把译作《佐治刍言》纳入晚清社会变革的行动者场域，这样就能很好地描述和解释我们提出的翻译研究问题。我们认为，译书一经出版，将以物行动者的身份在社会历史环境中游走，后续的发展流变将很大部分脱离译者控制，其接受效果在社会环境中发酵，甚至超脱时间和空间的局限，在不同历史时期将有不同表现。译著本身具有行动者网络理论赋予的"确实改变了事态发展"的功能。我们还认为，译作作为非人行动者，同样具有惯习，可称其为"译作惯习"。首先，场域是行动者关系的网络，行动者皆有惯习与资本。译作作为物行动者具有文化资本，而文化资本有一种身体化形态，表现为气质、性情等品质，译著作为行动者，随着时代的变化，会自动获取时代差赋予的资本和气质。对比一下任何一部古代经典和现代的任何一部同类著作，我们便能感觉到两者所透露的"气质"的巨大差异。这与作为人的行动者惯习的"性情倾向系统"的概念内涵无异。其次，惯习可以转置（需要引用相关文献），译者将一部分惯习（文如其人）倾注到译作中，随着社会结构的变化，译者会通过译作产生一定的影响（甚至可能超乎译者本人的预期），这便是译作惯习生效的结果。最后，非人行动者（actant）和人类行动者一样也具备主动性。不仅是行动者网络理论持这种观点，庄子在《齐物论》中也持有相似的看法，以批判实用导向的、功利性的、人类强加的物的意义。庄子认为"物无非彼，物无非是。是亦彼也，彼亦是也"（2006：66）。海德格尔对东方老庄之学曾有过深刻的研究，还曾译过《道德经》，在对待物的态度上他认为"物就是诸多在其上现成的并同时变化着的特性的现成的承载者，物具有历史性"（2010：31–40）。作为新物质主义文学批评的代表人物，比尔·布朗（Bill Brown）的"物论（Thing Theory）"又在海德格尔的"物性（Thingness）"基础上更多关注到物体的存在方式及其如何影响和参与人类经验和社会互动。宁一中（2020：133）认为"微观世界里物的存在方式与宏观世界里物的存在方式形成物存在的双重性"。布朗对"物性"的这一揭示，使我们对物的隐性和显性存在，以及物的"同时双重性存在"有了更为清楚的认识。译作亦具有"物性"和"物的力量"。

通过从古至今东西方哲人的不同视角，我们可以看到译作不仅是翻译行为的结果，它本身也是具有"历史性"和"力量"的"非人行动者"。译作惯习因此不仅是翻译者个人的实践结果，也是社会历史过程中物化的文化产品，它可以影响社会并被社会结构所影响，在不同的文化和社会环境中发挥不同的作用。译著的这种特性又与社会实践理论的"迟滞效应（Hysteresis）"相贯通。布迪厄认为，当"惯习与场域结构之间的关系断裂与不相符"（Cheryl, 2008: 130），或发生延时（time lag）时，迟滞效应也随之发生。通过对《佐治刍言》译作惯习形成后近十年相对迟缓的传播，甲午战争后又广为人知的一系列过程的分析，我们可以对译作惯习发挥作用的方式有深入的了解。

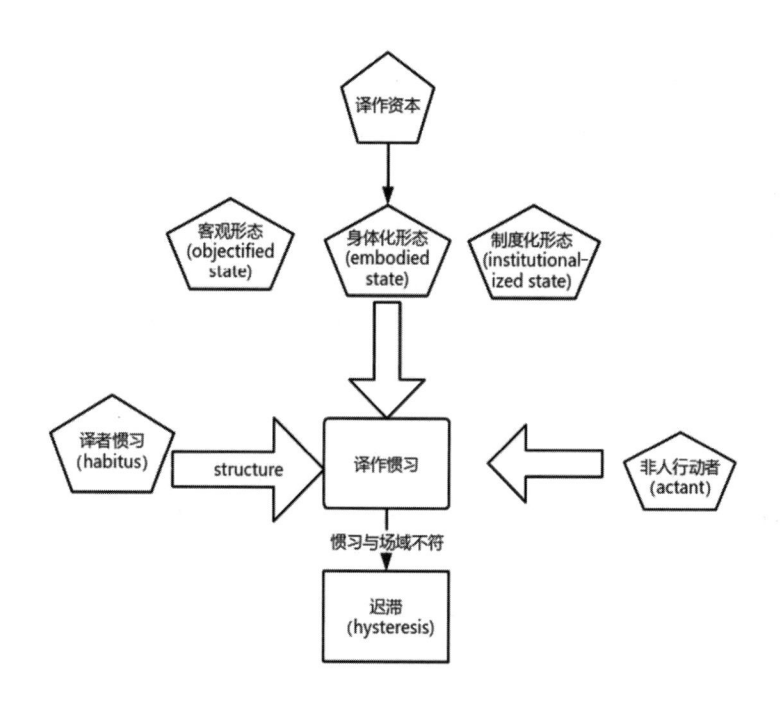

图 1　译作惯习生成机制示意图

四、《佐治刍言》译者惯习的倾注与译作惯习的形成

《佐治刍言》采取中西合译的翻译模式，合译者差别巨大的译者惯习在不同方面塑造着《佐治刍言》最终的文本呈现和整体气质。

7

（一）西译中述的合译模式，外儒内法的精神气质

傅兰雅会讲广东话、上海话以及官话，还曾任中文报刊编辑，可以说，他的中文水平是来华传教士当中最优的。以他对英文的熟练和对中文的熟悉，完全可以掌握译书的主动权并指导与他合译之人。而华人应祖锡作为他的助手，负责将其口授的中文加工润色，转化为书面文字。虽有进士的学位身份，但当时译书时应祖锡并无官职，处于中国官僚体系中的末端。因此，有着广方言馆西文教习、江南制造局翻译馆负责人和三品官衔持有者等多重身份的傅兰雅凭借其良好的中文水平和相对较高的社会地位，在与应祖锡组成的译者场域中占主导地位。

(1) 主译者傅兰雅的译者惯习：介绍西方的诉求

《佐治刍言》底本为 Political Economy, For Use In Schools, And For Private Instruction（以下简称 Political Economy）。该公司在出版此书之前，已有多部图书出版完成。该系列丛书涉及语言、科学、艺术等多个方面，涵盖面广，无所不包。钱伯斯兄弟在地理绘图方面更是享有盛名，1962年出版的《钱伯斯世界历史地图》如今看来依旧相当精妙。该公司多关注初级教育，所出之书多为简明易懂的入门读本。Political Economy 以教科书的形式编写。正文每段以阿拉伯数字为序，字数在几百字以内，可以一口气看完一节内容，符合低年级学生的阅读习惯。

时值救亡图存的洋务运动时期，国人自上而下均有着强烈了解西方的愿望，但碍于语言问题，需通过传教士这一媒介将西文传于国内。傅兰雅考虑到这部书内容深入浅出，在介绍了西方诸强国的政治经济情况，开拓中国人视野的同时，对社会政治方面措辞相对委婉，又不主张暴力革命，与统治者的利益冲突并不剧烈，决定将其引入国内。

原书前言中说："当人们对个人义务如此无知，公民社会的坚实基础也被试图破坏，在关系国家福祉这类至关重要的事情上引导青年人实在是十分重要的。因此，用简单的语言解释迄今为止被忽视的研究分支——社会经济，是现在交给教育工作者的主要目标。人们注意到，从道德和社会问题开始，政治经济学的原则会逐渐自然地摆在学生面前，并且可以毫不费力地掌握。"（1852：8）这段话所体现的情况切合晚清社会状态，政治经济学对社会的塑造作用吸引了统治阶级和知识分子的目光。另外，书中所体现的社会责任感，与傅兰雅早年所学师范专业形成的教育惯习和对于中国未来的期望也可以说不谋而合。故引入此书，既合情又合理。

(2) 应祖锡的译者惯习：保持政论文规范

傅兰雅（2010:546）在《翻书事略》中谈到华士润笔的职责作用："译后，华士将初稿改正润色，令合于中国文法。有数要书，临刊时华士与西人核对；而平常书多不必对，皆赖华士改正。因华士详慎郢斫，其讹则少，而文法甚精。"应祖锡等士子的职责主要是更正讹误和润色文笔。修正润色后的效果要达到"合于中国文法"甚至"文法甚精"的程度，这无疑对润笔之人的政论文写作功底提出很高要求。

而应祖锡则正是符合要求，能做到使译书"文法甚精"之人。应祖锡，字韩卿，出生在浙江永康，家学渊源深厚。曾入官办上海广方言馆攻读英文与西文。他与傅兰雅合译西书共两本。其一是《银矿指南》，该书由江南制造局于 1869 年出版，主要介绍了水银分矿的方法，对银矿挖采也有详细解释，保留原书序言目录，图文并茂，有较强的科学性和指导性。其二即是本书《佐治刍言》。后随清使任二等参赞于西班牙。回国后，先任江苏省南通、高邮四品知州，民国建立后，改任句容县知事。在任上著有《洋务经济通考》《增广尚友录》等。

值得注意的是，晚清时文章学承继传统政论文规范的同时，将八股文作为科考选拔人才的主要文体。以四书五经原句为出题内容，行文风格庄重严肃。每篇文章包括从起股到束股四个部分，每部分有两股排比对偶的文字，合起来共八股。应祖锡则在译书期间（1885—1890），考取了光绪十四年（1888）"光绪戊子科"举人（齐君，2017:49）。在 39 位有记录的译员中，正式考取功名者共 10 人，举人仅有 5 人，而应祖锡正是其中之一（元青、齐君，2016:35）。可见其古文功底深厚，在馆内笔述译员中应属于佼佼者。应祖锡在润色《佐治刍言》的时候，来自翻译馆官方对于中国文法的鼓励和举子的行文惯习达成一致，形成合力，使得文本落脚时，在形式上体现出文法严密、儒家文化浓厚的特点。

（二）西译中述的合译模式，外儒内法的文本显征

"译作惯习"体现在译作本身的结构化特性上，这些特性可能包括语言用法、文体选择、话语表达等及其背后映射的情感、思想。它们反映出翻译活动在特定社会文化语境下的规范和趋势。

考虑到《佐治刍言》由官办江南制造局出版，翻译馆有着相对明确的预设读者。主要是官员士大夫阶层、学生以及有阅读能力的普通人，这些人都是接受旧式教育的读书人。因而，傅兰雅介绍西方政治经济情况的内在诉求和翻译西书制订的八股文法以及政论文文法时，双重要求落实到文本上，使得译文较原文发生多处形变，风格也大为改变。主要体现为章节删减、加强政论文文体特征、资产阶级思想本土

化柔化和术语专项解释性翻译等特点。

(1) 删减章节，保留思想精华

Political Economy 英文原本共 35 章（除 introductory 外），476 节，《佐治刍言》共译三卷 31 章，418 节，删去（或失落）最后 4 章的内容。这四章标题分别为 "Commercial Convulsions" "Accumulation and Expenditure" "Insurance against Calamities" "Taxes"。发生这样重大删节（失落）的原因推测为应祖锡在译书期间考取举人，译书事业潦草结尾。这在江南制造局翻译馆也是常有之事，《翻书事略》中就有佐证。"另有数君，译书之时暂久不定，或因嫌译书为终于一事者，或因升官而辞职者。但此常换人之事，自必有碍于译书。盖常有要书译至中途，而他人不便续译；或译成之原稿，则去者委人收存，至屡去屡委，则稿多散矣"（傅兰雅，2010：536）。应祖锡中举后，或因升官离馆而弃译最后几章，或将译稿委托他人留存，最终丢失，这都大有可能。《佐治刍言》的翻译骤然截止，傅兰雅本可以请他人续译，但他没有这样做，正是个人惯习使然，他不愿文脉断裂，书中的思想遭到误读误译，因而索性放弃最后四章，直接付梓出版。

(2) 虚词反证，加强文体特征

政论文中常用虚词表达语气和情感。为符合文体规范，原文增译一部分虚词。如"夫"用于政论开头，"乎"用于疑问句或反义疑问句结尾。"也""矣"表示议论结束。同时，为符合政论文要求，除增加虚词外，《佐治刍言》中还大段插入与上句语义大致相同，但实为反证的语句，以增强说服力。

例1：

"To frame and execute laws, as well as for other useful ends, a GOVERNMENT becomes necessary" (Chambers, 1852: 21)

"夫欲设立律法　并执掌律法　以办理一国公事　必有若干人出为维持"（傅兰雅、应祖锡，1885：37）

例2：

"An improvement in the means of finding it out is one of the things which may be reasonably expected as civilization advances." (Chambers, 1852: 7)

"新法岂病民乎"（傅兰雅、应祖锡，1885:22）

例3：

"The blunders which have been committed hitherto have been caused by despising the knowledge of political economy, and following the guides of prejudice and habit instead of it." (57)

"其有办理国政　往往误事者　皆因未明此理　不肯考究学问　徒泥成法　徇众人妒嫉之心　逞一己贪婪之念　卒至徒劳无功　贻羞覆辙"（162）

例1中，"夫"的作用不只是开启议论，还可理解为"你"的指代与原文动词不定式作主语暗合。但原文中大写 GOVERNMENT 意在对专有名词的强调，译文却完全忽略这一点。例2中，译文言简意赅，把于国家有益的做法统称为"新法"，将"新法"一词基本与进步、发展画上等号。且用"乎"字将陈述语气改为反问，在对应原文的强调句型的同时，在句意上表现出对新法于民大有裨益的绝对信心。此外，例3说明译文多使用对仗工整的四字格结构，短促有力，便于诵读，强化呼吁效果。上述各例，均反映了译文无论是字词选择、节奏语序，还是说理策略均仿效政论文文体，以突出表达效果。

(3) 换例合儒，本土化资产阶级思想

在内容层面，为更多体现出原文意旨，两位译者对资产阶级思想进行释解，使其通俗化。译文使用换例和合儒的翻译方法，通过替换原文中生疏的例子和西方的基督教观念拉近译文与目标读者的心理距离，增强可读性。

例1：

"These are calculated to consume daily 300 bullocks, 2126 sheep, 700 lambs, and a like number of calves and pigs; bread amounting to 175,350 quartern-loaves." (Chambers, 1852: 52)

"每日所需食物共計牛六百隻　小牛一千四百隻　羊四千隻　小羊一千四百隻　豬一千四百隻　饅頭三十五萬塊"（傅兰雅、应祖锡，1885:156）

例 2:

"The patriarchs, whose history is founded in the Bible" (Chambers, 1852: 14)

"旧学全书　言其风俗　一家之中　有一首领　管理家事　不巽家长。"（傅兰雅、应祖锡，1885：43）

例 1 中，译者将民众不熟悉的"面包"译为馒头，缩短了阅读距离。另外，译文的数字也较原文增加了许多。究其原因，译文较原文所描述的年代相隔 30 年，资本主义国家人口增长，居民生产、消费水平也大有变化，而译者将其简单处理为翻倍，说明对于资本主义经济的发展速度并无确切认识。因而换成虽不真实但寓意美好的数字，使底层市民对资本主义社会产生向往之情。而在例 2 中，译者将 Bible 译为"旧学"显然是为目标语读者考虑，是对基督教思想极致的归化。"旧学"是我国未受近代西方文化影响前固有的学术，主要指四书五经等儒家经典。译文将基督教经典的《圣经》包裹上儒家文化的外衣，以增加译文的接受效果。

(4) 增删并改，柔化资产阶级思想

此外，为应对政治审查，两位译者不得不使用增译、省译、合并等翻译方法，对原文进行模糊处理。"省译"是指译者为了贯彻翻译事件场域中的规范以及各种规范性的关系，而有选择性和倾向性地删除文本形式或内容的某个部分的策略（刘晓峰，2017：187）。而在原文言尽之处，译者又常有大段增译，借此委婉地向上表达治国的高见。

例 1:

"Merely to possess knowledge while others are ignorant, is to possess power over those other persons." (Chambers, 1852: 8)

例 2:

"Vanity and selfishness may sometimes mislead at the commence, -will generally find the public too strong for him" (Chambers, 1852: 12)

例 1 原文是关于"知识就是力量"的言论，过于尖锐，与洋务运动"中学为体，西学为用"的指导思想无关，甚至直戳封建阶级的统治实质，如果译出可能会加深普通民众对统治阶级的对立情绪，故略去不译。另外，两位译者常增加政治诉求以及理想国家形象的译评，此类增译在段后常见，多以"盖"引出。如例 2，译文简要说明原文内容，并增译"盖国中每有一种人，孳孳为利，但求于己有益，至人之受害与否，置之不问。或有性情僻傲，往往一事方行，而弊端已随其后。况损人益己之事，纵勉强获利，亦必指摘交加，渐成怨府，又安能久享其利耶？所以文教之国所行之事必彼此俱能获利，其事方可举行"（傅兰雅、应祖锡，1885：35）。增译部分完全为译者自身的政见，期盼国家文教臻盛。译者期盼统治阶级行事不仅要利己，还需扩大市民阶层，广惠民生。这一翻译策略以柔化的方式减少了直白的民主思想和落后的封建统治直接冲突的可能，增加了译文的接受效果。

(5) 政治经济类术语的隐性深度翻译

虽然在《佐治刍言》前，日本明治维新时期著名学者福田谕吉介绍并翻译了 *Political Economy*，即《西洋近事》。但有学者已经对此和《佐治刍言》进行了比较，并否定了前者对后者的译名产生了显著影响。"《佐治刍言》所选用的翻译词汇，已充分反映当时中国思想界对欧美思想的认识和吸收，也在中国学术传统上消化传播，其中并无受到日译本的影响"（梁台根，2006：340）。在撰写《佐治刍言》时，傅兰雅对于政治经济类术语的翻译，体现出隐性深度翻译的倾向。"所谓深度翻译，就是深入历史文化语境的翻译"（曹明伦，2023：177）。傅兰雅用既存的概念术语替代新概念、新术语，用二字或四字词语甚至于整句话来解释术语内涵。在不添加注释、不创造新译名的情况下，让原意传达得明白晓畅。

表1 部分政治经济术语英汉对照一览表

原文	译文	译法
civilization	文教	替代
the fruits of industry	工资	替代
rights & duties	分所应得之端，分所应当之事	释译
grades and ranks	名位；贤愚贵贱；类聚群分；轻清重浊	释译
feudalism	欧洲各国内，数百年前，其国皆有大诸侯	替代；释译
stock	公款	替代
share	支用	替代
representative system	于众人中举其才德兼备者，以为官长。办理地方公事。其国主并办理国事之人。俱从民间保举而起，法至善也	释译
political economy	国家扩节财用之事；治民与节用	释译

（续表）

原文	译文	译法
The Wealth of Nations	《万国财用》	替代
production, accumulation, distribution and consumption	盖谓凡人日用所需物料，何者有益于人，何者使人颐养性命，及各物何以能生，何以能俱能散	释译
supply and demand	各人日用必需之物并如何能得各物	释译

综上，众多译文文本表征均为译者惯习产生的结果。译者在翻译过程中将长久以来形成的译者惯习，投射到译作之中，以"转置"的方式形成译文的译作惯习。针对《佐治刍言》而言，有两位译者发挥了作用。傅兰雅自身在资产阶级社会成长教育的经历，应祖锡举子的阅读惯习、审美惯习使得《佐治刍言》成书之时就具备了"外儒内法"，即"规范的政论文外衣，资产阶级政治思想内核"的特点，这也就是其译作具有的惯习。

译作惯习的概念可分两个方面来理解。首先，根据行动者网络理论，译本作为非人行动者拥有人类行动者，比如译者所具备的惯习属性，是动态的，具有结构和被结构双重形式。其次，惯习属性的叠加使得译作文本能更具有自主性地行走于网络之中，在特定的社会结构下，产生影响，拉长了或拓展了非人行动者的时空范围。译作惯习是对社会实践论和行动者网络理论的灵活运用，亦是对社会翻译学理论弹性融合的创新尝试。"译作惯习"是指部分由译者注入，但译作本身亦具有的，随时空、社会背景变化所呈现出来的稳定模式和特性，这些模式和特性在一定程度上独立于译者个人的惯习，并能够在不同的社会文化历史语境中产生影响。

五、迟滞与译作惯习的沉寂

"拉图尔构想的人类与非人类相互构建的行动者网络，适用于分析翻译与生产传播的全过程，因为该过程涉及作者、译者、出版商等人类行动者，也依赖文本、观念等非人类行动者"（汪宝荣，2017：114–115）。事实上，译介与传播的过程并不是静态的，而是受文本、意识形态等诸多因素影响，处于动态变化中的。"当实践实际面对的环境与客观上他们适合的环境相去甚远时，实践会容易招致消极的负性制裁"（Bourdieu, 1977: 78）。在翻译馆成立之初，清政府要求傅兰雅"特译紧要之书",李中堂"数次谕特译某书"(傅兰雅,2010:539)。当时洋务派重视介绍器物科技、服务军工的西书,而像《佐治刍言》之类蕴含资产阶级经济思想和民主思想的政经书籍则被当时的社会环境所轻视。另外,受官府态度影响,民间和知识分子对《佐治刍言》的内涵价值也认识不足。康有为在1886年,也就是《佐治刍言》出版后第二年,曾对傅兰雅所译之书发表看法,认为傅译西书中政书过少,表现出对翻译馆的政书关注不多。他托人向张之洞转达建议,希望中国能自行翻译西方的政书。"中国西书太少,傅兰雅所译西书,皆兵医不切之学,其政书甚要,西书甚多新理,皆中国所无,宜开局译之,为最要事"(2011:17)。徐维则在《东西学书录》序言中道:"言政以公法公理之书为枢纽……傅兰雅在局最久译书最多,究其归旨,似长于格致制造诸学。算学之书可云备矣,惟公法公理各致之书,中国极少……"由此可见,《佐治刍言》蕴含的政治经济学思想在首次出版后受到冷遇的原因主要是洋务派强调学习强国的器物,忽视甚至漠视政经方面中国的落后。中国进步分子对傅兰雅所译的格致之书比较推崇,但对其所译经济政治类图书关注度不够,评价不高。换言之,《佐治刍言》的译作惯习被译者惯习遮蔽,被迫隐性发展。但同时,晚清进步人士表现出对当时政学类图书不足的不满,并期待此类图书的数量和质量能有所突破。这说明,社会对具有政治经济方面启发意义的译作其实有很大需求,这为《佐治刍言》译作惯习的后续发挥奠定基础,也就是说,虽然译作惯习沉寂,迟滞效应产生,但等到特定社会结构形成,译作惯习会发挥结构效果,即对社会的建构作用。

六、场域变迁诱发译作惯习

"惯习迟滞的影响会赋予行动者适应新场域、抓住契机的能力"(Cheryl, 2008:135)。甲午中日战争中国战败,宣告了洋务运动的破产,同时,中国人普遍觉醒了救亡图存的反侵略反封建意识。权力场域发生变动,统治阶级思想松动,1898年张之洞提出"中体西用,政艺兼学"的治学思想,对"中体西用"思想进行修正。这为《佐治刍言》译作惯习显化,发挥建构作用提供了契机。另外,康梁维新派主张资产阶级君主立宪政体,《佐治刍言》的内涵同维新派发生思想共振,隐而不发的译作惯习和恰逢的社会结构产生共鸣,在特殊时期发挥作用,助推晚清政治经济学成形。

《佐治刍言》是戊戌以前介绍西方社会政治思想最为系统、篇幅最大的一部书。在戊戌变法时期,晚清整个思想界对书中内容进行了慎重挖掘。《新学书目提要》

收录了《佐治刍言》，编者赵祖惪论及中国向欧洲学习时间已久，但内容局限于艺学，到甲午之后政学才得到机会后来居上，肯定了如《佐治刍言》之类西学书籍对近代政学形成的积极作用。梁启超对《佐治刍言》透彻谈论国与国相处，国与家同频，国内公民应尽之责的特长十分欣赏，在湖南时务学堂的参考书目中，梁启超不仅将《佐治刍言》选入通识课程，还将其列为宪法课程的必读书目，多次强调该书的重要性。这相当于直接将《佐治刍言》和旧学古法割开，而与新法宪政联系起来，提升了其指导性的理论地位和历史地位。

《佐治刍言》在1895年后至1902年和译西书[①]传入期间大放异彩，在多部西学书目中均有所收录。如1896年的《西学书目表》，1897年的《西政丛书》，1899年的《东西学书录》，1902年的《增版东西学书目》。阅读量大，流传甚广。《望山庐日记》记载，徐宝瑄在1901年读到《佐治刍言》并受启发，挖掘出该书中的维新思想从而大谈新旧之别。"人人有维新性质，无守旧性质。何以言之？人之心皆利是趋，而害是避。彼守旧者，惧新之足以害己，恐失其旧利，故坚不肯变革。使一旦知新之利，察旧之害，未有不谈新者也。然则维新者，亦人之本性然也。"（2015：340）在百日维新后，慈禧下令禁毁梁启超等人所编书籍，在一定程度上影响了《佐治刍言》的传播。另外，随着和译西书的数量大大增多，翻译馆所译西书逐渐式微。

由此可见，《佐治刍言》的译作惯习，即其内涵思想，不仅源自译者，也随社会结构变革而焕发生机，译作惯习和维新派的政治追求多处契合，可为其变法张目，从而推动社会进步。

七、结语

《佐治刍言》的译介和传播过程经历时间长，社会环境变化复杂，体现着被社会建构，同时又建构社会的双向互动。本研究发现，在翻译和早期传播阶段，主译者傅兰雅负责传达原作思想，而应祖锡负责在形式上将其合理化。傅、应二人的译者惯习通过《佐治刍言》中资产阶级民主思想的文本显征，转置为译作惯习得以存续，隐性发展。《佐治刍言》成书后传播的第二阶段，主要指甲午战争后，当权力场域发生变化，译作惯习得以触发，和维新派产生思想共振，因此在戊戌维新时期作为思想武器，为政治改革起到宣传作用，从而推动社会进步和现代政治学学科建构。文章以《佐治刍言》译介传播的历时考察为例，探讨了译作惯习的名与实，及

[①] "和译西书"即日本所译西学书籍。

其迟滞效应的具体体现，指出在翻译活动中，与社会结构双向互动的不仅有译者惯习，亦有文本本身的译作惯习，希望能够启发社会翻译学领域对"非人行动者"特性的进一步探讨。

【参考文献】

[1] 曹明伦，2023．再谈"深度翻译"和"隐性深度翻译"[J]．中国翻译 44（1）：174–177.

[2] 戴吉礼编，2010．傅兰雅档案第 2 卷 [M]．弘侠译．桂林：广西师范大学出版社．

[3] 方维规，2021．历史的概念向量 [M]．北京：生活·读书·新知三联书店有限公司．

[4] 傅兰雅、应祖锡，1885．佐治刍言 [M]．上海：江南制造总局翻译馆．

[5] 郭庆藩撰，王孝鱼点校，2006．庄子集释 [M]．北京：中华书局．

[6] 康有为，2011．我史 [M]．北京：中国人民大学出版社．

[7] 梁启超，1897．读西学书法 [M]．长沙：时务报社．

[8] 梁台根，2006．近代西方知识在东亚的传播及其共同文本之探索——以《佐治刍言》为例 [J]．汉学研究（2）：323–351.

[9] 刘晓峰，2017．*Manual of Political Economy* 汉译本《富国策》翻译研究 [D]．北京：北京外国语大学．

[10] 刘晓峰、惠玲玉，2023．社会翻译学理论融合问题再思考 [J]．中国翻译（1）：13–18.

[11] 骆雯雁，2022．行动者网络理论的名与实及其对社会翻译学研究的意义 [J]．外语学刊（3）：55–61.

[12] 马丁·海德格尔，2010．物的追问：康德关于先验原理的学说 [M]．赵卫国译．上海：上海译文出版社．

[13] 宁一中，2020．比尔·布朗之"物论"及对叙事研究的启迪 [J]．当代外国文学（4）：131–136.

[14] 齐君，2017．近代"笔受"译员群体探析——以江南制造局翻译馆为中心的考察 [J]．历史教学（22）：46–58.

[15] 孙青，2009．晚清之"西政"东渐及本土回应 [M]．上海：上海书店出版社．

[16] 汪宝荣，2017．社会翻译学学科结构与研究框架构建述评 [J]．解放军外国语学院学报（5）：110–118+160.

[17] 汪宝荣，2022．中国文学译介与传播模式研究：以英译现当代小说为中心 [M]．杭州：浙江大学出版社．

[18] 王峰、乔冲，2023．行动者网络理论对翻译研究的方法论启示 [J]．中国外语，20

（05）：88–95.

[19] 王洪焕，2014.《佐治刍言》译本论体文文法研究［J］. 蚌埠学院学报（3）：123–125.

[20] 王林，2008.《佐治刍言》与西方自由资本主义思想的传入［J］. 甘肃社会科学（6）：193–196.

[21] 王涛，1995. 中国近代法律的变迁（1689—1911）［M］. 北京：法律出版社.

[22] 熊月之，2010. 西学东渐与晚清社会［M］. 北京：中国人民大学出版社.

[23] 徐宝璜，2015. 忘山庐日记［M］. 上海：上海人民出版社.

[24] 徐维则编，1899. 东西学书录［M］. 石印本.

[25] 元青、齐君，2016. 过渡时代的译才：江南制造局翻译馆的中国译员群体探析［J］. 安徽史学（2）：32–43.

[26] 张登德，2009. 求富与近代经济学中国解读的最初视角《富国策》的译刊与传播：英汉对照［M］. 合肥：黄山书社.

[27] 张燕，2012. 从交际翻译理论视角看《佐治刍言》［J］. 长春工程学院学报（社会科学版）（3）：69–71.

[28] 周洁，2013. 从改写理论视角看《佐治刍言》［J］. 淮海工学院学报（22）：75–77.

[29] Bourdieu, P & J. D. Wacquant. (1992). *An Invitation to Reflexive Sociology* [M]. Chicago: University of Chicago Press.

[30] Bourdieu, P. (1977). *Outline of a Theory of Practice* [M]. R. Nice (trans.). Cambridge: Cambridge University Press.

[31] Bourdieu, P. (1986). The Forms of Capital [C]. In Richardson (ed.). *Handbook of Theory and Research for the Sociology of Education.* New York: Greenwood, 241-258.

[32] Bruno, Latour. (1996). On Actor Network Theory: A Few Clarifications[J]. *Soziale Welt,* (47), 369-381.

[33] Bruno, L. (2005). *Reassembling The Social: An Introduction to Actor Network Theory*[M]. Oxford: Oxford University Press.

[34] Cheryl, H. (2008). Hysteresis [C]// Grenfell (ed.). M. *Pierre Bourdieu Key Concepts.* London: Routledge, 126-145.

[35] William. & Robert. Chambers. (1852). *Political Economy, For Use In Schools, And For Private Instruction* [M]. Edinburgh: Chambers.

[36] Wolf. M. (2007). Introduction: The emergence of a sociology of translation [C]// W. Michaela & A. Fukari (eds.). *Constructing a Sociology of Translation.* Philadelphia: John Benjamins Publishing Company, 1-36.

The Emergence and Induction of Target-text Habitus: A Socio-Translation Study of *Zuozhi chuyan's* Translation and Dissemination

Xi'an International Studies University　FU Na, LIU Xiaofeng

Abstract: Zuozhi chuyan, translated by John Fryer and Ying Zuxi, introduced Western politics, economy, education, and ethics, and it had a profound impact on the development of late Qing society, with Liang Qichao calling it "the most comprehensive book on politics". Based on the Habitus Theory and Actor Network Theory, this paper traces the positive effects of the book on the evolution of late Qing society by analyzing the process of translation and dissemination of Zuozhi Chuyan. The study concludes that Zuozhi Chuyan, as an actant, also possesses habitus. It simultaneously constructs and is constructed by society. Influenced by the Hysteresis Effect, the Translation Habitus of Zuo first survived implicitly by virtue of its own symbolic capital, which was manifested in the mediocre response to the bourgeois ideological interpretations in the book, and then triggered to appear in a specific field. After the First Sino-Japanese War, Zuozhi Chuyan resonated with the ideology of the Reformists, and thus played an important role in the period of the Hundred Days' Reform.

Keywords: *Zuozhi Chuyan*; target-text habitus; hysteresis and induction; socio-translation studies

基于文献计量的中国典籍翻译研究概况及趋势（2011—2021）可视化分析

曲阜师范大学　谢文琦[①]

【摘　要】 本文以中国知网期刊论文数据库（CNKI）收录的2011年至2021年间国内典籍翻译研究的学术期刊文献为数据来源，借助CiteSpace可视化工具，并结合传统的文献计量方法，绘制出中国典籍翻译研究近10年发文统计图、发文期刊来源分布图、关键词聚类图谱、时间线图谱和突现关键词图谱，从发文总体趋势与分布、研究热点演变、文献前沿动态分析等方面进行数据分析与可视化呈现，较为客观地揭示了近十年来国内典籍翻译研究的发展趋势，从关键词聚类分析和突现关键词谱探析了研究热点和前沿动态，旨在助力典籍翻译研究发展，推动中华文化不断走出去。

【关键词】 典籍翻译；研究热点；CiteSpace；可视化分析

一、引言

中国典籍承载着中华民族五千多年的知识财富，记录着中华文明的传承与变迁。开宗明义，典籍可以定义为"中国清代末年，1911年以前的重要文献和书籍"（王宏，2021）。据此，典籍不仅包括古典文化作品，还包括古典医药、军事、法律等作品；不仅包括汉语典籍，还包括少数民族典籍。可见，中国典籍涵盖内容极其丰富，涉及文史哲社、天文地理、宗法礼数、美术建筑、音乐歌舞等（陈梅、文

[①] 谢文琦（1998—），曲阜师范大学翻译学院硕士研究生，研究方向为典籍翻译。邮箱：wenqix@foxmail.com。

军，2011），对世界文明做出的贡献不容置疑。全球化时代，中国正与世界加强政治、经济往来，并积极推动中华优秀传统文化走出去，与其他国家和民族的文化进行广泛交流，不断增强文化软实力。典籍翻译作为中华文化走出去的一个重要环节，对于弘扬民族文化，保持中国固有的文化身份十分必要（霍跃红，2005），同时也能促进中华文化与世界文化的平等对话与融合。

我国自20世纪末起，启动了向世界介绍、弘扬中华优秀传统文化的《大中华文库》工程，随后又先后启动了"经典中国对外出版工程""中国图书对外推广计划"等项目（王宏，2012），在国家层面积极推动典籍翻译事业发展。同时在学界，典籍翻译研究也逐渐得到学者们的重视，从译本研究、译者主体研究、翻译策略研究、传播情况等不同的视角展开讨论，但是尚少有学者对典籍翻译进行整体性和系统性研究，分析典籍翻译的研究热点和发展趋势。当前，国内学者对典籍翻译的关注度如何，取得了怎样的研究进展？未来的研究趋势应往哪个方向展开？本文借助文献计量学的可视化软件CiteSpace挖掘文献数据，形成多种可视化图谱，梳理近十年典籍翻译研究的基本态势，对我国典籍翻译的研究热点和前沿动态进行追踪，借此推进中国典籍翻译的深入研究。

二、研究方法及数据来源

本研究使用文献计量工具CiteSpace对数据进行统计分析。CiteSpace软件能够根据节点类型呈现多种可视化图谱，直观地展现科学知识领域的信息全景，识别某一科学领域中的关键文献、热点研究和前沿方向（侯剑华、胡志刚，2013）。该软件主要通过高频关键词、突现术语以及关键词聚类分析等功能挖掘学科的发展趋势和走向，研究某一学科领域的研究热点及前沿，绘制学科发展的可视化知识图谱。

本文以中国典籍翻译作为研究对象，聚焦2011年至2021年间刊载的国内典籍翻译研究的学术期刊文献。期刊是重要的学术信息交流平台，期刊论文与其他文献类型（如报告、著作、会议和学位论文等）相比，通常可以较快地呈现某一领域的研究热点和前沿（杨艳霞、王湘玲，2019）。本研究以"典籍""翻译""英译""外译""阿译""俄译""西译""葡译""德译""日译""韩译"为主题，统计收录在CSSCI中的期刊论文，时间限定为2011年至2021年，通过中国知网期刊论文数据库（CNKI）详细统计，经过人工筛选，剔除与典籍翻译主题不相关的检索结果后，共获得有效文献 571 篇。

三、数据分析

（一）发文总体趋势与分布

文献发布数量的历时变化能够直观地体现出学界对该主题的关注热度，笔者根据检索结果绘制了典籍翻译研究近 10 年发文统计图（如图 1）。图 1 显示，近十年国内学者对典籍翻译的关注度总体处于上升趋势，近三年来发文量虽出现上下波动的情况，但仍保持在较高水平。自 2011 年至 2017 年，呈现逐年递增的趋势，在 2017 年发文篇数达到峰值后，2019 年至 2021 年关注热度逐渐趋于平稳。可见，典籍翻译在国内正受到学者的重视，研究成果相应增多。

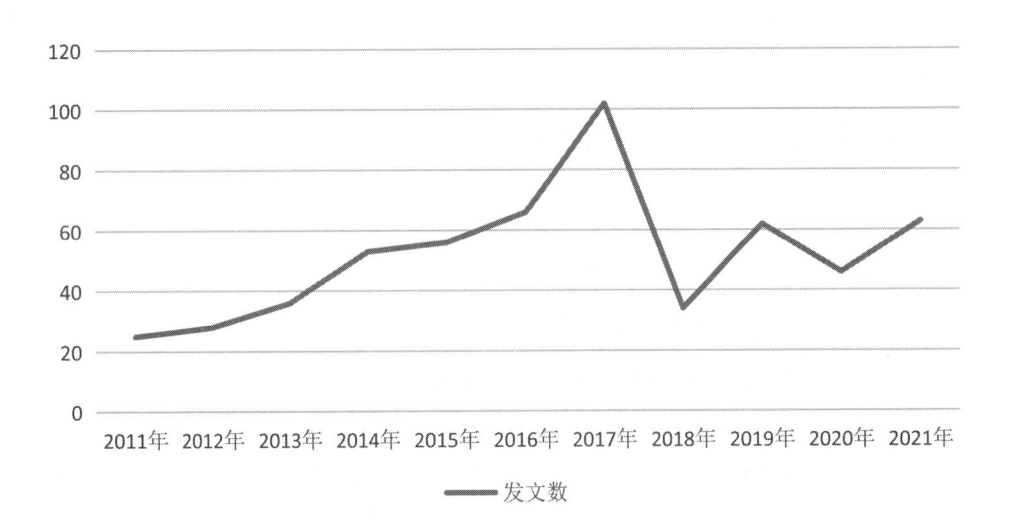

图 1 典籍翻译研究文献近 10 年发文统计图

究其原因，1994 年至 2016 年，是《大中华文库》发展的第一阶段，国家在约 20 年的时间内完成了汉英对照版 110 种的译介出版，在此期间不断有学者对相关典籍的译本进行研究，发文数量持续增加。在 2007 年，国家立项启动《大中华文库》多语种版编纂出版工作，"截至 2018 年，多语种对照版 193 种已经陆续出版 170 多种，以法语、阿拉伯语、俄语、西班牙语、葡萄牙语、德语、日语、韩语等 8 个文种出版中国最经典的典籍作品"（李子木，2019）。多语种的典籍翻译作品出版也使得典籍翻译不仅局限于英译，而成为真正意义上的典籍翻译。研究俄语、德语、法语等多语种典籍翻译极大地丰富了典籍翻译的研究内容及范畴，拓宽了研究视角及广度，相关研究发文随之逐渐增多。随后在 2017 年举办的"一带一路"国际合作高峰论坛上，习近平总书记提出将"一带一路"建成"和平之路、繁荣之路、开放之路、创新之路、文明之路"，这正与《大中华文库》在"一带一路"的传播目标紧密契合。"一带一路"的蓬勃发展成为典籍翻译研究的强大动力，最直观的体现是 2017 年典籍翻译研究发文量达到近十年的峰值。归根到底，这一切离不开我国经济实力、文化软实力及国际影响力的增强，这将进一步促进国内典籍翻译研究的发展，促进中华文化与世界相互沟通、交流。

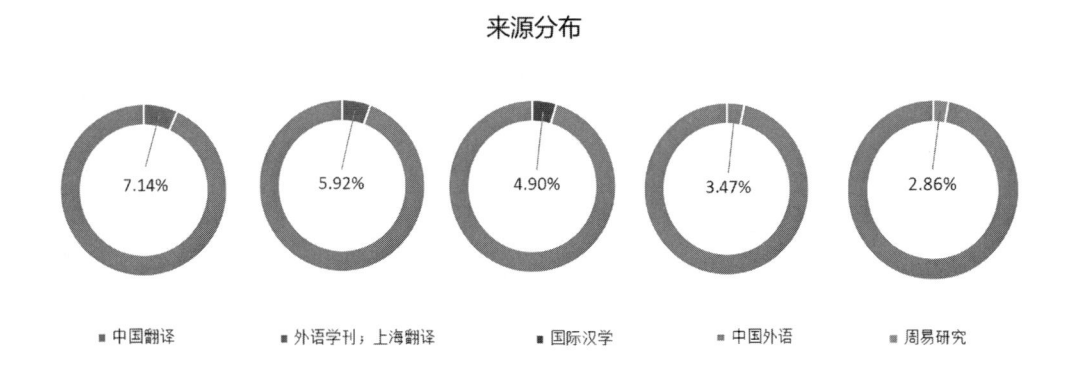

来源分布

中国翻译	外语学刊；上海翻译	国际汉学	中国外语	周易研究
7.14%	5.92%	4.90%	3.47%	2.86%

图 2　典籍翻译研究发文期刊来源分布图

除发文数量外，典籍翻译研究的发文期刊分布也能反映出当前学界的研究方向，分布情况如图 2 所示。排名靠前的期刊多为外语类核心期刊，发文量排名第一的是《中国翻译》，共有 35 篇发文，涉及方向主要是研究译本的翻译策略、比较译本差异、分析译者风格等方面。其中，《国际汉学》和《周易研究》虽不是外语类期刊，但其中不乏典籍翻译相关研究的出现，说明当前典籍翻译已与文化学、哲学等学科互通发展，交叉融合，具有强大的发展潜力。图 2 中没有显示的《贵州民族研究》排名也比较靠前，其中刊登的文献绝大部分与民族典籍的翻译有关，中国作为拥有五十六个民族的多民族大国，民族典籍蕴含着丰富的文明财富，具有鲜明的中国特色，说明民族典籍翻译也是典籍翻译的重要组成部分，已得到学者的关注。观察典籍翻译的研究发文期刊来源分布发现,发文期刊分布在外国语言文学、文化学、哲学等学科,说明当前对典籍翻译的研究已呈现出跨学科、多领域的态势,研究视角及研究内容已得到拓宽和提升。

(二)研究热点演变

聚焦典籍翻译的研究热点能够帮助学界了解典籍翻译研究的核心议题和关注重点,利用 CiteSpace 可视化工具绘制关键词知识图谱,可以即时生动地反映出研究领域的热点话题,进一步揭示研究领域的关注重点和发展前沿,以此为依据进一步拓展研究领域、拓宽研究视角、提升研究层次。

这一部分将从关键词聚类分析、时间线图和突现关键词等知识图谱揭示近十年典籍翻译的关注重点、发展演变和前沿领域。

1. 关键词聚类分析

关键词通常是文献的高度浓缩和概括,能够全面直接地将文献的核心内容体现出来(张晓雪,2017),在某一特定时间段内以较高的频次反复出现,可以显示出较高的关注度,从而揭示某一学科领域的研究热点和重要主题。CiteSpace 软件能够自动计算每一关键词的中心性,并对部分高频关键词进行聚类,生成基于关键词共现网络的知识图谱(李红满,2014)。

表 1 是由 CiteSpace 软件统计得出的高频关键词及高中心度的关键词表。图 3 是近十年国内典籍翻译研究的关键词聚类图谱。图中节点代表关键词,节点越大表示该关键词在文献中出现的频率越高。关键词的字体大小则表明其中心性的强弱,即该节点在连接其他节点上发挥的作用,中心性越强表明通过该关键词开展的研究越多,其在共现网络中的影响力就越大(高振宇,2016)。

结合表 1 关键词表和图 3 关键词聚类图谱中可以看出,除主题词"英译""翻译"之外,关注度较高的关键词是"《论语》""翻译策略""红楼梦""理雅各""副文本""传播"等,这些关键词反映了国内典籍翻译研究的重要研究领域。根据主题,这些关键词可以分成四类:典籍翻译的研究主题("翻译""英译""典籍英译""典籍翻译"),译本研究("《论语》""红楼梦""翻译策略""副文本""《诗经》""《易经》""《中庸》"),译者主体研究("理雅各""汉学家""林语堂""宇文所安"),外部研究("传播""意识形态")。

表 1 典籍翻译高频关键词和高中心度关键词表

排名	高频关键词		高中心度关键词	
	关键词	频次	关键词	中心度
1	英译	54	《论语》	0.31
2	翻译	48	翻译	0.24
3	《论语》	45	英译	0.22
4	红楼梦；典籍英译	31	翻译策略	0.21
5	翻译策略	29	红楼梦；典籍英译	0.14
6	典籍翻译	18	典籍翻译；理雅各；译介	0.08
7	理雅各	16	副文本；汉学家	0.07
8	副文本	15	典籍外译；民族典籍 林语堂；诗歌翻译	0.05
9	译介	13	传播；语料库；《诗经》	0.04
10	传播	12	—	—

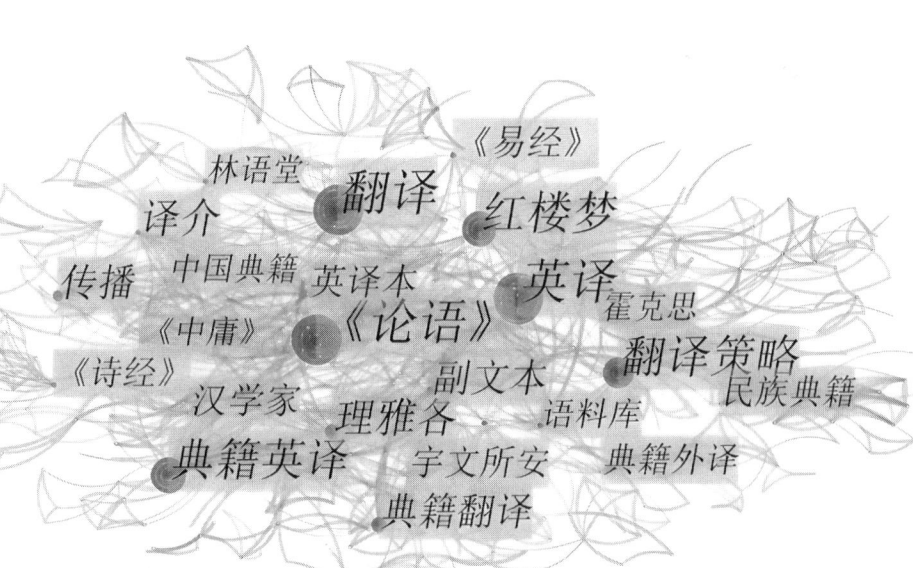

图 3 典籍翻译研究关键词聚类图谱

译本研究不仅是翻译界普遍关注的方向，也是典籍翻译研究领域关注的热点问题，越来越多的学者对不同典籍译本进行了多角度的深入研究。其中，《论语》《中庸》《红楼梦》等作品最受关注。如黄国文（2012）以《论语》英译为例，探讨了语内翻译和语际翻译的过程；宋晓春（2014）以21世纪初三种《中庸》英译本为例，分析了典籍翻译中的"深度翻译"倾向；闫敏敏（2005），文军、任艳（2012）等人梳理了不同阶段的《红楼梦》的英译史；刘泽权（2011，2012，2013）从对比四个英译本的译者风格，探究虚义动词结构的使用与成因以及从叙述视角下看《红楼梦》英译本等多角度切入典籍翻译研究。

近十年，译者主体性逐渐得到学者的关注，由此针对译者主体的研究也成为典籍翻译研究的重点领域之一。图3显示，英国汉学家理雅各、美国汉学家宇文所安和我国的翻译家林语堂成为近十年典籍翻译研究中获得关注最多的译者主体。王东波（2012）从"译名之争"到中国经典翻译，探讨了理雅各对中国文化的尊重与包容；张萍、王宏（2018）分析了理雅各的三版《诗经》译本中宗教观在不同阶段所发生的变化；滕雄、文军（2017）则从副文本着手，分类比较了理雅各《诗经》三种版本的副文本之间的异同，对差异产生的原因进行分析。许渊冲（2017）针对美国汉学家宇文所安独自完成杜甫诗全译，真切发问道："中国经典外译只能靠汉学家吗？"并且，他据此提出了汉学家与中国译者各自的优势与局限。

外部研究主要指典籍翻译内部要素之外的其他制约因素，如意识形态、诗学因素、社会、历史、文化背景等（王宏、刘性峰，2015）。近十年，文化转向之后，外部研究已逐渐得到学界的重视。如杨平（2015）调查发现《易经》在西方的翻译与传播已呈现出多元化趋势，对西方文化的影响越来越大；汪庆华（2015）从传播学视域出发，分析了《红楼梦》英译本中翻译策略的选择与中国文化走出去的问题；李宁（2015）以《孙子兵法》为例调查分析了《大中华文库》国人英译本海外接受状况；陈梅、文军（2011）则通过对亚马逊图书网上中国典籍英译本的调查，揭示中国典籍英译本在国外阅读市场的传播现状。"传播""意识形态"等关键词的高频出现说明当前典籍翻译的研究关注到了文化传播这个方向，这与国家倡导的中华文化走出去紧密契合，是文化自信的最直观体现，深入研究典籍翻译或对国人坚定文化自信多有裨益。

2. 关键词历时演进分析

CiteSpace软件绘制的关键词时间线图谱可以直观地展示研究领域的热点变化趋势以及文献间的相互影响（杨艳霞、王湘玲，2019）。图4显示的是2011年至2021年中国典籍翻译研究的历时变化趋势。"英译""翻译"和"《论语》"节点最大，中心性最强，向外发散的时间线最多，说明十年期间，不断有学者对典籍翻译这一领域进行研究，有关《论语》的研究在典籍翻译研究领域中获得的关注度最高，典籍翻译的语言本体研究仍是关注焦点。从关键词的时间分布来看，在 2011 年，典籍翻译研究领域更多地关注语言的本体研究，如翻译策略、翻译方法等。到 2016 年左右，学界对典籍翻译外部研究的关注度有所提升，传播、出版等方面的研究逐渐增多，从文化传播、文化自觉和文化自信等方面探讨典籍翻译的研究，注重社会背景对典籍翻译的影响。由此可以看出，中国典籍翻译研究的演进趋势可以概括为，从关注翻译的语言本体研究逐渐转向到基于社会背景对典籍翻译研究领域的拓展，是从内部研究向外部研究的逐渐转变，外部因素能够对于语言机制本身发挥更深刻的作用，这些值得高度重视，为未来研究的发展提供新方向。

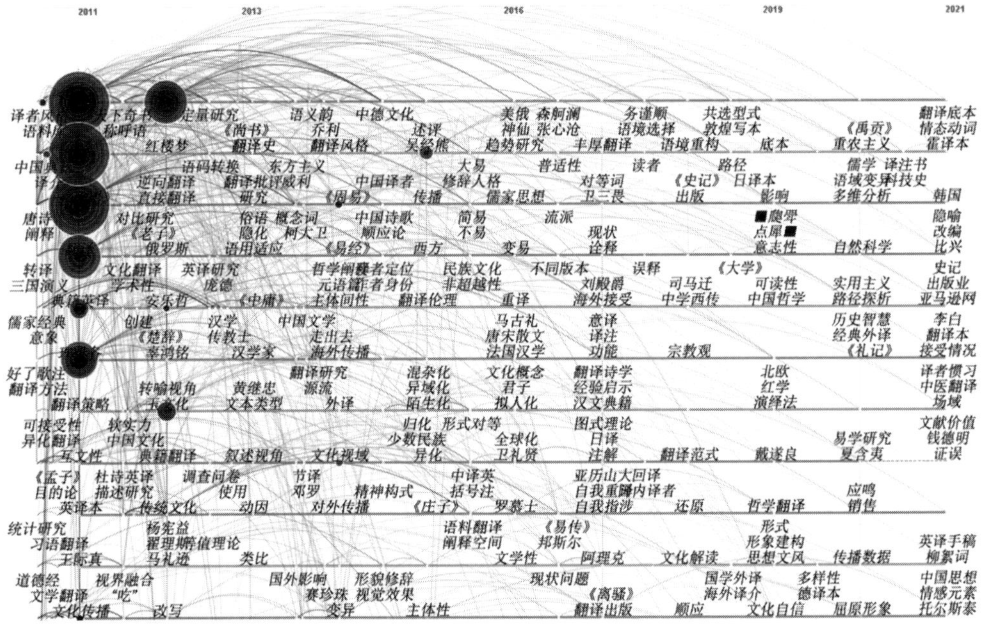

图 4　典籍翻译研究时间线图谱

3. 文献前沿动态分析

突现关键词能够分析关键词频次在不同时期的阶段性变化，如在某一时间突然增多或者突然减少，频次的突然增多通常显示出某一主题在特定时间段内成为研究热点。通过 CiteSpace 可视化工具绘制出排名前 25 的突现关键词图谱，如图 5 所示。典籍翻译在 2011 年至 2021 年十年间前期，关注重点为"译者""英译""《论语》"等主题，大多关注的是典籍翻译的内部研究。"民族典籍"和"少数民族"从 2014 年到 2017 年左右呈现出研究热度持续增长的态势，说明学界在这个阶段对民族典籍翻译研究格外关注，研究少数民族典籍的翻译有利于促进民族团结，彰显中国特色。"罗慕士""阿理克"等突现关键词在2017年左右先后突现，说明该译者所翻译的译本在2017年前后受到学者关注较多。罗慕士是美国翻译家，他翻译的《三国演义》于1992年在美国出版，在英语读者中引起了强烈的反响（董琇，2016）。阿理克是苏联汉学家，他将《聊斋志异》译成俄语，该俄译本被公认为是《聊斋志异》最经典、影响最大的俄译本（王晔，2017）。这两位译者的突现说明在2017年左右对《三国演义》和《聊斋志异》及其译者的研究发文数量激增，受到学界关注，说明古典文学典籍翻译研究热度依旧不减，并有扩大语种范围和研究内容的倾向。

Top 25 Keywords with the Strongest Citation Bursts

Keywords	Year	Strength	Begin	End	2011 – 2021
译者	2011	2.45	2011	2012	
理雅各	2011	3.31	2012	2013	
英译	2011	2.07	2012	2013	
《论语》	2011	1.23	2012	2013	
红楼梦	2011	1.14	2012	2013	
译者风格	2011	1.28	2013	2014	
民族典籍	2011	1.38	2014	2017	
翻译研究	2011	1.27	2014	2016	
林语堂	2011	2.04	2015	2017	
少数民族	2011	1.56	2015	2017	
异化	2011	1.19	2015	2016	
典籍翻译	2011	1.81	2016	2017	
《易经》	2011	1.46	2016	2019	
罗慕士	2011	1.46	2016	2017	
译介模式	2011	1.21	2017	2019	
翻译出版	2011	1.21	2017	2019	
阿理克	2011	1.21	2017	2019	
典籍外译	2011	1.19	2017	2018	
传播	2011	1.89	2018	2021	
意识形态	2011	1.51	2018	2021	
《诗经》	2011	1.56	2019	2021	
文化自信	2011	1.47	2019	2021	
影响	2011	1.47	2019	2021	
《庄子》	2011	1.27	2019	2021	
变异	2011	1.27	2019	2021	

图5 典籍翻译研究前25位突现关键词图谱

在2011年至2021年十年间的后期，"传播"和"意识形态"这两个关键词从2018年到2021年呈现研究热度增长的态势，说明典籍翻译的外部研究在这个阶段受到学界的关注，传播效果研究逐渐成为新的生长点。《易经》《诗经》《庄子》等单一书目的突现，不仅代表着该阶段学界对此书目的研究有增加趋势，还说明在该阶段该书目所在的典籍类别受到学界的关注。《庄子》是道家的经典著作，《诗经》是儒家经典，《易经》既属于儒家经典，也属于道家经典，说明当前不只儒学典籍得到了学界的关注，道家典籍的研究也逐渐成为典籍翻译研究的热点领域。值得注意的是"文化自信"于 2019 年至 2021 年突现，这说明典籍翻译开始与国家信念相联系，积极推动中华优秀传统文化走出去，坚定文化自信，加强典籍翻译研究至关重要。

三、中国典籍翻译发展趋势及不足

经过上文的数据分析，可以总结出近十年典籍翻译的研究热点、发展趋势以及存在问题。当前我国典籍翻译研究，对典籍翻译的内部研究依然是热点话题，如译本研究、译者主体研究、翻译策略研究等方面；民族典籍研究发展趋势良好，呈现多元向好的倾向；典籍翻译的研究内容更加丰富，研究范畴更加广阔，哲学典籍的翻译研究不再仅局限于儒家经典，中国传统哲学多家学派的经典已得到关注，且研究视角更加多元，研究层次逐渐提升；传播、出版等翻译研究的外部研究正受到学界的关注，传播效果研究成为新的生长点，配合国家"一带一路"的宏伟倡议，保持持续增长的态势。当前，我国典籍翻译研究的演进趋势可以概括为，从关注翻译本身的内部研究逐渐转向基于社会背景对典籍翻译研究领域的拓展，是从内部研究向外部研究的逐渐转变，外部研究中的意识形态、社会、历史、文化背景等因素为未来典籍翻译的研究和发展提供新思路和新方向。

当前，典籍翻译的研究内容更加丰富，调查研究更加深入，但其中也还存在一些问题，如当前的研究重点依然集中在文学典籍和哲学典籍领域，虽然科技典籍和民族典籍的发展势头向好，但与之相比，仍然处于相对弱势的地位；同时在文化典籍方面，儒家经典的关注度较高，其他经史子集类典籍翻译研究相对较少，各个典籍子类的翻译研究尚待开拓；民族典籍的翻译研究关注度虽有所提升，但研究涉及的地域、民族和类型仍然需要继续开拓，民族典籍翻译中的民族政治意识和文明意识问题仍待改善（刘艳春、赵长江，2017）；典籍翻译的传播与接受效果研究尚不够广泛，调查研究尚不够深入，同时当前多数研究只关注到了英语世界的典籍翻译的传播与接受，其他语种的接受情况调查有待开展等。

根据以上分析出的中国典籍翻译的发展趋势及存在问题，笔者提出几点对策：（1）相关学者应当继续加大在典籍翻译领域的研究力度，从以文学典籍为中心，逐渐转向文学典籍、哲学典籍、科技典籍、民族典籍多中心发展研究（王宏，2021），拓宽科技典籍和民族典籍的研究范畴，持续从中挖掘研究价值，在理论研究和实践研究的广度和深度上协同发展，继续创新研究视角，拓宽研究视野，提升研究层次，丰富研究内容，激发研究活力。（2）传播与接受效果研究空间广阔，相关学者可以在不同文化背景中对各类语种和译本的传播与接受情况进行调查，紧密契合国家鼓励优秀传统文化"走出去"和"一带一路"倡议的时代精神（王宏，2021），从文化传播与交流的意义出发，探究中国优秀典籍译本在国际市场的发展，适应新时代发展的新需要。（3）有关部门应继续加大支持力度，采取具体有效措施，主动宣传与推介典籍翻译作品，不断拓展交流途径，系统地向国外介绍中国文化（许多、许钧，2015）。并出台相关政策，制定合理的报酬支付细则，鼓励更多专业译者与出版社参与到典籍翻译这一事业中来。结合"一带一路"倡议，重视典籍翻译研究，坚定文化自信，积极推动中华文化走出去。

四、结语

本文采用文献计量工具 CiteSpace 对国内近十年发表的有关典籍翻译研究期刊文献进行数据梳理与分析，揭示了近十年国内典籍翻译研究的发展趋势，从关键词聚类分析和突现关键词谱探析了研究热点和前沿动态。分析发现，我国当前的典籍翻译发展趋于稳定，发文量总体呈现上升趋势，发文期刊呈现跨学科和多领域的态势；研究热点依然聚焦在典籍翻译的内部研究，如译本研究、译者主体研究、翻译策略研究等方面；民族典籍研究发展呈现多元向好的倾向；典籍翻译的研究内容更加丰富，研究视角更加多元，研究层次逐渐提升；传播、出版等翻译研究的外部研究正受到学界的关注，传播效果研究成为新的生长点。当前，我国典籍翻译研究的演进趋势可以概括为，从关注翻译本身的内部研究逐渐转向基于社会背景对典籍翻译研究领域的拓展，是从内部研究向外部研究的逐渐转变，外部研究中的意识形态、社会、历史、文化背景等因素为未来典籍翻译的研究和发展提供新思路和新方向。但目前我国典籍翻译研究仍然面临诸多挑战，有关部门应加大支持力度，相关学者应团结协作，努力创新，为典籍翻译研究贡献力量，推动中华文化不断走出去，更有力地在世界舞台上讲好中国故事。

【参考文献】

[1] 陈梅、文军，2011．中国典籍英译国外阅读市场研究及启示——亚马逊（Amazon）图书网上中国典籍英译本的调查 [J]．外语教学 32（04）：96–100.

[2] 陈悦、陈超美、刘则渊等，2015．CiteSpace 知识图谱的方法论功能 [J]．科学学研究 33（02）：242–253.

[3] 董琇，2016．罗慕士英译《三国演义》风格之探析——以邓罗译本为对比参照 [J]．中国翻译 37（04）：93–99.

[4] 高振宇，2016．国际课程研究的现状与未来趋势——基于 Citespace 知识图谱方法的实证分析 [J]．华东师范大学学报（教育科学版）34（04）：89–97+120.

[5] 韩星、韩秋宇，2016．儒家"君子"概念英译浅析——以理雅各、韦利英译《论语》为例 [J]．外语学刊（01）：94–97.

[6] 侯剑华、胡志刚，2013．CiteSpace 软件应用研究的回顾与展望 [J]．现代情报 33（04）：99–103.

[7] 侯羽、刘泽权，2012．《红楼梦》英译本中虚义动词结构的使用与成因研究 [J]．红楼梦学刊（04）：221–236.

[8] 黄国文，2012．典籍翻译：从语内翻译到语际翻译——以《论语》英译为例 [J]．中国外语，9（06）：64–71.

[9] 霍跃红，2005．典籍英译：意义、主体和策略 [J]．外语与外语教学（09）：52–55.

[10] 李红满，2014．国际翻译学研究热点与前沿的可视化分析 [J]．中国翻译，35（02）：21–26+127.

[11] 李宁，2015．《大中华文库》国人英译本海外接受状况调查——以《孙子兵法》为例 [J]．上海翻译（02）：77–82.

[12] 刘艳春、赵长江，2017．国内民族典籍英译现状、成就、问题与对策 [J]．西藏民族大学学报（哲学社会科学版），38（02）：140–145.

[13] 刘泽权、谷香娜，2013．冷眼看世界：叙述视角关照下的《红楼梦》英译 [J]．外语学刊（02）：103–109.

[14] 刘泽权、刘超朋、朱虹，2011．《红楼梦》四个英译本的译者风格初探——基于语料库的统计与分析 [J]．中国翻译，32（01）：60–64.

[15] 宋晓春，2014．论典籍翻译中的"深度翻译"倾向——以 21 世纪初三种《中庸》英译本为例 [J]．外语教学与研究，46（06）：939–948+961.

[16] 滕雄、文军，2017．理雅各《诗经》三种英译版本的副文本研究 [J]．外语教学，38（03）：79–85.

[17] 王东波，2012．理雅各对中国文化的尊重与包容——从"译名之争"到中国经典翻译 [J]．民俗研究（01）：44–49.

[18] 王宏、刘性峰, 2015. 当代语境下的中国典籍英译研究 [J]. 中国文化研究（02）：69–79.

[19] 王宏、沈洁、王翠、刘性峰, 2021. 典籍英译新发展研究 [M]. 北京：清华大学出版社.

[20] 王晔, 2017. 苏联汉学家阿理克的《聊斋志异》俄译本研究 [J]. 国际汉学（02）：87–94205.

[21] 文军、任艳, 2012. 国内《红楼梦》英译研究回眸（1979—2010）[J]. 中国外语, 9（01）：84–93.

[22] 许多、许钧, 2015. 中华文化典籍的对外译介与传播——关于《大中华文库》的评价与思考 [J]. 外语教学理论与实践（03）：13–17+94.

[23] 许明武、王烟朦, 2017. 中国科技典籍英译研究（1997—2016）：成绩、问题与建议 [J]. 中国外语 14（02）：96–103.

[24] 许渊冲, 2017. 中国经典外译只能靠汉学家吗？[J]. 国际汉学（03）：5–9+2.

[25] 闫敏敏, 2005. 二十年来的《红楼梦》英译研究 [J]. 外语教学（04）：64–68.

[26] 杨君君、张辩辩, 2016. 从"一带一路"战略看典籍英译的重要性——以19世纪"侨居地翻译"为例 [J]. 湖北经济学院学报（人文社会科学版）, 13（10）：126–127.

[27] 杨平, 2015.《易经》在西方的翻译与传播 [J]. 外语教学与研究, 47（06）：923–934+961.

[28] 杨艳霞、王湘玲, 2019. 中外机译应用研究的可视化分析（1998—2018）[J]. 上海翻译（05）：33–39+95.

[29] 张丹丹、刘泽权, 2014.《红楼梦》乔利译本是一人所为否？——基于语料库的译者风格考察 [J]. 中国外语, 11（01）：85–93.

[30] 张继光, 2016. 国内语料库翻译学研究状况的科学知识图谱分析（1993—2014）[J]. 上海翻译（03）：34–40+61+93.

[31] 张萍、王宏, 2018. 从《诗经》三译本看理雅各宗教观的转变 [J]. 国际汉学（02）：52–57+205.

[32] 张晓雪, 2017.《论语》英译研究热点、领域构成及展望——基于CNKI学术期刊2001至2017年文献的共词可视化分析 [J]. 上海翻译（05）：69–74+95.

Visual Analysis of the Overview and Trends of Research on Translation of Chinese Classics (2011—2021) Based on Bibliometrics

Qufu Normal University   XIE Wenqi

Abstract: This paper takes the academic journal literature of translation of Chinese classics from 2011 to 2021 collected in China National Knowledge Infrastructure (CNKI) as the data source, with the help of CiteSpace and traditional bibliometric methods, draws a statistical map of research on the translation of Chinese classics in the past 10 years, a distribution map of journal sources, a knowledge map of keyword clustering, a timeline evolution map. The visualization and data analysis reveal the development trend of research on the translation of Chinese classics in the past ten years from the overall trend and distribution of publications, the evolution of research hotspots, and the analysis of literature frontier dynamics. The research hotspots and frontier dynamics from keyword clustering analysis and burst term spectrum are also discussed, aiming to help the development of research on the translation of Chinese classics and promote Chinese culture to go out continuously.

Keywords: Translation of Chinese classics; Research hotspots; CiteSpace; Visualization

《2024年政府工作报告》的文体特征和译文分析[①]

重庆文理学院　陈友勋[②]

【摘　要】本文结合语料数据，从句子数量、词汇数量、平均句长、词语密度等方面对《2024年政府工作报告》的中英文版分别进行了详细的文体分析，认为它不同于其他以说理见长的政论文，而是兼顾了口语汇报和书面表达的双重特征。其英文版则很好地保留了中文版的文体特征，但在词语、句子层面都出现了明显的译文显化倾向，而这也是得到学界公认的翻译共性之一。

【关键词】政府工作报告；译文显化；平均句长；翻译共性

一、引言

对于语言与政治的关系，田海龙（2002：23）曾做出精辟的总结："语言与政治的密切联系可以从两个方面进行研究，一方面是研究语言的政治问题，一方面是研究政治的语言问题。"二者的关系在翻译领域就表现为"翻译的政治"和"政治的翻译"（谢旭升，2018：1），尤其以时政翻译为典型代表。至于时政翻译，一般认为它是以国内外权威机构、主流媒体、专家学者等发布的政治评述、文献及相关译本为主要对象，涉及党政会议记录、领导人重要讲话、领袖著作、政府工作报告等文件实体，其翻译作用不可小视，正如习近平总书记（2014：162）总结的那样，优秀

[①] 基金项目：本文系教育部产学合作协同育人项目《以人工智能技术助力高校人才培养——外语学院翻译实训平台建设》（项目编号：230904647183543）和教育部产学合作协同育人项目《基于信息技术的翻译教学实践基地建设》（项目编号：230906342184930）的部分研究成果。

[②] 陈友勋（1975—　），男，重庆永川人，副教授，硕士，主要从事翻译理论与实践研究。

的时政翻译能够"提高国际话语权""加强国际传播能力建设，精心构建对外话语体系，增强对外话语的创造力、感召力、公信力"。当然，鉴于时政翻译的这些特殊性和重要性，它必然要求译者具有较强的政治敏锐性，不但能够坚持本国的文化取向和政治导向，而且不局限于语言转换表象，善于将政治内涵融入外语文本，将其不折不扣地传递给译文读者（龙新元、李秋霞，2020）。在我国，对时政翻译颇有研究的专家学者主要包括过家鼎（外交部）、贾毓玲（中央编译局）、王平兴（新华社）和杨明星（郑州大学中国外交话语研究中心）。其中杨明星曾发表多篇文章对时政材料的翻译原则进行讨论。他基于时政文本的特殊性和奈达的"等效"理论，认为在这一领域，译者应当遵循一套复合性的翻译标准，即"政治等效＋意象再现"（杨明星、齐静静，2018）。从实践效果而言，应当说杨明星的这些观点对时政翻译带来了积极影响，在理论层面具有指导价值。

最近，"中国网双语文件库"公布了李强总理在两会上作的《2024年政府工作报告》中英对照版，为我们学习和探讨时政翻译提供了宝贵的资料。下面本文将结合该双语报告在词语和句子层面的对照特征，剖析译者进行时政翻译时要遵循的理论原则以及实践技巧。

二、原文特征

（一）宏观特征

首先，为了让读者对政府工作报告的语体特征有一个更明确的认识，我们把2021—2024年的政府工作报告的原文都导入雪人CAT标准版，统计出它们的总字数和句子数量；再将这四篇文章上传至"微词云"，获得它们的词语总数和特征词数。有了这些原始数据之后，我们进行简单的比例计算，就得到了它们的语料统计数据（表1）：

表1 2021—2024年政府工作报告的词句统计

类型 年份	总字数/个	总句数/句	每句平均字数/个	词语总数/个	特征词数/个	每句平均词语/个	词语密度/%
2024年	15 432	511	30.20	5 743	2 036	11.24	35.45
2023年	16 104	512	31.45	5 799	2 096	11.33	36.14

（续表）

类型 年份	总字数/个	总句数/句	每句平均字数/个	词语总数/个	特征词数/个	每句平均词语/个	词语密度/%
2022年	15 199	529	28.73	5 591	2 065	10.57	36.93
2021年	15 601	503	31.02	5 740	2 079	11.41	36.22

注释：

表中的其他数据都很简单，基本能够见文知意，但对于特征词数和词语密度则需要稍作解释。这两处数据都是借助"微词云"获取的。而"微词云"是把一篇文章的所有词语去重之后得到词语数量，或者我们类比西方的语料分析术语，可以说词语总数就是中文分词之后的形符数量（Token：包括重复的词语），而特征词数就是类符数量（Type：不重复的词语），至于词语密度当然就相当于西方语料分析中的类符/形符比（TTR: Type/Token Ratio），它能反映文本使用词汇的丰富程度。

分析：

我们从这些宏观统计数据中可以看出：政府工作报告作为每年例行的最重要时政文章，其长度一般控制在 17 000 字左右，大约包括 510 个句子，平均每句约为 30 个汉字，11 个词语，全篇文章的词语密度则在 35% 左右。

为了更好地提炼政府工作报告的文体特征，我们可以先在中文语篇内部进行横向比较。首先，政府工作报告的平均每句字数为 30 个汉字，而根据黄自然（2018）对 120 万汉字的语料统计分析，就整体水平而言，汉语的平均句长为 10.91 个汉字，其中最高频句长区间为 6～8 个汉字。这个结论和刘宓庆的观点不谋而合，他认为汉语句子的最佳长度为 7～12 字，超过此长度往往会给理解带来困难（刘宓庆，1990：190）。如此一来，我们发现政府工作报告的句子长度大大超过汉语表达的平均水平，已经体现出明显的书面语特征，而它较高的词汇密度（35% 以上）似乎也从另一个侧面印证了这一特征。

（二）微观分析

然而，鉴于统计均值容易掩盖某些重要细节，笔者又对 2024 年政府工作报告原文的每句字数进行了详细统计，并将其导入电子表格按升级排列，还生成了相应的柱状图（图1）。

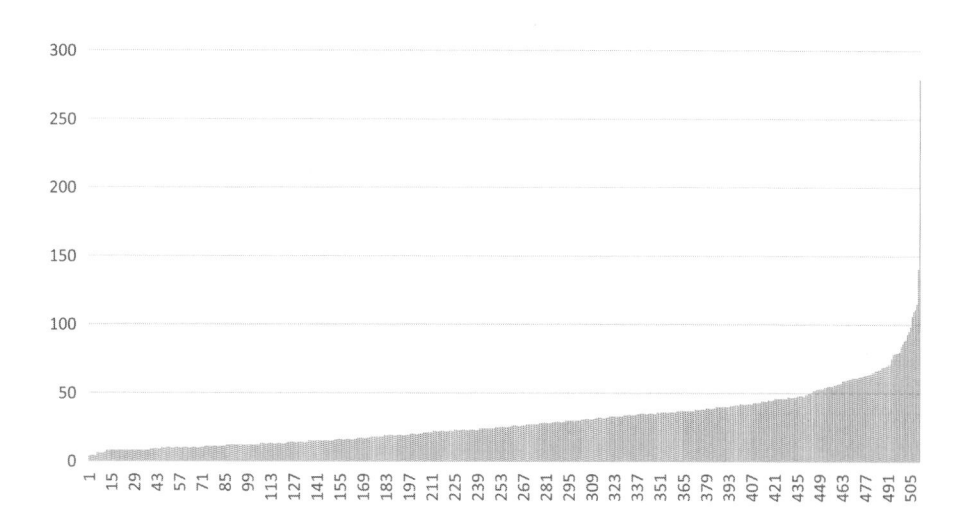

图 1 《2024 年政府工作报告》中文版的每句字数柱状图

结果发现：在 511 个句子当中，最短的句子只有 4 个汉字（称呼词：各位代表），内容不超过 11 个汉字的竟然有 85 句（主要表现为小标题、省略主语句以及动词短语句），这些短句在 2024 年政府工作报告的所有句子中占比为 16.63%。如果我们以每句平均字数为分水岭进行统计，会发现其中较短句子的数量略多于较长句子的数量：4～30 个汉字的共 302 句（59.10%）；31～279 个汉字的 209 句（40.90%）。也就是说，2024 年政府工作报告的句式其实长短交错，总体上具有时政文章严谨精准的书面语特征，但其中仍有不少句子和词汇表达，比较短小，符合我们的日常表达习惯，从而体现出政府工作报告面向全国代表进行直接宣讲的口语特征。张绍麒、李明（1986）曾统计政论文的平均句长为 67.01 个汉字，而 2024 年政府工作报告的平均句长只有 30.20 个汉字，与之相差甚远，更接近他们所统计的、大量使用口语和短句的小说的平均句长（28.7 个汉字）。综上所述，政府工作报告不同于其他纯粹以说理见长的政论文，而是兼顾了会议汇报的口语交流特征，注重在不失庄重的前提下发挥其呼吁、宣传功能。

三、翻译技巧

沿着同样的思路，我们对官方提供的 2024 年政府工作报告英文版也进行了语料分析，并试图从中总结出它所采用的主要翻译技巧。

（一）词语层面

下面列出的是我们对英文版进行语料统计的最终结果（表 2）。

表 2 《2024 年政府工作报告》英文版的语料分析

类别	总词数 / 个	特征词数 / 个	句子总数 / 句	每句词语数 / 个	词语密度 /%
原文	5 743	2 036	511	11.24	35.45
译文	13 946	2 298	638	21.86	16.48%

同样，我们也统计了英文版的每句单词数量，将其导入电子表格进行升序排列，并生成相应的柱状图（图 2）。

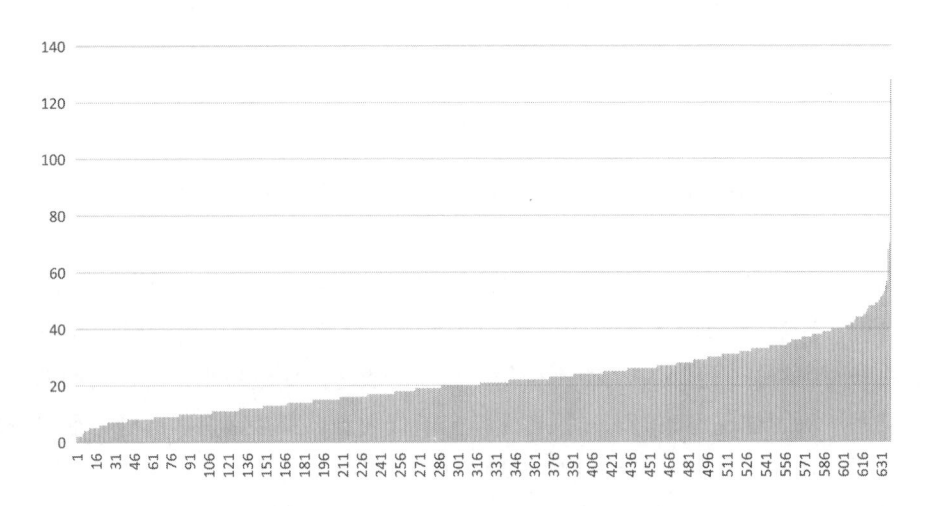

图 2 《2024 年政府工作报告》英文版的每句字数柱状图

分析如下：英语版一共 638 句，其中 372 个句子包括 2～22 个词语，占比 58.31%；剩下的 266 个句子包括 23～128 个单词，占比 41.69%。如果以每句平均词数为界，译文中较短的句子也是略多于较长的句子，句式上属于长短交错，这和原文的风格保持了一致。我们再来看译文的每句词语数量，即所谓的"平均句长（average sentence length）"。Olohan（2004）认为，与词语密度一样，平均句长也是反映译者风格的一般性标记。至于英语平均句长的具体数值，《写作之书》的作者保拉·拉罗克（Paula LaRocque, 2019）认为，一篇流畅文章中的句子的平均长度应该在 20 个单词左右。这和合众国际社提供的数据基本一致，后者认为，英语中一个标准句子大约包括 17 个单词；如果英语句子中的单词超过 20 个，就变得有些难读；如果英语句子中的单词上升到 25 个，则已经进入难句的范畴了。如此看来，2024 年政府工作报告译文的平均句长为 21.86，在英文中算总体流畅、但略微偏难的范畴，所以在这一点上，也和我们前面对原文的分析一致。

接下来我们结合译例具体分析，看英语版本在翻译重要关键词时采取了哪些主要方法，以及取得的表达效果如何。在这里，我们主要根据《经济观察网》列举的 41 个关键词，并在此基础上剔除往年出现过的表达，筛选出今年才出现的新词汇，将相应的英译表达以及其中使用的主要翻译方法和技巧列表如下（表3）。

表 3 《2024 年政府工作报告》新增关键词的双语表达

关键词	英译表达	主要使用的翻译方法和技巧
新质生产力	new quality productive forces	直译
超长期特别国债	ultra-long special treasury bonds	直译
结构性减税降费	structural tax and fee reduction	直译
低空经济	the low-altitude economy	直译
一揽子化债方案	a package of measures to defuse risks caused by existing debts	意译：增词解释
赤字率	the deficit-to-GDP ratio	直译
"投资中国"品牌	make China a favored destination for foreign investment	意译
第三支柱养老保险	third-pillar pension plans	直译
长期护理保险制度	insurance schemes for long-term care	直译
人工智能+	an AI Plus initiative	直译
中小企业专精特新发展	use specialized and sophisticated technologies to produce novel and unique products	意译：增词解释
银发经济	the silver economy	直译
基础教育扩优提质行动	upgrade basic education	意译：减词翻译
"三个区分开来"	the "three distinctions,"*(The three distinctions refer to those between errors caused by lack of experience in pilot reforms and deliberate violations of discipline and law; between errors made in conducting experiments that are not explicitly restricted by higher-level authorities and arbitrary violations of discipline and law despite higher-level authorities' explicit prohibition; and between unwitting errors made in pursuing development and violations of discipline and law for personal gains.)	直译+意译（增词翻译、尾注解释）

我们发现《2024年政府工作报告》英语版对中文关键词还是以直译为主，比如"新质生产力"就直接表述为"new quality productive forces"。究其原因，首先，这是因为中文关键词大部分都是专有名词，其结构紧凑、表达严谨、风格朴实，倾向于平铺直叙，很少采取文学修辞手法，因此不容易产生歧义，符合"直译优先"的翻译原则。其次，这也间接反映了我们越来越明显的文化自信，即在介绍具有中国特色的事物时，我们不再一味无原则地迁就老外，总是优先考虑他们的思维习惯和表达风格，而是让他们有意识地学会适应中国的语言特色和文化特征，这也是大国形象在语言领域的塑造。最后，则是考虑受众因素。能对政府工作报告感兴趣并阅读的外国人，一般都是政治、经济领域的专家学者，在这方面有丰富的背景知识和实践经验，其中甚至很多就是"中国通"，他们对我国的政治、经济术语早就耳熟能详，因此翻译的时候以直译为主，保持原汁原味，反而更符合这些读者的口味。

当然，也有少数关键词的英译是采取意译方法，翻译技巧上则采取增词解释，这方面的例子包括"一揽子化债方案"（a package of measures to defuse risks caused by existing debts）和"中小企业专精特新发展"（use specialized and sophisticated technologies to produce novel and unique products）。我们可以看出，这样的关键词在中文中是典型的简化说法，其完整表达由于在日常表达中高频使用而催生出了这种简单的缩略形式，虽然在汉语的语言环境中已经司空见惯，无须解释，但在英译版本中，鉴于外国读者不一定熟悉这些缩略形式背后隐藏的完整意义，所以保险起见，还是采取了解释性的翻译手法。但是直接在文中增词解释有一个前提条件，就是这样的解释不是太长，不至于对译文读者的阅读习惯造成太大干扰，甚至完全中断他们的阅读思维。

然而，如果在翻译关键词时，英语提供的解释说明的确太长，真的有可能出现上面所担心的极端负面效果，那我们就只能采取"直译＋注释"的形式，比如表3中列举的最后一个关键词"三个区分开来"，其译文就属于这种情况：它是在直译的基础上，又采取了"增词翻译、尾注解释"的处理方式，具体表达该缩略说法的完整含义，因此从基本的翻译方法上可以归类为"直译＋意译"。

当然，对于像政府工作报告这样严肃的时政文章，翻译其中的关键词肯定要做到慎之又慎。我们从上述关键词的英文表达也可以看出，它们绝大多数都符合杨明星等人提出的翻译标准："政治等效＋意象再现"。比如，"银发经济"被翻译成了"the silver economy"，而没有采取另一种在欧美较为流行的表达"the gray-hair economy"，是因为"gray-hair"（白发）无论在中英文化中都是衰老孱弱的象征，而"silver hair"（银发）则是一种更积极乐观的比喻。虽然同样是以头发颜色来象征老年人，但后者更能体现党和政府对老年人的关注，所以该措辞显示出为他们创造一个宜居社会以及提振社会经济发展的决心和毅力，具有很强的政治意义。不过，在上述关键词的译文当中，把"'投资中国'品牌"意译成"make China a favored destination for foreign investment"，应当说强调力度还不够，因为该关键词出现的上下文是"加强外商投资服务保障，打造'投资中国'品牌。"其中"投资中国"放在引号当中就是为了特别强调，显示了我们对吸引外资的高度重视，希望他们在选择投资对象时能条件反射式地想起中国，就犹如有一条宣传口号在头脑中回响一样。因此此处若采取直译，将其表达成"make 'invest in China' a brand in attracting foreign capitals"，似乎效果更好。

（二）句子翻译

我们在前面已经统计出《2024年政府工作报告》原文和译文的句子数量是511∶638，但这只是依据形式特征（表明结束标志的标点符号）统计出来的自然句的数量。事实上，在整理双语对照文件时，如果仍然仅根据自然句的数量来统计原文和译文之间的对应关系就显得有些粗糙，因为很多自然句虽然形式上只是一句，但从语法关系上分析，可能是两句或者更多，比如英文版有这样一个自然句"We have a long way to go in protecting and improving the environment, and weak links in workplace safety should not be ignored."，它其实是用并列连词"and"连接的两个简单句，所以应当算成两句。此外，我们在整理双语对照文件时，还发现原文和译文之间并非简单的一一对应关系，相反，很多时候，它们会呈现一对多、多对一和多对多等复杂关系。最终，我们把原文和译文一共整理出488处句级对应，并将每处句级对应中的原文-译文数量统计如下（表4）。

表4 《2024年政府工作报告》原文和译文之间的句级对应数量关系

对应	1—1	1—2	1—3	1—4	1—5	1—6	1—7	1—8	1—9	2—1	2—2	2—3	3—1
数量	223	135	67	22	6	5	1	1	1	10	11	5	1
比例	45.70%	27.66%	13.73%	4.51%	1.23%	1.02%	0.20%	0.20%	0.20%	2.05%	2.25%	1.02%	0.20%

从上表可以看出，《2024年政府工作报告》英文版在翻译句子时主要采取一一对应译法（原文、译文句级数量对应关系为1—1，占比45.7%）和拆句译法（原文、译文句级数量对应关系从1—2到1—9，占比48.77%），并且后者的比例还略高于前者。至于合句译法（原文、译文句级数量对应关系包括2—1、2—2、2—3以及3—1），加起来也才27处，占比为5.53%。

41

这些统计数据和原文的文体特征以及两种语言的个性特征基本吻合。首先，根据前文的分析，政府工作报告在文体上具有口语交流的特征，其平均句长接近于大量使用口语和短句的小说，所以整篇报告中较短句子占比很高。而对于原文中的简单短句，在翻译中的常规操作就是采取直接对译，反映到本例中就是 1—1 的句级对应在整个英译本中的占比高达 45.7%。这方面的例子如下。

例 1：
2023 年工作回顾
A Review of Our Work in 2023
技术合同成交额增长 28.6%。
The volume of contracted technology transactions grew by 28.6 percent.

其次，政府工作报告的原文是中文，属于典型的意合语言，不但习惯在语境中省略某些表达成分，而且喜欢以流水句的形式把大量意义融在一起，因此翻译中文长句往往难度很高，一般在英语中只能采取断句翻译，才能把原文的意思交代清楚，同时照顾英语的形合特征——力求让整个译文的表述逻辑清晰、主次分明。在前文的分析中，我们看到《2024 年政府工作报告》原文中的较长句子几乎占到一半的比例，因此其英语版中有 48.77% 的句子采取拆句译法也就不足为奇了。这里略举一例（句级对应数量关系为 1—3）。

例 2：
从国际看，世界经济复苏乏力，地缘政治冲突加剧，保护主义、单边主义上升，外部环境对我国发展的不利影响持续加大。
Globally, the economic recovery was sluggish. Geopolitical conflicts became more acute, protectionism and unilateralism were on the rise, and the external environment exerted a more adverse impact on China's development.

合句翻译的比例极少，因为要把几个汉语句子合在一起翻译，其前提相当严格：一是必须每句都很短小，句意单一；二是几个句子之间的意思具有非常紧密的逻辑关系。下面是一个合句翻译的例子（句级对应数量关系为 3—1）。

例 3：
加强重要江河湖库生态保护治理。持续推进长江十年禁渔。实施生物多样性保护重大工程。

We will promote the ecological conservation and improvement of important rivers, lakes, and reservoirs, continue to enforce the 10-year fishing ban on the Yangtze River, and carry out major biodiversity conservation programs. ①

(三）译文风格

如果我们把《2024 年政府工作报告》原文和译文的语料数据进行一个对比（表5），就能明显地发现英文版相对于中文版而言，具有一个显著的风格特征，即译文显化（explicitation）。

表 5 《2024 年政府工作报告》中英文语料的对比分析

	词语总数/个	特征词数/个	句子总数/句	每句词数/个	词语密度/%
原文	5743	2036	511	11.24	35.45
译文	13946	2298	638	21.86	16.48

在表 5 中，英文版无论是句子总数、词语总数、特征词数还是每句词数，都远远超过了中文版的统计数值，其中词语总数甚至差距翻倍。造成这些差异的直接原因已经在前文中进行了分析：比如词语层面，英文版对一些关键词采取了直译＋增词解释的方式；而在句子层面，分句译法也无疑大大增加了英文版的表达长度。

当然，译文显化现象早已存在，Baker 和 Chesterman 等著名学者甚至将其列为翻译共性之一，并深入探讨了造成译文显化的原因，比如 Vinay & Darbelnet（1958/1995：342）就明确提出，显化是指"在译语中，将原语中的隐含信息加以明示（的过程或结果），此类信息在原语文本中可以根据语境或情境获得"。Nida & Taber（1969：163–168）则对显化做了进一步分析，提出翻译中的信息涉及长度（length）和难度（difficulty）两个维度，译者通常会增加冗余度（redundancy）以降低难度，使接受者可以更容易地理解译文，从而客观上造成译文篇幅增加，所以优秀的译文往往或多或少会比原文更长。

鉴于前面已经列举了不少关于译文长度增加的例子，下面再摘录一个关于译文降低阅读难度的例子。

---

① 本文将此类译文视为简单句：只有一个主语，但包括三个并列谓语（promote、continue、carry out）。

例 4：

国家实验室体系建设有力推进。关键核心技术攻关成果丰硕，航空发动机、燃气轮机、第四代核电机组等高端装备研制取得长足进展，人工智能、量子技术等前沿领域创新成果不断涌现。

We made major headway in establishing a system of national laboratories and achieved fruitful results in developing core technologies in key fields. Substantial progress was made in the research and development (R&D) of high-end equipment, such as aircraft engines, gas turbines, and 4th-generation nuclear power units. A stream of innovations emerged in frontier areas such as artificial intelligence (AI) and quantum technology.

相对于中文版，英文版的阅读难度明显降低。首先，原文是两句，译文已经扩展成了三句。其次，原文第二句在结构上属于总分关系（关键核心技术攻关＝高端装备研制＋前沿领域创新成果），而分说部分覆盖了两个主题，并且每个主题有隐含的逻辑关系（航空发动机、燃气轮机、第四代核电机组等是高端装备研制的具体实例；人工智能、量子技术是前沿领域创新成果的具体实例），而这些信息在译文中则以独立句子（三个句子）以及衔接词汇（两个 such as）的方式得以明确体现，省去读者自己思索的麻烦，达到一读即懂的效果。

四、结语

本文结合大量的语料数据，从句子数量、词汇数量、平均句长、词语密度等方面对《2024 年政府工作报告》的中英文版分别进行了详细的文体分析，认为政府工作报告不同于其他纯粹以说理见长的政论文，而是兼顾了会议汇报的口语交流特征，注重在不失庄重的前提下发挥其呼吁、宣传功能，其英文版也很好地保留了这一文体特征。然而，鉴于中英版本在语言、文化方面存在巨大的语际差异，《2024 年政府工作报告》英文版不可避免地表现出了译文显化特征，这在词语、句子层面都有明显表现。尽管本文限于篇幅，未能联系前几年的更多双语版本的政府工作报告进行验证，但译文显化既然作为学界公认的翻译共性之一，在前几年的英文版本中应当也同样会有鲜明表现。

【参考文献】

[1] 黄自然，2018. 以"字"为单位的汉语平均句长与句长分布研究[J]. 齐齐哈尔大学学报（哲学社会科学版）（1）：133–138.

[2] 经济观察网. 41个关键词，经观带你读懂2024年政府工作报告[EB/OL].（2024-03-05）[2024-03-22］. https://www.eeo.com.cn/2024/0305/642015.shtml

[3] 刘宓庆，1990. 现代翻译理论[M]. 南昌：江西教育出版社.

[4] 龙新元、李秋霞，2020. "政治等效＋认知趋同"：认知翻译观视阈下的政治文本翻译研究[J]. 天津外国语大学学报，27（5）：104–120+161.

[5] 田海龙，2002. 政治语言研究：评述与思考[J]. 外语教学（1）：23–29.

[6] 习近平，2014. 习近平谈治国理政[M]. 北京：外文出版社.

[7] 谢旭升，2018. 翻译的政治性与有效性[J]. 翻译界（2）：1–3.

[8] 杨明星、齐静静，2018. 外交修辞的复合性翻译标准："政治等效＋审美再现"——以国家领导人外交演讲古诗文为例[J]. 中国外语，15（6）：89–96+109.

[9] 张绍麒、李明，1986. 小说与政论文言语风格异同的计算机统计（实验报告）[J]. 天津师大学报，6（4）：82–86.

[10] 中国网双语文件库. 2024年政府工作报告（全文）[EB/OL].（2024-03-14）[2024-03-22］. http://www.china.org.cn/chinese/2024-03/14/content_117057714.htm

[11] LaRocque, P., 2019. 写作之书[M]. 张铮，译. 南昌：江西人民出版社.

[12] Nida, E., & Taber, C. (1969). *The theory and practice of translation*[M]. Netherlands: E. J. Brill.

[13] Olohan, M. (2004). *Introducing Corpora in Translation Studies*[M]. New York: Routledge.

[14] Vinay, Jean-Paul and Jean Darbelnet. (1958, 1995). *Comparative Stylistics of French and English. A methodology for translation*[M]. Translated and edited by Juan C. Sager and M. J. Hamel. Amsterdam/Philadelphia: John Benjamins Publishing Company.

Stylistic Features and Translation Analysis of the "Report on the Work of the Government in 2024"

Chongqing University of Arts and Sciences Chen Youxun

Abstract: This article, in combination with corpus data, conducts a detailed stylistic analysis of the Chinese and English versions of the "Report on the Work of the

Government in 2024" respectively from aspects such as the number of sentences, the number of words, the average sentence length, and the word density. It is believed that this report is different from other political essays that are good at reasoning, but takes into account the dual characteristics of oral reporting and written expression. The English version well preserves the stylistic features of the Chinese version, but there is an obvious tendency of explicitation in the translation at the word and sentence levels, which is also one of the translation universals recognized by the academic community.

Keywords: Report on the Work of the Government; Explicitation in Translation; Average Sentence Length; Translation Universals

《丰乳肥臀》俄译本读者接受研究

俄罗斯人民友谊大学　王小琳[①]

【摘　要】2012年莫言获得诺贝尔文学奖，此后，其作品在俄罗斯开始正式译介，第二本被译为俄语的长篇小说《丰乳肥臀》于2013年首次出版，2023年再次出版。本文从文学翻译视角出发，结合阅读心理学，采用定量和定性研究相结合的方式，分析82位读者对该书的评分、评价、类比、推荐等数据，考察俄罗斯读者对《丰乳肥臀》俄译本的接受情况，旨在为中国文学在其他文化背景读者中的传播提供借鉴与参考。

【关键词】《丰乳肥臀》；俄语翻译；读者接受；阅读心理

一、引言

　　1988年中国导演张艺谋改编自长篇小说《红高粱家族》的电影《红高粱》在德国柏林国际电影节上首映，这对于莫言的作品在海外的传播是第一个里程碑事件，标志着国际社会开始认识中国作家莫言。随后，《红高粱家族》英文版（1989）、日文版（1989）、法文版（1990）相继出版，而俄文版于2018年才正式出版，也就是说，改编作品影视化并没有引起俄罗斯文学界和出版商的关注。2012年，莫言成为诺贝尔文学奖得主，这一事件成为俄罗斯文学界和出版方开始对其作品进行译介的决定性因素，此前，仅有部分作品段落和一些短篇小说出现在中国文学作品集和一些非文学杂志上，正如俄罗斯汉学家和译者叶果夫所说："2012年10月以前，除了一些研究当代中国文学的汉学家以外，谁也不认识这位著名的作家。"

[①] 王小琳（1997—　），俄罗斯人民友谊大学语言学博士，研究方向：历史比较语言学、类型语言学及对比语言学。邮箱：m18350272113_1@163.com。

（Егоров，2014）因此，中国文学在俄罗斯读者心中的弱势地位也成为中国文学作品在俄出版传播的极大阻碍，圣彼得堡 Hyperion 出版社社长 С. Смоляков 曾表示，莫言的小说《酒国》和《丰乳肥臀》在莫言获得诺贝尔文学奖很早之前就已经翻译完毕，但却没能找到出版社出版（Смоляков，2021）。2012 年，第一本长篇小说《酒国》俄译本被出版，这本讽刺中国官场蛀虫和黑暗现象的小说故事性不强，在叶果夫翻译的 446 页的俄译本中，共出现 200 多处注解，可见从译者的体感来看，需要额外解读的文化要素数量庞大，但注解越多就意味着篇幅越长，对于出版商来说，这种做法会导致出版物利润下降，因此，注解数量需控制在一定范围之内。除了文化差异，主人公幻想的大量的醉酒场景描写更是减弱了读者对于阅读的信心和接受程度，从读者反馈来看，读者对于这本书的接受程度是两极分化的，"一半读者欣喜异常，另一半说是垃圾，浪费时间"（Егоров，2014）。《丰乳肥臀》是莫言第二本被翻译成俄语出版的长篇小说，相较于《酒国》来说，这本小说故事性更强，曾一度被认为是莫言获得诺贝尔文学奖的代表作之一。

鉴于此，本文结合阅读心理学视角，研究《丰乳肥臀》俄译本在俄罗斯读者中的接受程度，从读者的评分、评价以及对该作品的定位角度进行数据整理和分析，总结读者在阅读该作品后的心理及所产生的对中国文学，即莫言文学作品形成的主观印象，为中国文学海外传播研究提供参考。

二、《丰乳肥臀》在俄语世界的传播和翻译

由叶果夫翻译的《丰乳肥臀》俄译本至今在俄罗斯共出版过两版，第一版于 2013 年由圣彼得堡 Амфора 出版社出版，文本总页数共计 831 页。这一版本的封面配图颇具迷惑性和视觉冲击力，封面总共包含 6 个元素，占据页面篇幅最大的元素是女性的胸部和臀部，和小说题目《丰乳肥臀》字面含义相呼应，其次是作者的姓名俄译"Мо Янь"，"18+"的年龄限制从分布位置来看，为封面上第三重要的元素，而"2012 年诺贝尔奖"和小说题目"Большая грудь, широкий зад"分别位于封面的最上端和最下端，虽然字体和文字大小相同，但从通常为"自上至下"的阅读习惯来看，位于页面上端的信息比下端信息更重要，出版商信息则占据最小的位置。对于这一版俄译本的封面设计和装帧风格，叶果夫曾表示他个人难以认同，无法接受，但却难以改变出版方的想法和做法（王树福，2013）。第二版俄译本于 2023 年由莫斯科 Эксмо 出版社出版，总页数 832 页，这一版的封面设计则摆脱了以敏感元素来吸引读者眼球的设计，封面共包含五个元素，占据篇幅位置最大的是极具中

国风格和时代特色的元素：母亲右手抱着男孩，左手举着麦穗，身后是粮食生产基地和工厂，头上是红灯笼，这些图案元素更符合小说真正的内涵和时代背景。小说题目位于图片上面，在文字元素中处于第一位，而作者姓名和"18+"的标识分别位于题目正上方和正下方，"诺贝尔奖得主"这一宣传性信息则位于封面右下角，处于最弱位置。从这一变化可以看出，经过时间的沉淀和俄罗斯读者对莫言的了解，出版方已经无须用传递错误的干扰信息的方式来达到推广的目的，而逐渐回归文学的本真。

图 1 左图为 2013 版俄译本封面，右图为 2023 版俄译本封面

三、俄语读者接受度

本文共选取 82 个《丰乳肥臀》俄译本读者书评，样本来自俄罗斯图书推荐门户网站 LiveLib.ru（《Живая библиотека》《Лайвлиб》），该网站具备读者书评收录、文学新闻发布及新书推荐等功能。

（一）阅读原因

从莫言作品在俄罗斯的传播历程来看，莫言在俄罗斯文学界和俄罗斯读者眼中是一位"新作家"，读者选择阅读莫言主要出于以下三个原因：（1）了解诺贝尔文学奖得主及作品；（2）阅读活动任务或推荐；（3）对中国文学／莫言感兴趣。毫无疑问，诺贝尔奖是一篇最成功的"宣传"，"莫言像一颗流星一样冲进了俄罗斯文学苍穹。大量的、各种各样的反响几乎爆棚了"（Егоров，2014）。相当一部分读者由于该奖项对莫言给予的肯定而想要了解他的作品。一部分读者对莫言获得诺贝尔奖表示认可，认为"他（莫言）完全值得获得，他书写了自己祖国的历史，而他的书也不是只有中国读者可以阅读"。有的读者则对作品本身完全没有兴趣——"选择这本书是因为想了解为什么作者会获得诺贝尔文学奖……非常失望，我必须强迫自己读下去，不管是语言还是所描写的历史，我都不喜欢……""这部作品只为对其本身感兴趣的读者而作，诺奖并不能说明什么"。此外，有32位读者因为参加Флэшмоб—2015，Долгая прогулка 2015等阅读活动而阅读该作品，出于自身兴趣或随机选择阅读的读者仅占极小比例，有读者在研究亚洲文学的背景下选择阅读莫言，将其看作亚洲文学的代表作家之一。从阅读原因占比来看，61%的读者出于主观意愿自发阅读，39%的俄罗斯读者在阅读活动框架内被动阅读，而被动接受的作品在一定程度上本就不符合某些读者的兴趣和阅读偏好，因此，在这部分读者中消极评价出现的频率大于自发进行阅读的读者。

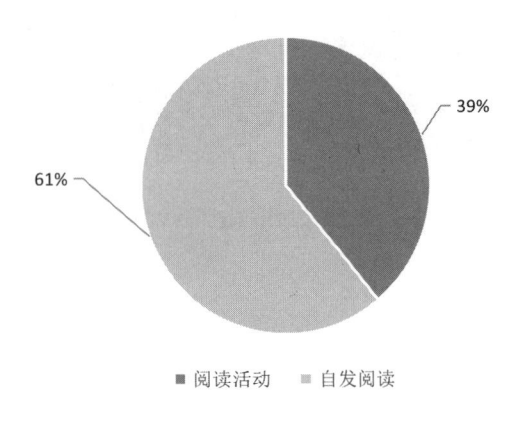

图 2　读者阅读原因

（二）读者评分

数据显示，在82位读者中，总共有34%（28人）对《丰乳肥臀》给出3.5分及更低评分，66%（54人）给出4分及更高评分。根据俄罗斯五分制评定法，5分为优秀，4分为良好，3分为及格，2分为不及格，1分为极差。基于该评定标准，15.8%读者认为该作品"不及格及更差"，84.2%读者认为作品达到"及格或更好的水平"，也就是说，绝大多数俄罗斯读者认可该作品。13.4%的读者给出评价为"极差",而 23.2% 的读者给出"优秀"的评价,从这两项较为极端的评价来看,俄罗斯读者对《丰乳肥臀》的认可多于否定。此外,一些读者对于自己的"不理解"或者"不喜欢"持怀疑态度,评价模棱两可,在主观上不接受该作品,但客观上认为该作品技艺高超,例如,"我的主观评价是 3.5 分,但我怀疑问题出在我身上,而不是作品上""我的评价是中立的,因为这毕竟是诺贝尔奖作品……毕竟我还是喜欢这个家族的历史",由此可见,诺贝尔文学奖对于作品和作者本人的加持作用也影响着部分读者的评价。

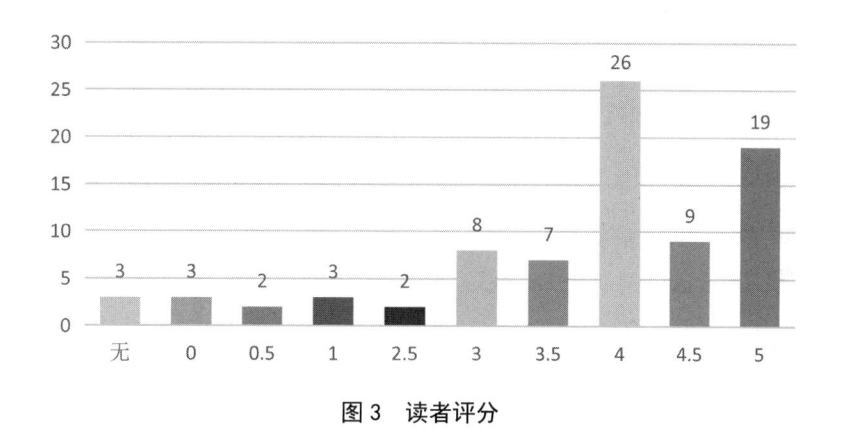

图 3 读者评分

表 1 读者评分占比

读者评分	占比 / %
≦1分,极差	13.4
2<X<3,不及格与及格之间	2.4
3≦X<4,及格与良好之间	18.3
4≦X<5,良好与优秀之间	42.7
X=5,优秀	23.2

(三) 读者评价

在读者的积极评价中,出现频率最高的关键词主要和作品内容相关,"有趣""内容丰富"等关键词共被提及 14 次,10 位读者认为作者"技艺高超""风格独特""值得获奖"。在描述主观阅读感受时,读者极少使用带有绝对积极色彩的形容词,只有 4 位读者明确表示"喜欢""阅读愉快";3 位读者认为作品读起来"轻松""文字易懂";1 位读者写道:"作者的语言和相当讽刺的幽默感使阅读这本书成为一次穿越时空的迷人旅程,阅读的过程是愉快的,我并不觉得这本书很长。"而在消极评价中,直观地描述整体感受的人明显增多,7 位读者表示"不喜欢"。5 位读者认为"主角/人物令人厌恶",有读者写道——"我不喜欢这本书,即便把它当作小说或带有讽刺含义的作品。阅读主人公的思想和生活也令人厌恶,尤其是书的后半部分,只描写主角金童""超自然的日常生活场景和人物的残酷命运使我无法享受阅读这本书……文中缺少吸引力的人物是主要负面因素"。5 位读者表示"阅读过程不愉快""奇怪的小说人物,还有这本书本身以及人物关系……一切都让我感到陌生、不理解和反感。说实话,对于在这本书上浪费的时间让我感觉可惜""尽管作者技艺高超,但是大量的血腥的细节描写和扭曲的现象击垮了我。我最近可能不会继续阅读莫言的书或者中国文学……和日本文学相比,我更喜欢日本文学";9 位读者表示在阅读的过程中产生了"生理不适""感觉恶心",而主要原因在于"画面血腥""暴力""变态",小说中充斥着集中的大量的负面因素和丑陋的场景描写,而作为主要线索的"女性胸部"也使读者产生抵触情绪,"对于女性胸部的不断赞美和描述令人厌烦""主角对于女性胸部的执着让人反感"。在消极评价中,10 位读者明确表示题目和封面引起反感,认为"标题具有挑衅性""标题暗示着色情""愚蠢的标题和封面掩盖了好内容";19 位读者表示"阅读困难""文章冗长"或"很难理解",庞大的篇幅使异国文学和极具个性的创作方法更加复杂,拉长了阅读时长,同时也在挑战着读者的承受限度。心理学研究表明,阅读文学作品会提高读者的认知共情能力,包括认知共情(Cognitive Empathy)和情感共情(Emotional Empathy)两个维度(陈丽娟,徐晓东,2020:434–44)。认知共情指的是对他人情绪状态、想法和意图的理解,情感共情是指对他人情绪的一种替代性分享,其核心是产生与他人情绪状态相一致或相匹配的情绪反应(Walter, 2012: 9–17),也就是在阅读过程中,读者心里同时进行理解人物情绪和共享人物情绪两个过程,这就说明了读者在阅读过程中跟随情节发展所产生的不愉快心理。而这种文学阅读的积极效应会随着时间的延长而增强(Appel & Richter, 2007: 113–134),在长达 800 多页的篇幅作用下,读者到阅读后期所产生的心理和情感负担逐步增强,尤其是随着作品人物的悲惨命运被逐步揭示,这进一步说明了部分读者到阅读后期产生的厌倦感增强的原因。

  对于一部分读者来说,在阅读这本书的过程中产生的感受是复杂和难以言说的。一方面,极具张力的画面、残酷的历史和悲惨的命运使读者心情沉重;另一方面,高超的写作手法和丰富的故事情节吸引着读者的注意力,"尽管有分娩、暴力、谋杀、肿胀的尸体和其他令人不快的现实,但它(这本书)很有趣,读起来轻松又令人兴奋""这是一本中国苦难史,作者以编年史的形式用一种超然的方式构建故事情节……对于这本书,无法用'喜欢'或'不喜欢'来评价"。

表 2　读者评价关键词

单位：次

积极评价		消极评价	
关键词	提及次数	关键词	提及次数
喜欢	2	不喜欢	7
愉快	2	失望/不愉快	5
文字易懂	3	生理不适/恶心/不舒服	9
内容有趣/丰富	14	阅读疲惫/难懂/冗长	19
风格独特/手法高超	10	人物不讨喜/主角令人厌恶	5
—	—	标题/封面令人震惊	10

"历史"和"女性"是《丰乳肥臀》的精神内核，也是所有国家和民族的共同主题，但各个国家的历史进程、社会环境及价值观存在明显的差异化，因此，同一个主题在不同的文化背景下表现的形式和所代表的内涵也会存在差异，而在莫言的作品中，文化的表现可以具体到"高密东北乡"这一具体地域，"也就是所谓的具有鲜明的在地性"（陈晓明，2013：35–54），这种遥远的异国文化可能远超读者的预期和想象。在82位读者中，有31位读者从民族主义和人类共性的角度对作品进行评判，其中，68%的读者提出"中国文学"和"中国作家"的概念，强调"俄罗斯人和中国人是不同的""如果肖洛霍夫来写这本书，将以完全不同的方式来呈现"。当谈到题目和文章中对女性胸部赤裸裸的过多描写时，出现"对于俄罗斯人来说是难以接受的，但是可能对于中国人来说很正常"的民族偏见，而怪诞的风格和出乎意料的人物命运被理解为"是中国人特有的幽默感和品格"。此外，除了"中国文学"的标签，俄罗斯读者也将其放在更大的范畴内观察，和欧美文学相对比，称其为"亚洲文学"，一些读者表示"很难读懂亚洲文学""不管是日本文学还是中国文学，风格上和欧美文学相差甚远"。和马尔克斯的拉丁美洲魔幻主义风格不同，莫言对魔幻现实主义进行了新的诠释，打破了读者对这种创作风格的固有认知，超出了读者的心理预期，有读者表示："我喜欢魔幻现实主义，但不是这种……文中不断提到绿色，血液呈绿色，还有鸟类的羽毛、肤色，几乎所有的东西都是绿色，这是某种中国象征主义还是作者对于色彩的异常感知？"绝大多数读者认为，这本书中所描写的事件是中国底层人民真实的生活，是20世纪中国的真实写照，这种认知在一定程度上加深了中国文学，即苦难文学的刻板印象，正如一条评论指出："这本书以和俄罗斯文学写作传统完全不同的方式完成，不敢想象如果是俄罗斯作家来

写这段历史，将会多么令人心碎……但中国作家是完全不同的，尽管内心所经历的痛苦丝毫不减，但是在中国作家手中，一切都是可以书写和描述的……"

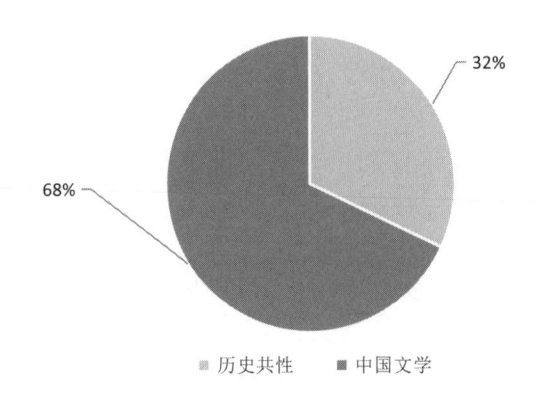

32%
68%

■ 历史共性   ■ 中国文学

图 5　读者评价中的文学标签

（四）读者类比

从写作风格和主题的角度来看，俄罗斯读者将《丰乳肥臀》与一些经典俄罗斯文学作品进行了对比，提及频率最高的是苏联作家米哈伊尔·肖洛霍夫及其代表作《静静的顿河》，两位作家的创作背景都是乡村，作品中充满乡土气息，主题都涵盖了革命和战争。从创作风格和故事发展结构来看，《丰乳肥臀》使读者联想到马尔克斯及其代表作《百年孤独》，两个作品都描述了一个家族的历史和几代人的更替，作者对家族中每一个人的命运都进行了刻画，而社会的变迁也通过家族的命运清晰地展现在读者眼前。魔幻现实主义的创作风格是两位作家之间的共性，马尔克斯将古老的印第安民间文化和西班牙巴洛克文化融合到马孔多镇，莫言则将中国民间神话和山东农村文化习俗融汇到高密东北乡这片虚构的土地。有俄罗斯作者将莫言称作"中国的马尔克斯"，但同时也指出了两位作家魔幻现实主义的差异化："众所周知，以一个家庭为例描述国家历史是许多作家长期以来都会采用的方式。我最喜欢的是加西亚·马尔克斯和他所描写的布恩迪亚家族，或许是因为这种文化、这段历史离我更近，或许是因为上官家族发生的一切让我感到反感。"从时代背景角度来说，读者联想到俄罗斯作家索尔仁尼琴的《古拉格群岛》、科钦的《女孩》、托尔斯泰的《战争与和平》、伊万诺夫的《永恒的呼唤》和《影子消失在正午》等作品，20 世纪的苏联和中国的历史及社会发展有诸多相似之处，充满变革与战争、痛苦与磨难，这也是俄罗斯读者对莫言的作品能够产生共鸣的重要原因。需要指出的是，在与《战争与和平》进行比较时，读者的意见存在分歧。一位读者指出："也许是我愚昧无知,但在阅读这本书时,始终思考着一个问题,诺贝尔文学奖为什么颁给他?这本书怎么能和《战争与和平》相提并论。"另一位读者的评论或许给出了答案:"这本书是《丧钟为谁而鸣》的一个非常生理化的版本,书中充斥着战争、毫无意义的死亡、盲目的激情,人就像动物一样。"

表3 读者类比作者及作品

作品	作者	国家	提及次数/次
《铁皮鼓》	君特·格拉斯	德国	1
《百年孤独》	加西亚·马尔克斯	哥伦比亚	5
《静静的顿河》	米哈伊尔·肖洛霍夫	苏联	9
《影子消失在正午》	阿纳托利·伊万诺夫	苏联	1
《永恒的呼唤》	阿纳托利·伊万诺夫	苏联	3
《普里亚斯林一家》	费奥多尔·阿布拉莫夫	苏联	1
《女孩》	尼古拉·科钦	苏联	2
《古拉格群岛》	亚历山大·索尔仁尼琴	苏联	2
《战争与和平》	列夫·托尔斯泰	俄罗斯	2
《丧钟为谁而鸣》	欧内斯特·海明威	美国	1
《午夜之子》	萨尔曼·拉什迪	印度	1

(五)读者推荐

65%的读者没有提及是否推荐,这部分读者更多地关注书中所描写的中国历史、中国女性、战争和人物的悲惨命运,并对其进行拆解和剖析。在35%涉及该问题的书评中,推荐阅读比例大于不推荐阅读比例,4%的读者表示强烈推荐:"只有才华横溢的人才能写出这样的作品……如果你喜欢《百年孤独》,一定要读这本书。"5%的读者表示推荐,4%的读者则认为这本书只适合一部分人看,原因多是由于血腥及暴力等"18+"阅读年龄限制因素——"《丰乳肥臀》不应该推荐给朋友和熟人,内容太痛苦、太血腥""总的来说,这个故事相当残酷,不建议儿童或胆小的人阅读""莫言是大师,这不是我敢反驳的事实。但他的作品并不适合所有人,强大的美学建立在怪诞、残酷和人道主义的象征之上,通过一个家庭的棱镜反映了一个复杂而模糊的历史时期……"等。还有4%的读者完全不推荐,主要原因在于阅读的过程中产生的心理不适和生理反感，有读者在第一次接触中国作家和中国文学时便选择了这部作品，阅读之后完全否定了中国文学本身，认为莫言的风格是中国作家的缩影，是中国文学的代表风格，因而提出"是否值得了解中国文学""尝试去喜欢中国作家是没有意义的事情"等偏激的想法。

四、结语

根据数据分析结果，俄罗斯读者对于《丰乳肥臀》的认可度达到84.2%，对读者阅读感受产生负面影响的因素多样复杂，包括内容引起生理性不适、篇幅冗长、语言及文化难懂、主人公不具备吸引力、对女性胸部描写过多等。仅有11%的读者推荐阅读该作品，5%的读者在推荐时强调书中包含暴力、血腥、色情场面。这表明，文学作品的走出去需要跨越的障碍除了市场因素，如商业价值、读者需求等，还包含文化差异、读者阅读偏好、个体接受差异等因素。在文学作品译介的初级阶段，选择合适的作品尤其重要，甚至对作者的其他作品在该地区的后续译介产生直接影响，这也是在译介的过程中叶果夫首选政治主题《酒国》及波澜壮阔的史诗性作品《丰乳肥臀》，英语译者葛浩文首选获奖作品《红高粱》及政治主题作品《天堂蒜薹之歌》的原因。而由于历史、社会、思维方式、价值观及个人经历不同，极具个性化及地域化的作品无法在读者中获得一致认同，从《丰乳肥臀》俄译本读者接受度研究中可以得到启示：中国文学走出去不仅要讲故事，还要讲好故事，和读者实现顺畅的沟通，达到高质量文学作品的持续输出。

【参考文献】

[1] 陈丽娟、徐晓东，2020．文学阅读如何影响读者的心理理论 [J]．心理科学进展，28（3）：434–442．

[2] 陈晓明，2013．"在地性"与越界——莫言小说创作的特质和意义 [J]．当代作家评论（1）：35–54．

[3] 第三次汉学家文学翻译国际研讨会．叶果夫：莫言的作品：文化差异和翻译 [EB/OL]．检索日期：2014年8月26日．网址：http://www.chinawriter.com.cn/2014/2014-08-26/215873.html．

[4] 俄罗斯卫星通讯社．俄罗斯读者能理解中国现代文学中的情节和主人公吗？[EB/

OL]. 检索日期：2022 年 1 月 26 日．网址：https://sputniknews.cn/20211023/1034692934.html.

［5］王树福. 热烈的与寂寥的：《丰乳肥臀》在俄罗斯［EB/OL］. 检索日期：2013 年 8 月 23 日．网址：https://epaper.gmw.cn/zhdsb/html/2013-08/28/nw.D110000zhdsb_20130828_5-23.htm.

［6］Appel M., Richter T. Persuasive effects of fictional narratives increase over time [J]. *Media Psychology*, 2007, 10 (1): 113-134.

［7］Рецензии читателей на книгу Большая грудь, широкий зад на сайте livelib.ru. [EB/OL]. https://www.livelib.ru/book/1007943334/reviews-bolshaya-grud-shirokij-zad-mo-yan. [2024-06-06]

［8］Walter H. Social Cognitive Neuroscience of Empathy：Concepts, Circuits, and Genes[J]. *Emotion Review*, 2012 (4): 9-17.

A Study of Readers' Acceptance of the Russian Translation of *Big Breasts & Wide Hips*

Peoples' Friendship University of Russia   WANG Xiaolin

Abstract: Mo Yan was awarded the Nobel Prize for Literature in 2012, after which his works began to be officially translated in Russia, and the second translated novel *Big Breasts & Wide Hips* was first published in 2013 and then republished in 2023. Starting from the perspective of literary translation and combining with reading psychology, this paper adopts a combination of quantitative and qualitative research to analyze the data of 82 readers' ratings, evaluations, analogies, and recommendations of the book, and to examine the acceptance of readers of the Russian translation of *Big Breasts & Wide Hips*, with the aim of providing references for the dissemination of Chinese literature among readers from other cultural backgrounds.

Keywords: *Big Breasts & Wide Hips, Russian translation, readers's acceptance, reading psychology*

翻 译 理 论
TRANSLATION THEORIES

军事典籍译者群体行为批评分析

——以《孙子兵法》为例[①]

曲阜师范大学 王文慧[②] 夏 云[③]

【摘　要】军事典籍的英译对于全球范围内中国古典文化的传播扮演着关键角色，其中《孙子兵法》尤为突出。本研究采用译者行为批评理论，将海外汉学家、军事人员和本土译者视为一个整体，对其翻译行为进行内外部批评分析。研究表明，译者的身份和赞助人等因素显著影响其行为模式。本土译者倾向于忠实性，力求译文忠实反映原文内涵；军事身份译者注重实用性，追求译文的实际应用价值；而海外汉学家译者的行为则更为复杂，在翻译过程中追求对原文的充分解释，同时在外部层面关注译文的实用性，平衡忠实性与实用性，既重视军事典籍的系统性与完整性，也考虑目标受众的接受程度。

【关键词】《孙子兵法》；军事典籍英译；译者群体；译者行为批评

一、引言

《孙子兵法》由春秋时期的孙武所著，位居《武经七书》之首，是中华优秀传统文化的精髓。它诞生于齐文化，孕育于吴文化（李宁，2015: 77-82）。这部作品不仅在中国被誉为"百代谈兵之祖"，而且在国际上也享有盛誉，被全球学术界公

[①] 基金项目：国家社科基金项目"儒学英译的海外认知与接受研究"（20BYY019）。
[②] 王文慧（2000— ），曲阜师范大学翻译学院硕士研究生，研究方向为语料库翻译学研究，邮箱：2948653141@qq.com。
[③] 夏云（1974— ），曲阜师范大学翻译学院教授，博士生导师，研究方向为语料对比与翻译、语料库语言学，邮箱：364078092@qq.com，本文通讯作者。

认为迄今为止最古老、最卓越的军事理论著作（吴如嵩、苏桂亮，2015：1）。《孙子兵法》蕴含了众多普适性原则，其价值跨越了时间的限制，成为不朽的智慧。它不仅在军事战略中占有一席之地，而且在商业竞争、企业治理、体育竞技和外交协商等多个领域都有着广泛的应用（吴如嵩，2019：5）。这部作品在西方世界同样受到了广泛的认可，成为中国文化向世界输出的杰出范例。

海外网站数据显示，在外译的中国典籍中，《孙子兵法》位列第二，其阅读和评价数量仅次于《道德经》，国外读者对《孙子兵法》的高度关注也促进了国内对其英译本的研究。《孙子兵法》英译本的研究往往结合理论，例如语篇分析、功能主义、对等理论、生态翻译学等（王琰，2022：83–88），对具体字词翻译分析比较。从译者角度研究《孙子兵法》英译的很少，且聚焦于单个译者的分析，而译者群体的译作特征及其成因都有很多可以研究的素材，值得深入挖掘（周领顺，2014b：165）。

周领顺（2021：87–93）将翻译分为译内行为（语言性行为）和译外行为（社会性行为），译者具有语言属性和社会属性。在翻译活动中，译者不仅要对原文进行语言层面上的处理，同时需要兼顾读者和社会的需求。译内行为研究译文和原文的求真度，译外行为研究译文服务社会的程度。从这两个层面可以使翻译批评更加科学、客观、全面。译者群体分为典型译者群体和非典型译者群体。典型译者群体指具备合作翻译关系的三个及以上的译者群体；非典型译者群体指由三个及以上的独立个体译者翻译同一原文构成的译者群体（周领顺，2023：16–23）。因此，本文选取《孙子兵法》的三位译者的译作，以译者行为理论为指导，探讨军事典籍的非典型译者群体的行为特征。

二、《孙子兵法》在英语世界的译介

自 1905 年首个英译本问世以来，国内外诸多译者对《孙子兵法》进行了英译，按照每位译者一种译本的方法统计，当前《孙子兵法》的英译本有 50 多种（孙志明，2021）。有的国内学者按照时间节点对《孙子兵法》的英译进行了阶段划分，主要为三阶段（李艺、谢柯，2014：127–132）或四阶段（吴莎，2012：25），或者按照翻译目的和侧重点将译本类型划分为文献型、军事型、哲学型、文化型和实用型五种类型（邱靖娜，2018：8）。

来自不同领域的专家对《孙子兵法》进行了英文翻译，这些译者拥有多样的文化背景、专业知识和个人信仰。在众多翻译者中，许多人同时拥有多重文化身份。下文对《孙子兵法》的英文译本进行了分析，重点关注其译介性质，将其他应用型和研究型文本排除在研究范围之外。本文主要将译者分为三类：中国本土译者、外籍汉学家译者以及军人译者，其他类型的译者，如宗教背景译者、商业背景译者等将不做讨论。整理结果见表1。

表1 《孙子兵法》译本分类

中国本土译者	军人身份译者	外籍汉学家译者
1945年，郑麐	1905年，卡尔斯罗普（E. F. Calthrop）	1910年，翟林奈（Lionel Giles）
1987年，袁士槟	1944年，菲利普斯（Tomas Phillips）	1981年，克拉维尔（James Clavell）
1993年，潘嘉玢、刘瑞祥	1963年，格里菲斯（Samuel Griffith）	1988年，克利里（Thomas Cleary）
1994年，林戊荪	2012年，维奈（Dalvi Vinay）	1993年，安乐哲（Roger T. Ames）
1996年，罗志野	—	1993年，黄柱华（J. H. Huang）
2003年，李庆山	—	2002年，塔弗（Dwayne E. Tarver）
—	—	2002年，闵福德（John Minford）
—	—	2007年，梅维恒（Victor H. Mair）
—	—	2011年，蒲华杰（James Trapp）
—	—	2018年，哈里斯（Peter Harris）

本研究选择英国汉学家翟林奈、美国军事家格里菲斯和国内翻译家林戊荪作为群体译者进行分析。翟译本史、评、译、注相结合，堪称《孙子兵法》学术型翻译范本，在英语国家流传较广。格译本被收录进联合国教科文组织的《中国代表作丛书》，并在美国军事学术界产生了显著影响。林戊荪的译作收录在《大中华文库》，被称为"最具代表性"的华人英译本。三位译者分别来自不同的国家和地区，他们的译作在各自领域内都产生了较大影响，具有较高的学术价值和参考意义。

本文旨在探讨非典型群体译者各自的特点和优势，探究不同背景的译者受翻译外哪些因素的影响对原文进行解读和再创造，进而影响译文的风格、表达和传播效果。此外，通过比较三位译者的翻译风格、翻译方法以及翻译外的影响因素，我们可以发现非典型群体译者在翻译过程中的共性和个性，同时推动军事典籍翻译事业的不断发展。

三、《孙子兵法》译者群体的译内行为

"翻译内"主要关注的是文本的求真效果。"通过文本中隐或显的意志性行为痕迹，可揭示译者行为的规律"（李鹏辉、高明乐，2021：55–60）。下文重点探讨译者对《孙子兵法》词汇和句子两个层面的翻译策略痕迹。

（一）章节名翻译

《孙子兵法》共有十三章，前三篇讲的是战略运筹，第四篇到第六篇主要讲解作战指挥，第七篇到第九篇涉及战场机变，第十篇、第十一篇讲的是军事地理，最后两篇是特殊战法。章节名的翻译能够反映出译者对原文的理解、翻译目的以及翻译策略见表2。

表 2　章节名翻译

《孙子兵法》	林戊荪	格里菲斯	翟林奈
计篇	Making assessments	Estimates	Laying plans
作战篇	Waging war	Waging war	Waging war
谋攻篇	Attacking by stratagem	Offensive strategy	Attack by stratagem
形篇	Disposition (xing 形)	Dispositions	Tactical dispositions
势篇	Momentum (shi 势)	Energy	Energy
虚实篇	Weakness and strengths	Weakness and strengths	Weak points and strong
军争篇	Contest to gain the initiative	Maneuver	Maneuvering

（续表）

《孙子兵法》	林戊荪	格里菲斯	翟林奈
九变篇	Varying the tactics (jiu bian 九变)	The nine variables	Variation of tactics
行军篇	Deploying the troops	Marches	The army on the march
地形篇	The terrain	Terrain	Terrain
九地篇	Nine regions	The nine varieties of rebound	The nine situations
火攻篇	Attacking by fire	Attack by fire	The attack by fire
用间篇	Using spies	Employment of secret agents	The use of spies

三位译者对《孙子兵法》章节名称的翻译各具特色，体现了他们对原文理解的不同角度和翻译策略。翟林奈的翻译则更注重在保留原文的文化内涵和语言美感的基础上，突出原文的实用性。他将"虚实篇"译为"Weak points and strong"，既传达了虚实变化的概念，又通过"weak points"和"strong"强调了军事行动中的关键点。此外，翟林奈会通过大量的译者评注来解释文本的内涵，更注重文本的文化深度，这与他汉学家的身份密切相关。而格里菲斯更加注重翻译的实用性，强调语言的清晰性和逻辑性，以适应军事学者的研究需求。他将"谋攻篇"译为"Offensive strategy"，通过将"攻"转化为名词，突出章节的实用价值。在"九变篇"中，他选择"The nine variables"，既准确传达了"九变"的概念，又通过"variables"这一名词强调了变化多端的特点。林戊荪多采用阐释的方法，在翻译时倾向于将文化内涵丰富的词通过译文+拼音+汉字的方式表达出来，忠实于原文，尽量保留原文的文化内涵。例如，他将"形篇"译为"Disposition（xing 形）"，既保留了原文的"形"字，又通过"Disposition"传达了军事部署的含义。在"势篇"中，他选择"Momentum（shi 势）"来传达"势"的概念，同时保留了"势"的拼音，在忠实于原文的基础上，促使读者探索原文的内涵，传播中华文化。

（二）军事术语翻译

军事术语在《孙子兵法》中占据了相当大的比重，裘禾敏（2019：87–90）将这些术语大致划分为兵制、兵器、兵略、地形、兵技、治军等六大类。本文将选取其中的三类术语，探讨其翻译策略。

(1) 兵制类

例1：

全**军**为上，破军次之；全**旅**为上，破旅次之；全**卒**为上，破卒次之；全**伍**为上，破伍次之。(出自《孙子兵法·谋攻篇》)

翟译：So, too, it is better to capture an **army** entire than to destroy it, to capture a **regiment**, a **detachment** or a **company** entire than to destroy them.（Giles, 1910）

格译：To capture the enemy's **army** is better than to destroy it; to take intact a **battalion**, a **company** or a **five-man squad** is better than to destroy them. For to win one hundred victories in one hundred battles is not the acme of skill.（Griffith, 1963）

林译：To have the enemy's **army** surrender in its entirety is better than to crush it; likewise, to take a **battalion**, a **company** or a **five-man squad** intact is better than to destroy it.（林戊荪，2011）

在原文中，"军""旅""卒""伍"这些术语代表了军队的组织结构，分别指代一万两千五百人、五百人、百人和五人的编制（曹操等，2012）。三位翻译家在翻译这些术语时，都选择了归化的翻译方法，以便译文更符合目标语言的文化习惯，但这种做法也意味着原文的形式被舍弃了。较为不同的是，翟林奈将旅译成"regiment"，即团，而格里菲斯和林戊荪将其译成"battalion"，即营。西方并无battalion这种编制，翟林奈是一种归化译法。但值得注意的是，翟译本在这句的译文下面加入了对这几个术语的详细解释，并不会成为误译。格译本在这一句后面，加入一句解释性的话语，使得译文更具可读性，使他的译文更具实用性。

(2) 兵略类

例2：

食敌一**钟**，当吾二十钟；总秆一**石**，当吾二十石。(出自《孙子兵法·作战篇》)

翟译：Hence the wise general sees to it that his troops feed on the enemy, for one **bushel** of the enemy's provisions is equivalent to twenty of his; one **hundredweight** of enemy fodder to twenty hundredweight of his.（Giles, 1910）

格译：Hence the wise general sees to it that his troops feed on the enemy, for one **bushel** of the enemy's provisions is equivalent to twenty of his; one **hundredweight** of enemy fodder to twenty hundredweight of his.（Griffith, 1963）

林译：Therefore, a wise general does his best to feed his troops on the enemy's grain, for one **zhong (tr: 1,000 litres)** of grain obtained from enemy territory is equivalent to 20 zhong shipped from home country, and one **dan (tr: 60 kilos)** of fodder from enemy territory to 20 dan from home.（林戊荪，2011）

钟和石是古代的容量单位，其中一钟等于六斛四斗，一石等于十斗。在历史上，这些单位常用于度量粮食等物资。在英文世界中，不存在此种计量单位，译者在翻译时要考虑到文化空缺的问题，酌情增加解释来帮助读者明白其文化内涵，避免造成阅读障碍。林戊荪在翻译这几个术语时，在译文后面采用音译＋换算的方法，在忠实于原文的基础上更有益于中华文化的国际传播。而翟林奈和格里菲斯译本采用直译的方法，将钟和石分别译成 bushel（蒲式耳）和 hundredweight（英担），bushel 是一种容量单位，而 hundredweight 是一种重量单位，存在一定程度的不对应情况。

（3）兵技类

例 3：

故兵有**走**者，有**弛**者，有**陷**者，有**崩**者，有**乱**者，有**北**者。（出自《孙子兵法·地形篇》）

翟译：Now an army is exposed to six several calamities, not arising from natural causes, but from faults for which the general is responsible. These are: **(1) Flight; (2) insubordination; (3) collapse; (4) ruin; (5) disorganization; (6) rout**.（Giles, 1910）

格译：Now when troops **flee**, are **insubordinate, distressed, collapse in disorder or are routed**, it is the fault of the general. None of these disasters can be attributed to natural causes.（Griffith, 1963）

林译：In warfare, there are six calamitous situations. namely, **flight, insubordination, deterioration, ruin, chaos and rout**.（林戊荪，2011）

兵技类术语主要涉及战争中常用的战术和技术，军队必须遵循明确的指令和具备相应的素质来应对战场上的不确定性，同时需要严格的纪律和规则来避免各种不利情况的发生。这里的"走、弛、陷、崩、乱、北"指军队内部关系问题造成的负面结果。通过对比分析原文，三位译者在翻译时，都采用了直译的翻译方法。原文语言精练、形式简练，但其内涵却极其丰富，三位译者的译文虽然没能完全体现出原文的文化和内涵，但其在文本形式和术语经济性方面得到了很好的表现，能够满足译语读者的接受度。

（三）修辞翻译

《孙子兵法》不仅是一部享誉全球的军事理论杰作，也具有深厚的文学价值。全书文风简洁、论述清晰易懂，并且巧妙地运用了多种修辞手法。接下来将探讨译者在处理这些修辞时选择的策略和方法。

(1) 比喻翻译

例 4：

故善出奇者，无穷如天地，不竭如江河。（出自《孙子兵法·虚实篇》）

翟译：Indirect tactics, efficiently applied, are inexhaustible as Heaven and Earth, unending as the flow of rivers and streams.（Giles, 1910）

格译：Now the resources of those skilled in the use of extraordinary forces are as infinite as the heavens and earth; as inexhaustible as the flow of the great rivers.（Griffith, 1963）

林译：The resourcefulness of those skilled in the use of *qi* is as inexhaustible as heaven and earth and as unending as the flow of rivers.（林戊荪，2011）

三位译者都试图传达原文的比喻意义，即善于出奇制胜的人拥有无穷无尽的资源和策略，就像天地和江河一样。在翻译这一比喻时，各位译者都保留了原文的结构，将比喻显化。通过比较发现这三例在"奇"和"江河"的翻译上各具特色，翟译将"奇"译成"indirect tactics"，在忠实于原文的基础上也比较易于西方读者理解，但"efficiently applied"可能限制了原文含义，用"rivers and streams"来翻译"江河"也稍显冗余。格译通过"extraordinary forces"传达了"善出奇者"的策略和智慧，但"Now"的出现造成语境上的不连贯，"the great rivers"也可能被误解为特指。林译虽然尽力保留原文的文化内涵，但"qi"需要借助副文本才能令不熟悉中国文化或哲学的读者理解。

(2) 对偶翻译

例 5：

水因地而制流，兵因敌而制胜。（出自《孙子兵法·虚实篇》）

翟译：Water shapes its course according to the nature of the ground over which it flows; the soldier works out his victory in relation to the foe whom he is facing.（Giles, 1910）

格译：And as water **shapes** its flow **in accordance with** the ground, **so** an army **manages** its victory **in accordance with** the situation of the enemy.（Griffith, 1963）

林译：As the water **changes** its course **in accordance with** the contours of the terrain, **so** a warrior **changes** his tactics **in accordance with** the enemy's changing situation.（林戊荪，2011）

《孙子兵法》频繁使用对仗修辞，以增强文势，紧密连接论点，提升论证的力度。在这对对仗句中，格里菲斯和林戊荪都保留了这种对仗结构，采用了相似的句式框架，且都使用"so"将原文的逻辑关系显化。翟林奈并未在形式上保持原文的对仗，而是根据个人表达习惯，采用了截然不同的句式和短语。尽管如此，他在语义上尽力贴近读者，反映了他以目标语言和读者为中心的翻译理念，即使用易于理解的语言，向西方读者介绍《孙子兵法》。

（3）顶针翻译

例6：

地生度，度生量，量生数，数生称，称生胜。（出自《孙子兵法·形篇》）

翟译：Measurement **owes** its existence **to** Earth; Estimation of quantity to Measurement; Calculation to Estimation of quantity; Balancing of chances to Calculation; and Victory to Balancing of chances.（Giles, 1910）

格译：Measurements of space **are derived from** the ground. Quantities derive from measurement, figures form quantities, comparisons from figures, and victory from comparisons.（Griffith, 1963）

林 译：Measurements of space **refers to** the difference in the territories of the opposing parties; **from that** derives estimation of quantity, which **refers to** the difference in the resources; **from that,** calculation of numbers, which **refers to** the difference in the size of their troops; **from that,** comparison of the relative strengths of their armies and finally, assessment of the material base for the chances of victory.（林戊荪，2011）

"顶针"修辞手法能够让句子的结尾与开头紧密相连，起到承上启下的作用，使得句子结构工整，语气流畅。翟林奈和格里菲斯在翻译时都弱化了原文中的顶针修辞，翟林奈使用了"owe to"，而格里菲斯使用了"be derived from"，这样的处理改变了原文的主宾关系，原文中首尾相接的词语在译文中被分别放置在前句的开头和后句的结尾，从而失去了连贯性。尽管如此，他们又都采用了相似的句型，使得译文呈现出排比的效果。这种翻译方式显示了他们对目标语言表达习惯的尊重，使得译文简洁清晰。相比之下，林戊荪的译文更注重充分表达原文的深层含义，虽然他也没有保留原文的顶针修辞，但他通过使用三组"refer to"和"from that"将原文的"度""量""数""称"四个要素相互连接，揭示了它们之间的逻辑关系。

四、《孙子兵法》译者群体的译外行为

译外行为主要表现为译者的社会人行为，"是其在翻译活动中融入自己意志性成分的行为现象"（周领顺，2014a：13），包括译者的翻译目的、翻译选材、译者身份、读者意识等（周领顺、张思语，2018：103–109）。下文主要分析《孙子兵法》译者群体在译者身份和赞助人两个外部因素作用下的行为表现。

（一）译者身份

英国汉学家翟林奈，在中国出生，并曾担任大英博物馆东方书籍馆副馆长，拥有深厚的汉学造诣。他的独特背景和经历让他对中国语言和文化有了深刻的认识。翟林奈认为卡氏（卡尔斯普罗）转译自日语底本的译本错误颇多，译文舍弃《孙子兵法》的中国语境而求诸日本语境，故于1910年推出了自己的译本。裘禾敏（2019：87–90）认为，与其他已出版的《孙子兵法》英文版本相比，翟译本在翻译格式、译文处理技巧和学术规范方面都表现出更高的严谨性和科学性，其权威地位稳固不可撼动。翟译本的突出特点是，在译文正文部分，同时包括中文原文、译文和译者评注。译者评注部分，结合前人研究说明自己对原文的理解及翻译理由。这一特点与其汉学家的身份密切相关，但过多的副文本可能会给读者造成阅读负担。

美国军人格里菲斯，一位海军陆战队准将，退役后进入牛津大学攻读汉学博士学位。1963年，他基于自己的博士论文，出版了译作 *Sun Tzu: The Art of War*。屠国元和吴莎（2011：187–191）指出格里菲斯的译本在军事战略层面上深刻阐释了孙子的思想，详细论述了孙子的战争观念。Corbett（2001：157–173）指出，格里菲斯被视为翻译《孙子兵法》的最优秀翻译家之一。实用性以及贴近军事自然是格里菲斯译本的首要选择，同时攻读博士学位的学术要求又驱动他对《孙子兵法》的原文内容和成书背景做大量的调查，采用大量注释和评注以便于读者理解。译者作为职业

军人兼学者的双重身份使其译本用词专业、表达地道,具有相当强的权威性(谢柯、李艺,2015:79-84)。

林戊荪,以其对中国古典文学和文化的深刻理解,以及对原文忠实而细致的翻译风格而著称。他的译作《红楼梦》和《水浒传》等经典作品,不仅在国内受到了高度评价,也在国际上产生了广泛的影响。林戊荪的翻译风格以忠实原文为基础,同时注重保持原文的语言特色和风格。这种翻译策略不仅准确传达了原文的意蕴,而且为推广和研究中国文化做出了重要贡献。林戊荪以推广中国文化、促进文化交流为目的翻译出版了《孙子兵法》英译本。他的目标是将孙子的思想传播到国际舞台,因此在翻译作品中保留了许多中国文化的特色(Zheng,2019:537–544)。林戊荪精湛的翻译工作在当前中国文化"走出去"的大背景下为我们提供了宝贵的经验,为翻译经典文献树立了榜样。

(二)赞助人

翟林奈的译本由伦敦的卢扎克公司于1910年发行。卢扎克公司成立于19世纪末,主要专注于东方语言、文学、历史和哲学等领域的研究和出版。作为一家商业性出版集团,卢扎克公司必须考虑经济回报,因此要求译作符合通俗读物的语言简明、文风顺畅的特征,以满足大众读者的阅读需求。因此,翟林奈多采用归化策略,增强了译文的"可接受性"。

格里菲斯译本主要面向西方军界和军事院校学生,他的赞助人主要是一些军界人士。因此,他的翻译专注于军事思想,频繁使用专业术语。他通过阅读中国历史上的著名战例来领悟、理解《孙子兵法》的军事思想和中国古代兵学体系,反思在朝鲜战争中失败的深层原因。格译本必须符合出版方国家的意识形态和主流文化风格才能为读者所接受,格译本彰显了浓厚的军事特色。

林戊荪的译本由中国外文出版社出版,这是一个肩负国家对外宣传使命的出版机构,主要任务是翻译和出版党政文件及中国古典文学等文化类书籍。出版社的宗旨是"用外文说明中国,以图书沟通世界",这影响了译本的风格,促使译者从文化交流和文化鉴赏的角度出发,面向国外读者宣传《孙子兵法》的基本精神,弘扬中国传统文化,忠实地传达原文的思想和精神,突出译文的文学性和艺术性,而非仅仅强调军事价值。这种定位强调了译本的"非战"思想,凸显了其文化传播意义,弱化了军事意义。

五、译者行为分化原因

"译者群体行为批评"既能解释译入行为,又能关照译出行为,要求译者既对原文求真,又要对社会务实,实现求真和务实的双向互动。《孙子兵法》英译中译者群体的行为痕迹有明显的差异性,这种差异性与译者的翻译目的有密切关系。

翟林奈作为一位汉学家,他的翻译目的主要是传播中国文化,让西方读者能够深入了解和欣赏《孙子兵法》的文化内涵。在翻译过程中,他通过大量的文化背景注释来解释文本的内涵,使西方读者能够更好地理解原文的文化背景和深层意义。这种翻译目的体现了他对文化交流的重视,以及他希望通过翻译工作促进中西文化的相互理解和尊重。

身为前美国海军陆战队准将的格里菲斯曾在驻中国美军中任职并学习过汉语,其翻译目的是通过对中国军事的研究,从中汲取经验,学习作战的精髓,更好地服务于美国海军陆战队并满足西方军界读者借鉴孙武兵学思想的需求。他的读者群体为西方军事学家或者军事院校的学生,因此,翻译时考虑更多的是译本的军事性,译文采用语义翻译,倾向于凸显军事特色,文中插入大段注疏、释义,内容翔实,善于运用专业术语表达转换古汉语兵学用语,兵学术语的准确性、简明性以及统一性在其译文中得到了很好的体现,尽可能地做到了忠实于原文和忠实于孙子的意图。

林戊荪翻译《孙子兵法》的目的是让西方普通的中国文化爱好者了解中国传统文化,发扬中国传统文化,有效地实现跨文化交际(王宏印,2011:7–10)。因此,林戊荪的"文化型译本"采用了音译并附加注释的方式,忠实地反映了中国历史文化的背景,并着重展现了中国兵学的宏伟气势,力求让读者在阅读译文时能够体验到与原文读者相似的感受。林译本充分发挥了本族语译者的优势,传达出古代兵学博大精深的哲学内蕴,同时又能考虑到译文读者的接受程度。林戊荪的翻译工作不仅准确传达了原文的意蕴,而且注重保持原文的风格和语言特点。

六、结语

军事典籍作为中华文明的瑰宝,《孙子兵法》的英译版本则成为传播中国古代军事文化的关键媒介。依托国内本土理论之一的译者行为批评理论,本研究从翻译内在实质与外在语境两个维度出发，对《孙子兵法》的三个代表性英译本进行了深入分析。

研究结果表明，不同译者群体均在其自身知识基础上，努力实现翻译内在真实性与外在实用性的双向互动。三位译者都忠实于原文，努力传达孙子的核心思想，他们都认识到《孙子兵法》不仅是一部军事著作，也是一部哲学作品，因此在翻译时力求保持原文的深邃和凝练。

但受翻译目的、自身文化背景和语言习惯的影响，他们在翻译选择和语言表达上有所不同。外籍汉学家译者将《孙子兵法》置于更广泛的文化和学术背景中进行解读，在文内添加大量的副文本，以帮助目标语言的读者更好地理解中国文化背景下的军事策略。军人身份的译者更加注重军事术语的准确性和实用性，格里菲斯在翻译时，结合自己的军事经验，对孙子的一些战术思想进行现代化的解读和应用。概括而言，"外籍"翻译家的翻译行为显示出对原文内容的忠诚以及对目标语言文化的适应性，他们重视原文意义的传递，并在译文形式上做出了一定的妥协。

另一方面，本土译者群体在翻译实践中更倾向于追求翻译的务实目的，译者采用杂合翻译策略，在确保内容准确传达的同时，译文也力求维持原文的文学性。这一行为倾向与本土译者的翻译动机紧密相关，旨在推动中国军事典籍在西方普通读者中的广泛传播和共生，通过翻译实践促进中外军事文化的交流与理解。不同身份的译者之间的差异不仅丰富了《孙子兵法》的翻译研究，也为不同背景的读者提供了多角度的理解和启示。

综上所述，译者群体行为的差异性主要源于其翻译动机，进而影响了译文在追求真实性与实用性之间的平衡。通过对翟林奈、格里菲斯和林戊荪的译本进行深入分析，本研究不仅揭示了译者行为背后的复杂性，也为未来军事典籍的翻译实践提供了参考。

【参考文献】

[1] 李宁, 2015.《大中华文库》国人英译本海外接受状况调查——以《孙子兵法》为例 [J]. 上海翻译（02）: 77–82.

[2] 李鹏辉、高明乐, 2021. 译者行为批评视域下 19 世纪英译群体行为研究——以《三国演义》为例 [J]. 外语学刊（6）: 55–60.

[3] 李艺、谢柯, 2014. 布迪厄社会学视野下的《孙子兵法》英译 [J]. 外国语文（04）, 127–132.

[4] 裘禾敏, 2019. 典籍英译与东方情调化翻译倾向 [J]. 西安外国语大学学报 (1): 87–90.

[5] 邱靖娜, 2018.《孙子兵法》英译文功能语境重构研究 [D]. 北京: 北京科技大学.

[6] 孙武, 2012. 十一家注孙子 [M]. 曹操等, 注; 杨丙安, 校理. 北京: 中华书局.

[7] 孙武、孙膑, 2011. 孙子兵法; 孙膑兵法: 汉英对照 [M]. 吴如嵩, 吴显林, 校释; 林戊荪, 英译. 北京: 外文出版社.

[8] 孙志明, 2021. 解构主义视角下的《孙子兵法》英译研究 [D]. 北京: 国防科技大学.

[9] 屠国元、吴莎, 2011.《孙子兵法》英译本的历时性描写研究 [J]. 中南大学学报 (社会科学版)（4): 187–191.

[10] 王宏印, 2011. 译品双璧, 译事典范——林戊荪先生典籍英译探究侧记 [J]. 中国翻译 (6): 7–10.

[11] 王琰, 2022. 西方学界的中国军事典籍英译: 回顾与展望 [J]. 外语研究 (4): 83–88.

[12] 吴如嵩、苏桂亮, 2015. 孙子兵学大辞典 [M]. 沈阳: 白山出版社.

[13] 吴如嵩, 2019. 孙子战略散墨 [J]. 滨州学院学报 (1): 5.

[14] 吴莎, 2012. 跨文化传播学视角下的《孙子兵法》英译研究 [D]. 长沙: 中南大学外国语学院.

[15] 谢柯、李艺, 2015. 传播学视域下中国文化"走出去"之译介模式研究——以《孙子兵法》在英语世界的译介为例 [J]. 外文研究 3 (3): 79–84.

[16] 周领顺, 2014a. 译者行为批评: 理论框架 [M]. 北京: 商务印书馆.

[17] 周领顺, 2014b. 译者行为批评: 路径探索 [M]. 北京: 商务印书馆.

[18] 周领顺、张思语, 2018. 翻译家方重的译者行为批评分析 [J]. 外国语文 (4): 103–109.

[19] 周领顺, 2021. 译者行为研究方法论 [J]. 外语教学 (1): 87–93.

[20] 周领顺, 2023. 译者行为研究及其理论建设 [J]. 中国翻译 (1): 16–23.

[21] Corbett, J. The Seafarer: Visibility and the translation of a west Saxon Elegy into English and Scots [J]. *Translation & Literature*, 2001, 10 (2): 157-173

[22] SUN Tzu. *Sun Tzu on the Art of War* [M]. GILES Lionel, tr. London: Luzac & Company, 1910.

[23] SUN Tzu. *The Art of War* [M]. GRIFFITH Samuel B, tr. Oxford: Oxford University Press, 1971.

[24] Zheng, J. N. A Comparative study on English translations of military terms in Sun Tzu: The Art of War. [J]. *Theory and Practice in Language Studies*, 2019, 9 (5): 537-544.

Military Classics Translation Community Behavior Critique Analysis
— A Case Study of "The Art of War"

Qufu Normal University   WANG Wenhui, XIA Yun

Abstract: The translation of military classics plays a crucial role in the global dissemination of classical Chinese culture and *The Art of War* is one of the most prominent. This thesis employs the theory of translator behavior criticism, integrating perspectives from overseas sinologists, military personnel, and native translators, to analyze their behaviors through internal and external critiques. The findings indicate that factors such as translators' identity and sponsors significantly influence their behavior patterns. Native translators tend to prioritize fidelity, aiming to reflect the essence of the original text in their translations. Military translators focus on practicality, pursuing the practical application value of their translations. In contrast, overseas sinologists' behavior is more complex, seeking a comprehensive interpretation of the original text during translation, while also considering the practicality of the translation at the external level, balancing fidelity with practicality. They not only emphasize integrity of military classics but also take into account the receptivity of the target audience.

Keywords: *The Art of War*; translation of military classics; translator groups; translator behavior criticism

蓝诗玲《猴王：西游记》节译本的中国形象建构与阐释研究[①]

江西师范大学 北京外国语大学 张 汨[②]
江西师范大学 阳思雨[③]

【摘 要】2021年出版的《猴王：西游记》颇受读者好评，而蓝诗玲对原文选择性的删减和保留为现代英语读者构建了特定的中国形象。本文采用描述-解释性研究方法，分析蓝译本中的形象建构并解释背后的各种规约因素。首先通过文本对比，从宗教、心学、人物和官僚方面呈现和分析译者的形象建构，发现蓝诗玲趋向于用具有现代话语风格的西方叙事方式建构《西游记》的文化形象，此种建构方式得到了Goodreads读者的广泛赞赏和好评。然后，从译者认知、译入语读者的阅读期望和赞助人的出版要求对这种选择性的形象建构进行解释。研究发现，蓝诗玲重构特定形象的目的是将原著的宗教旨归和心学要义显明化，并通过改写放大对人物及官僚的批评讽刺态度，以建构一个诙谐逗趣、主题鲜明而又颇具颠覆性的奇幻冒险世界。

【关键词】形象建构与阐释；《猴王：西游记》；蓝诗玲；中国文学

一、引言

《西游记》最新英语节译本 Monkey King: Journey to the West（中文译名为《猴王：

[①] 基金项目：本文为江西省高校人文社科青年"《射雕英雄传》在英语世界的传播接受与中国形象建构研究"（项目号：YY22212）的部分研究成果。
[②] 张汨（1988— ），博士，江西师范大学外国语学院副教授、硕士研究生导师，北京外国语大学英语学院在站博士后。研究方向为翻译史。邮箱：micanzhang@126.com。
[③] 阳思雨（1999— ），博士，江西师范大学外国语学院硕士研究生。研究方向为英汉翻译。邮箱：ysymtier@163.com。

西游记》，以下简称《猴王》）于 2021 年 2 月问世，由蜚声国内外的图书出版商——企鹅出版社出版并发行，英国著名新生代汉学家及翻译家蓝诗玲担纲翻译。蓝诗玲对原文进行了大刀阔斧的删节，由一百回缩减到三十六回。《猴王》一经出版，便受到海外读者的广泛好评，不仅英美文艺界、出版界、众多作家、评论家以及海外汉学家和海外华人学者对该译本给予高度评价（朱明胜，2021），国际知名书评网站 Goodreads 上也是好评如潮，读者喜爱率更是高达 98%。新时代下，中国文学走出去成为热点话题，蓝诗玲的《猴王》无疑能够有效推动中国优秀古典文学作品的海外传播，并向世界介绍中国优秀文化，展示中国良好形象。翻译领域学者针对蓝译《猴王》的研究有从内外副文本分析当中体现的传播学理论，并借以探讨企鹅出版社的传播策略和产生的传播效果（崔子涵，2022），还有基于译文考察蓝诗玲使用的译述翻译策略之于中华典籍外译的重要意义（朱嘉春、罗选民，2022）。然而，现有研究并未涉及蓝诗玲节译本中为西方读者建构的特定形象。

二、形象学与翻译研究

形象学与翻译研究的结合可以追溯到 20 世纪 80 年代，当时翻译研究在比较文学的影响下经历着"文化转向"。在早期的研究中，Bassnett 和 Lefevere（1990）指出，翻译作为一种改写的手段，可以起到构建作者和来源文本形象的作用。Lefevere（1992）之后指出翻译具有保存和改变源文化形象的双重功能，这进一步表明翻译是形象建构的有效手段。然而，直到 20 世纪后期，翻译研究开始从社会学、形象学、历史学等其他学科中汲取新的理论视角和研究方法，翻译形象学研究才得以真正兴盛起来。在过去几十年中，电影（Gentile & van Doorslaer, 2019）、文学（Beller & Leerssen, 2007）和新闻（van Doorslaer, 2012）等方面的形象建构研究日益突出。

在研究内容上，Soenen（1997）和 Kuran-Burçoğlu（2000）分别分析了形象对翻译过程的影响以及应对方法，为翻译形象研究开辟了新的研究路径。还有学者探讨了影响译文形象（再）建构的社会文化因素，强调形象和身份不再是一个民族的固有特征，而是在社会生产和传播过程中逐渐形成的，并与特定群体相关联（王运鸿，2018）。此外，译者在形象（再）建构过程中的作用也引起了广泛关注（Flynn, Leersen & van Doorslaer, 2015）。

然而，目前的研究鲜少关注译入语读者对译文中所建构形象的接受和反应。王运鸿（2019：92）认为"目标语文化群体对中国文学、文化的形象认知亦反作用于经典英译活动"。在这方面，"不同类型读者对译文的接受度和相关反馈进一步揭示了预设形象与真实形象之间的重合度及差距,以此回答读者形象建构是否成功、翻译目的是否达成等读者中心取向的问题"(宋凯彤、蓝红军,2021:107)。本文以蓝诗玲《猴王》的节译本为例,通过文本对比分析"呈现了怎样的文学和文化形象"(孟华,2001:9),并结合 Goodreads 上的读者评论,探讨这种形象建构如何被译入语读者所接受和认可。最后,总结影响形象建构的各种因素,并揭示翻译与形象的多维互动关系。

三、蓝诗玲《猴王》节译本中的形象建构

本文将结合 Goodreads 上相关的读者评论,分析《猴王》中所建构的宗教、心学、人物、官僚等形象,并与吴承恩《西游记》原文所呈现的形象进行对比,探究其中出现的形象变异,并据此揭示翻译活动中制约形象建构的各种规约因素。

(一)宗教形象建构——凸显三教合一的教旨

《西游记》是中国神魔小说的经典之作以及中国古典四大名著之一,是古代长篇浪漫主义小说的巅峰,在中国乃至世界都颇负盛名。"原著的宗教主题不仅是这部文学作品的价值以及趣味所在,而且反映了明朝的社会风貌以及宗教生活风貌"(刘珍珍,2017:43)。《西游记》成书于 16 世纪的明朝中叶,这一时期奉行三教融合的宗教制度,将儒家作为主流哲学和统治思想,并以佛道二教为治国之辅(何孝荣,2014)。然而,在《西游记》这样的神魔小说中,儒教无法与佛道二教相提并论,因为儒教本身没有自己完整的神话系统。因此,作为三家之一,儒家的形象刻画通过以下三个方面间接呈现:人物语言引用儒家经典,人物行为遵守儒家规范,事物评判标准遵守儒家的伦理道德准则(兰拉成,2004)。

译者蓝诗玲在副文本和正文中都有意显化《西游记》三教合一的教旨,同时她也注意到原文中透露的宗教淡漠化倾向,并在导读中指出"西游记对三种教义的混用体现出明朝后期宗教信仰的融合",然而"书中对三种宗教代表的讽刺和贬抑表明,这本小说对任何一种信仰都不感兴趣"(Lovell, 2021: 19)。Goodreads 网站上的读者也对此给出有力印证,比如网友 Dan Knorr 就评价"节译本有效突出了原文主题,比如对儒、道、佛'三教'略带嘲讽的语言处理"。[①] 蓝诗玲在译本的正文中直

[①] Customer Review by Dan Knorr [EB/OL].(2022-01-16)[2022-03-07]. https://www.Goodreads.com/book/show/53403847-monkey-king.

接强化"三教合一"的宗教主题的例子如下：

例1：

原文：一日，祖师登坛高坐，唤集诸仙，开讲大道，真个是：<u>天花乱坠</u>，<u>地涌金莲</u>。妙演<u>三乘教</u>，精微万法全。慢摇麈尾喷珠玉，响振雷霆动九天。说一会道，讲一会禅，三家配合本如然。开明一字皈诚理，指引无生了性玄。（吴承恩，2006：12）

蓝译：Eventually, Subodhi climbed back onto his rostrum and summoned his immortals for a lecture on doctrine: a synthesis of Taoism, Buddhism, and Confucianism.（Lovell, 2021: 36）

在《西游记》第二回中，孙悟空向菩提祖师拜师学艺，一心渴望长生之术。译文则将菩提祖师讲经论道的内容和场景描写删除。《西游记》将菩提祖师塑造为兼容并包，百家皆通的高人形象，其本身也是"三教合一"的典型象征，既拥有佛道合一的号象，又表露道家的气质打扮，同时还兼具儒家的行事思想。菩提祖师传道授业的内容实则也是三教思潮的融合，但原文的韵文部分对于三教的着墨有所侧重。根据吕薇芬在2006版的世德堂本《西游记》校注，韵文中的"天花乱坠，地涌金莲""三乘教"均是佛教用语。其中"三乘教"即指佛教，佛教根据人的根性不同，有三种不同的修炼方法。菩提祖师讲经说法的内容是以三乘佛法为总纲，并配合儒家及道家的学说，而蓝诗玲选择将这些具有佛教意蕴的用语省去不译。原文虽说明"三家配合"，却只明确其中两家为"道"和"禅（即佛教）"，而译者蓝诗玲采用明晰化的翻译策略，补充儒家（Confucianism）为三家之一，并对原文删繁就简，省略文化信息高度稠密并与作品主题无直接关联的因素，以强化"三教合一"的中心教义。

蓝诗玲对宗教形象的建构还体现在对名称和称谓的处理上。名称与称谓一直被认为是最简单和直接的人物刻画手段之一（Chatman, 1980; Rimmon-Kenan, 2002）。《西游记》中的人物名称和称谓多为文化专有项（Culture-specific Items）。艾克西拉（Aixelà, 1996: 58）将之定义为"由于在译语读者的文化系统中不存在对应项目或者与该项目有不同的文本地位，因此其在源文中的功能和含义转移到译文时发生翻译困难的语言项目"。并且，艾克西拉还按照"跨文化操纵"的程度提出十一种处理文化专有项的策略，分为保留法（包括重复、转换拼写法、语言翻译、文外注释、文内注释）和替代法（包括同义词翻译、有限泛化、绝对泛化、归化、删除、自创）两大类。蓝诗玲深受西方主流诗学观影响，注重译入语读者的阅读体验，多采用替代的翻译策略以提高读者的接受程度。例如，蓝诗玲使用有限泛化（Limited

Universalization）将目的语文化中难以理解和接受的"太上老君"处理成译入语读者更为熟悉的另一个原语文化专有项"老子"（Laozi）。再如"三藏"的译名，蓝诗玲曾在翻译札记（A Note On The Translation）中表示，"韦利的版本仍然具有巨大的魅力和活力；因为他为三藏等取经人所起的名字为人熟知"（Lovell, 2021: 25），因此蓝诗玲沿用韦利译本中的多个人物译名，将"三藏"通过英语和梵文转写词组合并重构成 Tripitaka，向译入语读者明确唐三藏的宗教归属。由此，蓝诗玲在《猴王》中构筑起一个宗教文化多元而宗教立场鲜明的西游世界。

（二）心学形象构建——凸显心猿归正的历程

《西游记》的成书正是处于阳明心学发展的鼎盛时期。王阳明提出"至善者心之本体"，认为心学的最终追求便在于使人复归到本初的至善状态，摒除物欲和私我之心，这就需要加强个人的德性修养，做到"克己明德""诚意正心"（易翔宇，2004）。《西游记》的主线故事叙述的是唐僧师徒的取经之路，这同样也是师徒"求心"的心路历程，九九八十一难的设置不仅是对意志的磨炼，同样也是对求取真经的诚意考验。杨俊（1993：95）认为，"孙悟空从齐天大圣到孙行者、斗战胜佛，猪八戒从野猪精、悟能到净坛使者，唐僧从玄奘到旃檀功德佛，均形象地说明，西行取经的'经'就是修心向善、格物致良知"，并认为原作者吴承恩正是通过这些人物形象的塑造来诠释心学的基本思想。

而蓝诗玲对于心学形象的构建主要是通过凸显心猿归正的历程实现，译者通过对原文内容有目的地加以选择，更加强调"西天取经的根本目的是通过艰辛的求经之路磨炼和安定孙悟空的心性"（Lovell, 2021: 18），而弱化甚至屏蔽了其他角色的心灵发展。这也在 Goodreads 的读者评论中得到了印证，其中署名为 Charlie Corn 的网友评论道："孙悟空的真心在这个版本中（指蓝译本）体现得淋漓尽致。"而对比起来，"三藏是一个引人入胜的中心人物——但作为一个朝圣的僧人，在心灵上却似乎没有得到任何发展"。[1] 另外，署名为 Dan Knorr 的网友也认为"（蓝诗玲的）节译始终围绕孙悟空的发展展开叙述"。[2]《西游记》以心猿作为孙悟空的别称，用心猿比喻浮躁不安的人心，只有通过取经路上的无数磨难修行，才能降伏心猿，达到"明心见性"，而译者选取了多个具有代表性的情节来建构孙悟空（心猿）心性转变的过程。蓝诗玲在第七章中选译了孙悟空大闹天宫的情节，在原文的第七回中，孙悟空历经太上老君的八卦炉七七四十九日的锤炼，

---

[1] Customer Review by Charlie Corn [EB/OL]. (2021-01-12) [2022-03-07]. https://www.Goodreads.com/book/show/53403847-monkey-king.

[2] 同上。

反而炼成"火眼金睛",他从炉中逃出来之后更是大杀四方,无法无天。原文在此处以一首七律阐述"心""意",而蓝诗玲则在译文中通过"再创造"重构了心意的内涵,对比如下。

例2:
原文:猿猴道体配人心,心即猿猴意思深。
大圣齐天非假论,官封"弼马"是知音。
马猿合作心和意,紧缚牢栓莫外寻。
万相归真从一理,如来同契住双林。(吴承恩,2006:59)
蓝译:With discipline, he might become a force for supernatural good; without it, he was pure animal—a wrecking ball in Heaven.(Lovell, 2021: 77–78)

原文中的"心猿意马"出自汉代道典《参同契》:"心猿不定,意马四驰。"比喻人心如同猴子一样流荡散乱,思维意念像野马一样难以控制,"心猿意马"本是道教修炼心性的专用语,后来为儒释道三教通用,所谓拴住心猿即是三教修心的共同所指(沈欣,2012),在原文中则表明修行者须把握心神,才能去除蒙蔽,实现平定安和,最终修成正果。译者蓝诗玲则将原文的修心炼性之说转化为西方哲学中自由意志与自律精神的辩题,表明毫无节制的自由意志足以构成一种毁天灭地的破坏性力量,而真正的自由须是建立在自律的基础上,这对于身处西方文学场域和深受西方哲学思维影响的译入语读者而言更容易引起思考和共鸣。

大闹天宫之后,孙悟空(心猿)被如来佛祖压在五行山下以定心养性,而后蓝诗玲还选取了原文的第十四回"心猿归正 六贼无踪"、第七十八至七十九回孙悟空在比丘国挖心降妖救群童以及第八十七回"凤仙郡冒天止雨 孙大圣劝善施霖"以反映孙悟空重塑心性的过程,并在导读中评价道:"在书的最后几章,孙悟空明显变得更加沉稳、仁慈、爱护生命。"(Lovell, 2021: 18)

正如读者在译文最后所见,经历"魔划尽""道归根"而"心猿归正",孙悟空最终修成正果并被封为斗战胜佛。因此,蓝诗玲在译文中构筑的"求心"历程,其实际构架是围绕孙悟空,即心猿"放心""定心""修心""正心"的过程,而弱化了书中其他主要角色的心性转变。此外,蓝诗玲将中国诗性哲学这一他者形象映照并改写为西方更为熟知的自由意志与自律精神的哲学思辨,淡化了心学原有的主观唯心主义色彩。蓝诗玲在译文中对心学做出了西方化的诠释,体现出对译入语读者思维习惯的关照。

（三）人物形象构建——凸显师徒人性的弱点

蓝诗玲在《猴王》中还有意通过塑造唐三藏及其弟子的人物形象来凸显人性的弱点，她在导读里指出，"每个取经人都代表人性的不同方面。猪八戒耽于声色；沙僧忧郁孤僻；唐三藏胆小畏怯；孙悟空性情不定，需要经过锻炼（即取经之难的考验）来挖掘向善的潜能"（Lovell，2021：17）。

一方面，蓝诗玲对于人物形象的构建通过有意识地选择原著的某些情节来实现。不同于英语世界另一部具有代表性的《西游记》节译本，即阿瑟·韦利（Arthur Waley）的《猴》（Monkey），两种节译本在内容的选择上大相径庭，Goodreads 网站上署名为 Charlie Corn 的读者也认为"与韦利相比，蓝诗玲选择了西行取经之旅中不同的情节片段，只是在与神仙的一系列较量中情节的实质有所重复"。韦利在原著师徒历经的九九八十一难中仅仅选择了乌鸡国、车迟国和通天河三个故事，这是因为孙悟空在这些故事中表现得尤为英勇和充满智慧。出于迎合"二战"时英国读者的心理需要，韦利对原著展开有意识的、富有创造性的裁剪，将孙悟空塑造成一个几乎战无不胜的个人英雄主义形象（王文强，2019），而蓝诗玲所选择的情节中，不乏妖魔与孙悟空势均力敌甚至直接让孙悟空落于下风的情节，比如孙悟空被红孩儿的三昧真火烧伤，先是求助东海龙王，后不敌再去求助观音菩萨，最终才降服红孩儿。再如孙悟空被蝎子精的倒马毒桩蜇伤，最终求助昴日星官才得以降妖除魔。在一次次的战斗中，孙悟空经常需要搬救兵才能够渡过难关，这在一定程度上削弱了孙悟空无所不能的英雄主义光芒，放大了他身上人性的弱点，但这种缺点的保留反而让孙悟空的人物形象更加有血有肉，真实可信。孙悟空身上人性、神性与猴性的结合，也更能引起译入语读者在审美体验中的情感共鸣。

另一方面，蓝诗玲建构师徒形象是通过改写凸显人性弱点的，以唐僧为例：

例3：
原文：三藏闻得此言，愈加放怀无虑。（吴承恩，2006：124）
蓝译：All this was <u>music</u> to Tripitaka's <u>easily frightened ears</u>.（Lovell，2021：118）

例4：
原文：三藏心中不快，口里骂道："你这猴子！想你在两界山，被如来压在石匣之内，口能言，足不能行，也亏我救你性命，摩顶受戒，做了我的徒弟。怎么不肯努力，常怀怠懒之心？"行者道："弟子亦颇殷勤，何尝懒惰。"三藏

道:"你既殷勤,何不化斋我吃?我肚饥怎行?况此地山岚瘴气,怎么得上雷音?"(吴承恩,2006:246)

蓝译: Tripitaka now turned petulant. "Are you forgetting who rescued you from that stone casket beneath the Mountain of Two Frontiers? You owe me, Monkey! Get me something to eat before this pestilential mountain finishes me off." (Lovell, 2021: 146)

例3讲述的是孙悟空与唐僧经过两界山后忽然遇见一只猛虎,孙悟空轻松打杀猛虎后与唐僧的对话。蓝诗玲在画线部分对唐僧的反应做了明显的改写处理。Hermans(1999: 128)指出:"改写与社会文化有着重要的关联,因为在读者不能直接读到某部文学作品或该作品不存在的时候,改写就决定了这部作品的'形象'。"原文将唐僧听到孙悟空神通广大之后的反应描述为"放怀无虑",而蓝译使用的music和easily frightened ears则充满了戏谑和调侃的意味,强化了唐僧胆小懦弱的人物形象。

例4则是《西游记》中最为脍炙人口的情节之一——孙悟空三打白骨精,由于唐僧受到妖魔蒙蔽,导致最终"恨逐美猴王"。原文选取的对话则发生在白骨精出现之前,师徒赶路时行经嵯峨高山,三藏忽感肚中饥饿,便要求孙悟空前去化斋。唐三藏在原文的话语表达主要以陈述句和反问句的形式出现,且情绪上只是"心中不快",而蓝诗玲则加深程度,将其改写为"暴躁易怒"(petulant),此外还将原文的话语表达形式改写为语气更为强烈的反问句、感叹句以及祈使句,一句"You owe me, Monkey!"更是将唐僧塑造成一个专横跋扈的师父,将唐僧所代表的人性弱点暴露无遗。在Goodreads网站上,署名为Charlie Corn的读者评论道:"译文中有几处充分暴露了唐三藏的缺点,特别是对孙悟空的不信任和怨恨,这使人物形象更加丰满。"[1]读者Benjamin则认为"唐僧总是一遇到困难就哭泣"[2],另一位读者Mike Cheng也表明"书中每个主要角色的缺陷似乎都代表了人类的不完美:……三藏软弱无能,道貌岸然,盲目轻信,胆小怯懦"[3],这些评论对于蓝诗玲刻意凸显唐僧的人性缺点是有力的印证,人性暴露的缺点在一定程度上掩盖了唐僧作为佛教徒所具备的佛性特质。

---

[1] Customer Review by Charlie Corn [EB/OL]. (2021-01-12) [2022-03-07]. https://www.Goodreads.com/book/show/53403847-monkey-king.
[2] 同上。
[3] 同上。

（四）官僚形象构建——凸显官僚阶级的黑暗

探究《西游记》的政治意蕴时不难发现，原著作者吴承恩以夸张幽默的笔调暗讽了当时的官僚阶级。原作所构筑的奇幻神魔世界实际上是对人类社会的映照，《西游记》中的天庭以当时的明代朝廷为原型，尊卑有序的阶级制度符合儒家的伦理秩序和传统世俗眼光，从吴承恩笔下塑造的天庭形象中可以窥见他对当时政治制度的深刻反思和辛辣批判（王银宝，2015）。在《西游记》的世界体系中，无论是人界、神界，还是幽冥界都存在黑暗腐败现象，原作者塑造的人间帝王多昏庸残暴、轻信奸佞，译者蓝诗玲也在导读中附言道："取经人遇到的每一个国王都轻信、愚蠢、懦弱、残暴。"（Lovell, 2021: 16）除此之外，天界的玉皇大帝也是反复无常，刑罚严酷。

蓝诗玲在其译本中也有意识地将对官僚的讽刺凸显为主题之一，然而与原作的文言文、白话文杂糅的语言风格不同，蓝诗玲使用的是地道的现代英语，从而在一定程度上也折射了现代的官僚体系，正如署名为 Charlie Corn 的网友在 Goodreads 网站上的评价："蓝诗玲的译本对官僚主义的讽刺非常出色，让我想起了《是，大臣》这部电视剧，多亏它的翻译采用了现代官场语言，而没有完全采用行话。"蓝诗玲用现代主义话语建构官僚形象可在下例中窥见一二。

例 5：

原文：正在欢饮之间，猴王忽停杯问曰："我这'弼马温'，是个甚么官衔？"众曰："官名就是此了。"又问："此官是个几品？"众道："没有品从。"（吴承恩，2006：33）

蓝 译：While the others were merrily drinking away, Monkey suddenly set down his cup. "What grade am I in the civil service here?" "You don't have one," his colleagues replied.（Lovell，2021：56）

原文讲述的是齐天大圣孙悟空官封"弼马温"后，众监官为其接风贺喜，孙悟空在宴饮期间询问监官自己被任命的头衔和级别。蓝诗玲采用现代主义的话语将其译为"What grade am I in the civil service here?"（我在这里的公务员队伍中属于什么级别？）。其中 civil service 的选用尤为亮眼，因为它指代的多是政府的文职部门和行政机构，或者用来统称政府工作人员或公务员，而公务员是现代的人事行政制度，采用现代的管理模型。蓝诗玲将其用在成书于 16 世纪明朝中叶的《西游记》当中，为作为古典文学的《西游记》披上了一层现代主义的外衣。通过将《西游记》以现代的方式重新叙述，蓝诗玲在新时代呈现了一部焕然一新的《西游记》删节版本。

四、蓝诗玲《西游记》节译本中的形象阐释

形象学翻译研究既注重文本内部的分析，又强调置于特定社会历史文化语境下的文本外部研究。"对于翻译研究者而言，重建他者形象的形成过程，也就是重建特定历史文化语境下某些或某类翻译的生产、流通和传播过程"（王运鸿，2018：90）。以下从多个角度探究蓝诗玲建构《猴王》形象的原因及影响因素。

（一）译者认知

王树槐（2020：90）认为，"翻译家的情感融入往往取决于他们的生活阅历、译者惯习和翻译理念"，这也适用于蓝诗玲的翻译生涯。蓝诗玲于1994年入读剑桥大学中文系，1998年到南京大学的约翰斯·霍普金斯大学中美文化研究中心交换学习1年，此后又因为研究的需要曾在北京和上海短居，与中国结下了不解之缘。蓝诗玲热爱中国文化，对中国有着深厚的感情，她曾在访谈里坦言，自己对于外语学习和小说阅读的兴趣加之对中国文化的喜爱促使她走上翻译中国文学作品的道路（张汨，2019）。蓝诗玲身兼学者、翻译家、专栏作家、大学教师等多重身份，作为学者，她的学术关注点主要是文化（包括文学、建筑、史学）与现代中国国家建构的关系（吕奇，2021），因此对于中国的社会和历史有着较为深入的研究和了解。她在重译《西游记》前阅读过大量的相关材料，并在书中的注解（Notes）部分列出了所有参考文献。

此外，在《猴王》一书的导读部分，蓝诗玲详细地介绍了历史上唐玄奘的真实取经故事、作者吴承恩的生平及《西游记》的成书背景（明代的政治、经济、文化状况），她还在这一部分描述了她眼中的《西游记》所呈现的形象，如"这部小说打破了人们长此以往对古代中国形成的偏见，该书笔下所描绘的中国，没有闭关锁国，不奉行孤立主义，也不盲目排外""《西游记》是中国小说的基石，可以以此书为参考，研究早期现代中国的文化、思想以及历史"（Lovell, 2021: 13）。这些描述有力地重塑了中国形象，帮助译入语读者对《西游记》有了更为深入的理解。蓝诗玲对《西游记》的主题进行多角度的阐释和细致的分析，她在节译本《猴王》中着意将"三教合一""心猿归正"凸显为全书的主题，便于译入语读者把握原作的精髓，这也是受到她翻译理念的影响。蓝诗玲在访谈中表明，就翻译理念而言，作为译者需要忠实于原作和译作读者。译者应该尽可能认真、准确地进行翻译以忠实于原作。与此同时，译者在翻译时又是在对某一部文学作品进行解读，因此需要用目标语将

原著的文学精髓传递给译文读者（张汨，2019）。

（二）目标读者

王运鸿（2019）认为，目标语文化群体在中国文学及文化的形象认知会反作用于经典文学的英译活动，影响译者对于文本选择以及翻译策略的采用等。作为身处西方文学场域的译者，在选择翻译文本的内容和主题时，也需要考虑译入语读者的阅读喜好和接受能力。比如，同为汉学家与翻译家的葛浩文（Howard Goldblatt）就曾在 2013 年对欧美读者的阅读喜好和审美趣味做出概括，认为欧美读者"更喜欢批评现状而非一味赞扬的中国文学"（姜玉琴、乔国强，2014）。因此，蓝诗玲在重译《西游记》时，就通过师徒形象的建构着重突出人性的弱点，并通过官僚形象的塑造表达对现实官僚主义的批判，以此激发西方读者的阅读兴趣，更加贴合西方读者的审美偏好。

此外，为了提高叙事的流畅性，降低阅读的难度，蓝诗玲通常省略《西游记》中文化信息高度稠密而与作品主题不直接相关的元素，或者向目标语读者直接阐明不熟悉的背景知识，使译文更易为普通英语读者所理解。同时，蓝诗玲对于《西游记》的现代主义改写也考虑到了当代读者所处的历史语境。正如朱明胜（2021）所言，时代的进步和语言的更新呼唤新译本的出现。总之，蓝诗玲以读者为导向的翻译理念体现在她关注目标读者的审美期待，注重译文的流畅性和可读性，从而获得读者的青睐，提高译本的接受度。

（三）赞助人因素

作为赞助人的出版商也会对翻译的形象建构造成影响。出版《猴王》节译本的企鹅出版社是世界最著名的英语图书出版商之一。企鹅出版社曾购入蓝诗玲所译的《色·戒》在英国的版权，后又委托其翻译了《鲁迅小说全集》，这两者以及《猴王》都收入象征荣誉的"企鹅经典"丛书中。蓝诗玲重译《西游记》的契机源于 2012 年企鹅出版社在纽约一位编辑的邀约，虽然《西游记》在此之前已有多个译本，但企鹅出版社认为"语言在变，人们对语言的态度也与时俱进，因此有时重译是很重要的"（汪宝荣，2013：152）。蓝诗玲就曾在中国作家协会举办的"汉学家文学翻译国际研讨会"上表示，企鹅出版社以迎合市场与提高销量为目标，中国经济的蓬勃发展促使西方读者渴望了解当代中国，包括中国的文化。

尤其是在北京奥运会后，中国受到了包括企鹅出版社在内的许多著名出版商的关注，这些出版商纷纷出版发行了一系列中国文学方面的图书，当然他们也因此获得收益。由于资金的流入和大量宣传，这些出版社可能会助力中国文学走向世界，并成为以英语为首选语言的文学界的主流。企鹅出版社的市场定位与营销理念也对译者蓝诗玲所采取的翻译策略、目标读者定位、主题筛选与语言风格等造成影响，同时蓝诗玲也曾在与英国社会学者何越的访谈中透露，企鹅出版社对她重译《西游记》给出的字数限制是 10 万字（何越，2021），而原著总字数为 90.8 万字，这就要求蓝诗玲在节译本中做出适当取舍，从而为呈现书中特定的形象、凸显特定的主题提供了可能。

五、结语

蓝诗玲的《猴王》节译本利用有限的篇幅，在宗教、心学、人物、官僚四方面为读者建构了特定的西游世界形象，她对原文有意识地筛选与操纵考虑到自身认知、目标读者以及赞助人等多重因素。蓝诗玲有意识地选择了原文的特定部分，并采用译创策略。蓝诗玲深谙普通英语读者的阅读习惯及审美偏好，以其幽默生动的笔调、流畅地道的语言和现代主义的行文风格赢得英语世界读者的广泛好评，这也对中国文学外译有所启示。

【参考文献】

[1] 崔子涵，2022．传播学视阈下蓝诗玲英译《西游记》的副文本研究[J]．传播与版权（1）：99–101+105.

[2] 何孝荣，2014．论明朝宗教的特点[J]．福建论坛（人文社会科学版）（1）：98–103.

[3] 何越．英国汉学家蓝诗玲谈新译《西游记》[EB/OL]．（2021-03-27）[2022-06-25]．https://mp.weixin.qq.com/s/7ziL4GtkfRnU_L5H3gE5lw

[4] 姜玉琴、乔国强，2014．葛浩文的"东方主义"文学翻译观[N]．文学报 03-13 (018).

[5] 兰拉成，2004．《西游记》"三教合一"思想分析[J]．西安建筑科技大学学报（社会科学版）（3）：27–31.

[6] 刘珍珍，2017．译者宗教意识形态与《西游记》译介中的文本重塑[J]．中国翻译（3）：41–46.

[7] 吕奇，2021．汉学家蓝诗玲译者风格多维研究[M]．武汉：武汉大学出版社．

[8] 孟华，2001．比较文学形象学论文翻译、研究札记（代序）[A]．比较文学形象学[C]．

孟华主编．北京：北京大学出版社，1–16．

[9] 沈欣，2012．悟空尽知"心"里事——从"悟空"看《西游记》中的修心历程 [J]．文学界（理论版）（8）：223–225．

[10] 宋凯彤、蓝红军，2021．国内形象学视域下的翻译研究：过去、现状与未来 [J]．中国外语研究（1）：102–108+139．

[11] 汪宝荣，2013．鲁迅小说英译面面观：蓝诗玲访谈录 [J]．编译丛论（1）：141–161．

[12] 王树槐，2020．小说翻译的情感批评——以《祝福》英译为例 [J]．外语学刊（5）：86–92．

[13] 王文强，2019．倾听译者的心声——阿瑟·韦利的《西游记》英译本研究 [J]．山东外语教学（1）：115–124．

[14] 王银宝，2015．《西游记》政治意蕴探微 [J]．安徽文学（下半月）（2）：73–74．

[15] 王运鸿，2019．形象学视角下的沙博理英译《水浒传》研究 [J]．外国语（上海外国语大学学报）（3）：83–93．

[16] 王运鸿，2018．形象学与翻译研究 [J]．外国语（上海外国语大学学报）（4）：86–93．

[17] 吴承恩，2006．西游记 [M]．北京：作家出版社．

[18] 杨俊，1993．试论《西游记》与"心学" [J]．云南社会科学（1）：92–96．

[19] 易翔宇，2004．心化"西游"——论明代阳明心学在《西游记》中的投影 [J]．五邑大学学报（社会科学版）（2）：41–45．

[20] 张汨，2019．中国文学的海外传播：译者主体视角——汉学家、翻译家蓝诗玲访谈录 [J]．外语学刊（1）：110–115．

[21] 张汨、廖振庭，2024．《射雕英雄传》英译本的江湖形象建构研究——以《盘蛇欲出》为例 [J]．外语教育研究（1）：47–53．

[22] 朱嘉春、罗选民，2022．《西游记》蓝诗玲英译本中译述策略的运用——兼论译述对典籍外译的意义 [J]．外国语（上海外国语大学学报）（3）：111–120．

[23] 朱明胜，2021．蓝诗玲的《西游记》新译 [N]．中国社会科学报：04-26 (7)．

[24] Aixela, J. (1996). Culture-specific Items in Translation [A]. In R. Alvarez & M. Vidal (eds.). *Translation, Power, Subversion* [C]. Clevedon: Multilingual Matters, 158-175.

[25] Bassnett, S., and A. Lefevere. (eds.) (1990). *Translation, History and Culture* [C]. London: Pinter Publishers.

[26] Beller, M., and J. Leerssen. (eds.) (2007). *Imagology — The Cultural Construction and Literary Representation of National Character* [C]. Amsterdam: Rodopi.

[27] Chatman, S. (1980). *Story and Discourse: Narrative Structure in Fiction and Film* [M]. London: Cornell University Press.

[28] Flynn, P., J., Leerssen, and L., Van Doorslaer (eds.). (2015). *Interconnecting Translation Studies and Imagology* [C]. Amsterdam: John Benjamins.

[29] Gentile, P., and L., van Doorslaer. (2019). Translating the North-South Imagological Feature in A Movie: Bienvenue Chez Les Ch'tis and its Italian Versions [J]. *Perspectives* 27 (6): 797-814.

[30] Hermans, T. (1999). *Translation in Systems: Descriptive and System-Oriented Approaches Explained* [M]. Manchester: St. Jerome Publishing.

[31] Julia, L. (trans.). (2021). *Monkey King: Journey to the West.* [M]. New York: Penguin Books, 2021.

[32] Kuran-Burçoğlu, N. (2000). At the Crossroads of Translation Studies and Imagology [A]. In A. Chesterman, A., Salvador, N., and Gambier, Y. (eds.) *Translation in Context* [C]. Amsterdam: John Benjamins, 172-195.

[33] Lefevere, A. (1992). *Translating Literature: Practice and Theory in a Comparative Literature Context* [M]. London: Routledge.

[34] Rimmon-Kenan, S. (2002). *Narrative Fiction* [M]. London: Routledge, 2002.

[35] Soenen, J. (1997). Imagology and translation [A]. In N. Kuran (ed.). *Multi-culturalism: Identity and Otherness* [C]. Istanbul: Bogazici University Press, 139-158.

[36] Van Doorslaer, L. (2012). Translating, Narrating and Constructing Images in Journalism with a Test Case on Representation in Flemish TV News [J]. *Meta* 7 (4):1046-1059.

Journey to the West and Image to the West: Image Construction and Explanation in *Monkey King* translated by Julia Lovell

Jiangxi Normal University Beijing Foreign Studies University   ZHANG Mi

Jiangxi Normal University   YANG Siyu

Abstract: The abbreviated translation *Monkey King: Journey to the West* published in 2021 has enjoyed great popularity on Goodreads, and the selective abridgement and preservation of the original text by Julia Lovell has constructed specific images of China for modern English readers. Adopting the descriptive-explanatory approach, this article analyzes the images presented in Lovell's translation and explains reasons behind such construction. Through textual comparison, religion, heart philosophy, characters, and bureaucracy are firstly opted to present and analyze the translator's construction of images, and it is discovered that Lovell tends to construct the cultural image of *Monkey King: Journey to the West* by using a westernized narrative pattern in a modern style and such construction is widely accepted and appreciated by readers commenting on Goodreads.

Such option is then explained from the aspects of the translator's perception, the constraints of both the reading expectations from the target language readers as well as the publication requirements from the patron. In so doing, the aim to visualize the religious theme and essence of heart philosophy of the original text, to amplify the critical and satirical attitude toward the characters and bureaucrats through rewriting, and to construct a fantastic world realized.

Keywords: Image Construction and Explanation; *Monkey King: Journey to the West*; Julia Lovell; Chinese literature

中医术语英译的可行性研究[1]

湖北中医药大学 杨涵雅[2] 刘 锦[3]

【摘 要】中医术语及其概念为中国文化所特有，而四字格、三字格和双字格术语是构成中医语言体系的重要组成部分，它们不仅体现了中医理论的精髓，也承载着丰富的文化内涵。在英译中医术语的过程中，要准确理解和翻译中医术语，既要保证其专业性和学术性，又要兼顾其普适性和易读性。纽马克翻译理论中最重要、最具特色的两个部分便是语义翻译和交际翻译。本文以语义翻译与交际翻译为基本翻译原则，列举分析其在中医术语翻译中的应用案例，为中医术语英译提供新的翻译视角，拓宽研究思维。

【关键词】中医药翻译；语义翻译；交际翻译；中医术语

一、引言

中医术语是中医理论与实践的基石，融合了专业性与文化性。其专业性体现在精确表达医学概念、构建系统框架及指导临床实践上；文化性则深植于哲学思辨、历史传承与民族特色之中，展现了中医独特的医学智慧与文化底蕴。中医术语的翻译对于促进国际交流、推动中医发展及提高医疗质量至关重要。在翻译过程中，需深刻理解术语的专业与文化内涵，掌握精准翻译技巧，以桥梁之姿，助力中医文化

---

[1] 基金项目：本文为"2022年度湖北省教育厅哲学社会科学一般项目"（项目编号：22Y083），以及"2023年湖北中医药大学'中医药传承与创新计划'项目"的部分研究成果。
[2] 杨涵雅（2000— ），湖北中医药大学外国语学院硕士，研究方向为中医药翻译。邮箱：1115020831@qq.com。
[3] 刘锦（1998— ），湖北中医药大学外国语学院硕士，研究方向为中医药翻译。邮箱：2596798649@qq.com。

走向世界，同时促进中医学科的创新与发展，为全球健康事业贡献力量。

二、翻译理论概述

皮特·纽马克（Peter Newmark）根据德国语言学家卡尔·布勒（Karl Buhler）对语言功能所进行的分类（expression、appeal、representation），将文本分为三种主要功能，即表达功能、信息功能和呼唤功能（expressive function，informative function, vocative function）（Karl Buhler, 2011）。之后，纽马克在其著作 *Approaches to Translation* 一书中提出了语义翻译（semantic translation）和交际翻译（communicative translation）（Peter Newmark, 2001）。

纽马克认为，在翻译过程中，应该按照不同的文本功能，分别采取两种翻译方式：语义翻译和交际翻译。这两个概念的出现，使传统意义上的"直译""意译"等概念得到了扩展，从而为翻译实践与研究开辟了新的思路。纽马克本人认为，翻译研究以往的焦点都集中于字面意思和思想内容等矛盾之上，而未思考翻译时应综合考虑的翻译目的、受众特征以及语篇类型。纽马克认为翻译理论和实践中永恒的主题在于是以原作为主，还是以读者为主的矛盾，他认为这种矛盾是可调和的。纽马克采用了 V 字图形来展现不同翻译方法的差异，如图 1。

Word-for-word translation	Adaption
Literal translation	Free translation
Faithful translation	Idiomatic translation
Semantic translation	Communicative translation

图 1

（一）语义翻译

语义翻译指在译入语（Target Language）内涵和格式一致的背景下，努力把原作的感觉发挥到极致。当社交功能完全失去作用的时候，信息功能退居其次，这时候一般采取语义翻译。语义翻译要求尽可能地保持原作特色，以表现原作的思维过程，以此实现语言的表述目的。语义翻译强调表达原作者和原文信息，往往以原作和源语文化为主，从而使译文更加忠实于原文；而一般不对原文进行阐释性翻译，只有当其含义是最大的阻碍时，才能对其进行解释。

如果翻译中的语言脱离了原语的语体，那么翻译也应该反映在翻译中，也就是说，翻译的语言也不能脱离原文的文体标准。因此，语义翻译要比交际翻译更细致、更隐晦，它更注重表达作者的思想活动，而非其目的，有过译的倾向。

（二）交际翻译

交际翻译是指译文对译文读者的影响应该尽可能地与原作对原文读者的影响相等，强调读者的感受（Peter Newmark, 2001）。有些语篇与言语之间有着紧密的联系，而语言以交流为首要目的，因而该文本便是以交际为目标，且不需要在乎其思维过程，此类情况下可以采用交际翻译。交际翻译是一种主观性的翻译，它关注的是读者的反应，从而使得原语屈服于目的语和目的语文化中。交际翻译在一定程度上打破了传统翻译过程中的二元对立现象，发挥了译者的主体性。

交际翻译既能激发译者的主观能动性，又能使译者在译文中采取更加灵活的方式来达到交流的目的，并在需要的时候对原文进行阐释性翻译。然而，在交际过程中，交际翻译往往会故意迎合译者的阅读习惯、审美偏好并对一系列具有文化意义的词语、短语和句子进行淡化，从而造成文化意义和文体的丢失和扭曲。

三、中医翻译的难点探析

中医翻译面临显著挑战，主要源于中西方文化差异、术语的高度抽象性与专业性，以及蕴含的文化典故与独特结构（如双、三、四字格等）。这些特征要求译者在翻译过程中，不仅需具备深厚的医学专业知识，还需深入了解中医文化背景，以确保翻译既准确传达医学意义，又保留文化精髓。

（一）中医文化的独特性

随着全球化的到来，中国的对外文化交流活动也越来越频繁。值得注意的是，在中医药对外传播的过程中，中医药的翻译一直是阻碍其传播的主要问题。中医药文化富含独一无二的哲学性、文学性和历史性，并具有非常高的概括性以及深奥的抽象性。中医药术语同时属于医学范畴，具有极强的科学性和药理专业性。在翻译的时候如果未对其专业性把好关，便会导致内容的歪曲，给读者造成误解，给原文的传播带来限制，甚至可能会造成误导，对读者的生命健康造成有害影响。中医术语深受中国传统文化的影响，富含哲学和文学意义；且中医语言本身具有抽象与模糊、文学与人文共存，以及哲学与科学共存的特点。中医术语在格式上多为四字格或双字格，形式简练但内容深奥。

（二）中医术语翻译的字格特殊性

在中医中许多术语以及概念是中国文化中所特有的，比如说太仓（The great granary）、元气（Yuan-primordial qi）、邪气（Pathogenic qi）等等。此类术语富含文化内涵，概念复杂，在其他语言中很难找到对等词。在他国文化中虽可能有类似的词，但大部分虽然符合原文字面意义，但却不能表达清楚原文的内涵意义，往往不能将原文中所包含的知识和文化信息翻译出来。

中医术语主要源于中医典籍。它们不仅构成了中医语言体系的重要组成部分，还承载着中医理论的精髓和传统文化的智慧，在中医临床实践、文献研究、文化传播等方面都发挥着重要作用。"四字格""三字格""双字格"是分别由四个字、三个字以及两个字所组成的词组，比如"孤阴不生""心肾相交""肺藏魄""肝合胆""天癸"以及"命门"等。不同字格都在对仗结构、音韵、逻辑等方面彰显汉语的独特之处。在进行中医术语翻译时，应充分考虑其文化特殊性和结构独特性。

四、语义翻译与交际翻译在中医术语翻译中的应用

（一）语义翻译在中医术语翻译中的应用

纽马克提出，在翻译过程中，译者应根据文本不同的功能，有针对性和选择性地采用不同的翻译方法和技巧：采用语义翻译，在译语的语义和句法结构允许的条件下，尽可能准确地再现语境含义和原文形式；采用交际翻译，译作所产生的效果应力求接近原作，力图传译出原文确切的上下文意义，使译文无论是在内容上还是在语义形式上都能为读者所接受。

其中，语义翻译是指在保持源语文化和词汇特点的同时，保持对原著的忠诚度。这类翻译方法适用于中医术语中文化负载词的翻译。在翻译扎根于中华优秀传统文

化的中医术语时，语义翻译法能更好地再现中医术语的文化内涵，有利于目的语读者了解源语文化。

以下例子选于《WHO中医国际标准术语》（*WHO international standard terminologies on traditional Chinese medicine*）以及《中医药学名词》对中医术语的英译及解释。

表1　中医四字格术语英译

原文	译文一	译文二
阴阳互根	Yin and yang reciprocally root	Mutual rooting of yin-yang
	《WHO中医国际标准术语》	《中医药学名词》（2004）

《WHO中医国际标准术语》版本将中将其解释为"Yin and yang have reciprocal roots and cannot be separated"并翻译为"Yin and yang reciprocally root"（World Health Organization，2022）。"阴阳"采用零译法译为"yin and yang"，成分为主语；而"互根"则译为"root"，为谓语。"reciprocally root"虽然略显直白，但基本上传达了"互根"的概念，即相互依存、相互为根。

在《中医药学名词》（2004）中，其含义为阴阳相互依存、互为根本，其译文为"mutual rooting of yin-yang"。这一短语在结构上属于偏正短语（或称为修饰短语）该译本使用了"mutual rooting"来表达"阴阳互根"，其中"mutual"意味着"相互的"，而"rooting"则暗示了"生根、扎根"的动作或状态。"of yin-yang"作为后置定语，明确了"mutual rooting"的主体是阴阳，与原文的语境高度一致。

从语义翻译的角度来看，两个译本都较为准确地传达了"阴阳互根"的核心意义，即阴阳之间相互依存的关系。然而，在表达的流畅性和自然性上，"Yin and yang reciprocally root"可能略显生硬，而"Mutual rooting of yin-yang"则更为流畅和自然，更符合英语的表达习惯。

表2　中医四字格术语英译

原文	译文一	译文二
天人相应	Man–nature correspondence	Correspondence between human body and natural environment
	《WHO中医国际标准术语》	《中医药学名词》（2004）

译文一"Man-nature correspondence"简洁明了，直接传达了"天"与"人"之间的对应关系，且"nature"一词在广义上可包含自然环境，具有一定的灵活性。缺点是"man"一词可能过于泛指人类，未特指中医理论中的"人"（即身体、精神与社会环境的综合体）。同时，"nature"也可能不够具体，未明确指向"自然环境"。

而译文二"Correspondence between human body and natural environment"具体明确，直接指出了是"人体"与"自然环境"之间的对应关系，与中医理论中的"天人相应"概念更为吻合。它详细描述了中医理论中人体与自然环境的密切联系和相互影响。虽然相对于译文一来说，略显冗长，但在准确性和文化特色保留上更为出色。

从语义翻译的原则出发，译文二"Correspondence between human body and natural environment"更符合要求。因为它更准确地传达了"天人相应"中"人体"与"自然环境"之间的对应关系，且保留了中医理论的文化特色。

表3　中医三字格术语英译

原文	译文一	译文二
肺恶寒	The lung dislikes cold	Lung being averse to cold
	《WHO中医国际标准术语》	《中医药学名词》（2004）

译文一"The lung dislikes cold"直接明了地传达了"肺"对"冷"的不喜好，与原文意思相符。且使用了主谓宾结构，表达自然流畅。

译文二"Lung being averse to cold"，"averse to"同样表达了"不喜欢、厌恶"的意思，与原文意思相符。此译文使用了动名词短语结构，虽然这种结构在英语中不常用于直接表达某种特性或偏好，但在特定语境下（如科技文献、医学术语）可以接受。然而，它不如主谓宾结构直观易懂。

根据分析译文得出：译文一的主谓宾结构更为直接和常见，易于理解和接受；而译文二的动名词短语结构虽然在特定语境下可接受，但相比之下略显复杂。

表4　中医三字格术语英译

原文	译文一	译文二
脾藏意	The spleen stores intent	Spleen storing idea
	《WHO中医国际标准术语》	《中医药学名词》（2004）

译文一"The spleen stores intent"中"intent"在英文中通常指"意图、目的",与中医理论中"意"的概念不完全吻合。中医的"意"更多指的是神志、意识或意志活动,与脾的运化功能相关,但不仅限于"意图"。译文一虽为主谓宾结构,但"intent"的选词不够精准。

译文二"Spleen storing idea"中"idea"意为"想法、观念",同样与中医"意"的概念不匹配。中医的"意"并非简单的"想法",而是与心神活动密切相关的神志状态。虽然结构上是动名词短语,但"idea"的选择并不恰当。

从语义翻译的原则出发,两个译本都未能准确传达"脾藏意"的中医含义。然而,如果必须在两者中选择,译文一在结构上更为合理(主谓宾),尽管"intent"的选词仍有问题。

表5 中医双字格术语英译

原文	译文一	译文二
三焦	Sanjiao	Triple energy
	《WHO中医国际标准术语》	《中医药学名词》(2004)

译文一"Sanjiao"直接采用中文拼音"Sanjiao"作为英文翻译,保留了中医术语的原汁原味,避免了文化误解。作为专有名词的翻译,直接使用拼音在结构上是合理的,符合国际惯例。

译文二"Triple energy"试图解释"三焦"的某种功能或属性,但"energy"并不能准确涵盖"三焦"在中医理论中的复杂含义。中医的"三焦"不仅仅是一种能量,而是指人体上中下三个部位的脏腑和经络的综合功能区域。虽然"triple"和"energy"在英文中都是合理的词汇,但组合起来并不能准确表达"三焦"的概念。

从语义翻译的原则出发,译文一"Sanjiao"更符合要求,因为它直接、准确地传达了中医术语"三焦"的原意。

表6 中医双字格术语英译

原文	译文一	译文二
五运	Five movements	Five evolutive phases
	《WHO中医国际标准术语》	《中医药学名词》(2004)

译文一"Five movements"中的"movements"在英文中通常指"运动、动作"，而中医中的"五运"指的是自然界中木、火、土、金、水五种气运的化生与循环规律，不仅仅局限于物理上的运动。因此，"movements"虽能传达出"运"的动态性，但未能准确表达其深层的中医含义。从结构上看，"Five movements"是符合英文表达习惯的，但如前所述，语义上有所欠缺。

译文二"Five evolutive phases"中的"evolutive"表示"进化的、发展的"，"phases"表示"阶段、时期"。这个翻译试图捕捉"五运"中气运循环发展的特点，比"movements"更接近于中医"五运"的实质，即自然界中气的五种不同状态和变化阶段。"Five evolutive phases"结构上清晰，能够准确传达出"五运"的复数形式和其作为发展阶段的概念。

从语义翻译的原则出发，译文二"Five evolutive phases"更符合中医"五运"的实质。它不仅传达了"五运"的动态性和阶段性，还隐含了气运循环发展的深层含义。

（二）交际翻译在中医术语中的应用

交际翻译把目标读者看作是一个平等的沟通目标，同时也要考虑到读者在阅读过程中的期望经验和反馈。交际翻译超越了语言层次的限制，力求让译入语更接近译入语的文化和读者群，避免模糊、可疑，以便读者能够根据原文的原意做出回应，实现交际的目标。中医术语归根结底属于科学性和医学性文本，在对其进行传播的时候，应首先考虑其医学内容和意义的传播，且需要为目的语读者排除在阅读理解以及交际方面的阻碍，促进交际。

表7 中医四字格术语英译

原文	译文
罢极之本	The liver is the foundation for fatigue endurance
	《WHO中医国际标准术语》

《中医药学名词》暂未收集此术语。译文将"罢极之本"译为"The liver is the foundation for fatigue endurance"，准确地传达了肝脏在耐受和消除疲劳方面的核心作用，符合中医理论。译文的结构清晰，采用了"主语（The liver）＋系动词（is）＋表语（the foundation for fatigue endurance）"的句式，符合英文表达习惯，易于理解。

表8　中医四字格术语英译

原文	译文一	译文二
肺主皮毛	The lung is connected with the skin and body hair	Lung governing skin and hair
	《WHO中医国际标准术语》	《中医药学名词》（2013）

《中医药学名词》（2013）中的定义是"皮毛赖肺的精气以滋养和温煦，皮毛的散气与汗孔的开合也与肺之宣发功能密切相关"（《中医药学名词2013》，2014）。

译文一"The lung is connected with the skin and body hair"使用了"connected with"来表达中医中"主"的关系，虽然能够传达两者之间的关联，但可能不足以表达中医理论中"肺"对"皮毛"的滋养、调控等深层含义。英文句子结构清晰，主谓宾齐全，符合英文表达习惯。

译文二"Lung governing skin and hair"直接使用了"governing"，一个在英语中不常见但在中医翻译中常用的词汇，来传达中医中"肺"对"皮毛"的主导作用，更符合中医术语的特定表达方式和交际翻译的原则。整体上，该译文结构简洁，重点突出。

更符合交际翻译原则的是译文二"Lung governing skin and hair"。它更准确地传达了中医理论中"肺"对"皮毛"的主导作用，且结构简洁明了，易于目标读者理解和接受。

表9　中医三字格术语英译

原文	译文
女子胞	Uterus
	《WHO中医国际标准术语》

"女子胞"是一个偏正短语，"女子"修饰"胞"，"胞"即指子宫。这一术语体现了中医对人体生理结构的独特认识和分类方式。

《中医药学名词》暂未收集此术语。将"女子胞"译为"Uterus"在医学术语上是准确的，因为"Uterus"在西医中指的是子宫，与"女子胞"的生理功能有很大的重叠，都是女性生殖系统的关键部分。因此，从交际翻译的角度来看，这个译文是有效的，因为它能够清晰地传达出原文的含义。

译文直接进行归化翻译，并在目的语文化中找出了一项对等且意义相同的已有

99

词汇。这一翻译方法避免了译文因语言文化差异而产生理解障碍和文本歧义。

表10　中医三字格术语英译

原文	译文
急惊风	Acute infantile convulsion
	《WHO中医国际标准术语》/《中医药学名词》（2010）

《中医药学名词》（2010）中的定义是"以发病急骤、发热、抽搐、昏迷为主要表现的惊风"，译文与上面一致。"急惊风"是一个偏正短语，"急"修饰"惊风"，强调了病症的突发性和严重性。

结构上，译文采用了英文中常见的"形容词＋名词"短语结构，其中"acute"描述了病症的急性特点，"infantile"限定了病症多发的年龄段，"convulsion"则直接对应了中医中的"惊风"，即抽搐症状。整个短语结构清晰，易于理解。在医学术语的准确性上，"Acute infantile convulsion"与中医的"急惊风"在描述病症的紧急性、发病年龄和主要症状上基本吻合。

表11　中医双字格术语英译

原文	译文
溪谷	Muscle interspace
	《WHO中医国际标准术语》

《中医药学名词》暂未收录此术语。从交际翻译的角度来看，译文"Muscle interspace"可能未能完全传达"溪谷"在中医或传统中国文化中的丰富内涵。在中医理论中，"溪谷"可能指的是人体经络系统中的某些特定部位，或者是一种形象化的描述，用以说明气血流通的通道或空间。而"Muscle interspace"仅指肌肉间的间隙，可能过于狭隘，无法涵盖"溪谷"的广泛含义。因此，从交际效果上看，这个译文可能不够理想。

考虑到"溪谷"在中医理论中的特殊含义，一个更贴切的翻译可能是"Crevice-like channels"，这个短语既保留了"溪谷"作为通道或空间的概念，又通过"Crevice-like"传达了其狭窄、深长的特点，与中医理论中气血流通的细微通道相呼应。

表12 中医双字格术语英译

原文	译文一	译文二
黑睛	Cornea and iris	Black of the eye
	《WHO中医国际标准术语》	《中医药学名词》（2013）

《中医药学名词》（2013）中的定义是"眼球外壁前部中央占外层的1/6无色透明的组织，是光线透进眼内必经的通路，是通光体之一，有保护眼珠的作用"，译文为"black of the eye"。

译文一"Cornea and iris"将"黑睛"解释为角膜（Cornea）和虹膜（Iris），这在现代医学术语中是准确的。然而，在中医理论中，"黑睛"通常特指眼球前部的透明部分，即角膜，而不包括虹膜。对于熟悉现代医学的读者来说，这个译文可能易于理解，但可能会引入混淆，因为虹膜在中医中并不直接等同于"黑睛"。

译文二"Black of the eye"直接翻译为"眼睛的黑色部分"，虽然没有明确指出是角膜，但在中医语境下，这种表述通常被理解为"黑睛"，即眼球前部的透明且呈黑色的部分（主要为角膜）。这个译文更符合中医术语的表达习惯，能够将其内涵准确地传达给中医读者或对中国文化有一定了解的读者。

译文一采用了并列结构，将"黑睛"分解为两部分进行翻译，这在现代医学术语中是常见的，但在中医术语翻译中可能略显生硬。译文二则采用了简洁的偏正短语结构，突出了"黑睛"作为眼睛的一部分且颜色为黑的特征，更符合中医术语的表达方式。

以上术语也都是富含医学特色的词汇，在翻译时，应注重翻译其医学内涵。以上的"罢极之本"用来形容与肝相关的身体状况；其内涵意义是指肝能耐疲劳，是运动机能的根本，译文"The liver is the foundation for fatigue endurance"属于阐释性翻译，较好地描述了其意义，避免了给读者造成困惑。而"女子胞"，若按字面意思翻译为"cell of women"，则会给读者造成困惑，难以理解。因为在中医中，"女子胞"是指女生独有的器官，即子宫。"溪谷"和"黑睛"也是同样如此，若望文生义翻译成"valley"和"black eyes"都会造成原文意义的曲解，读者会不明所以，从而影响其交际功能。由于汉语具有丰富的表意功能，中医术语的内涵与外延需要译者准确的理解，不能仅按字面意思直译，只有如此，才能将中医术语中所包含的信息准确无误地呈现给目的语读者，从而不至于造成文化误解。

五、结语

在全球化的进程中，不同的文化观念和价值观相互影响、相互融合，作为中国传统文化精华的中医药文化的海外传播也面临着新的机会，因此，进行更大范围、更深入的中医药科学的跨文化传播是必然的。由于中医术语英译中存在许多问题，使得中医药的文化传播阻碍重重。对于中医翻译工作者而言，要将中医术语中的精髓和内涵准确无误、通顺清楚、简明优雅地传递出去，需要不断地加强自身翻译能力以及专研中医文化内涵。

【参考文献】

[1] 全国科学技术名词审定委员会，2005.《中医药学名词2004》[M]．北京：科学出版社．

[2] 全国科学技术名词审定委员会，2014.《中医药学名词2013》[M]．北京：科学出版社．

[3] 全国科学技术名词审定委员会，2011.《中医药学名词2010》[M]．北京：科学出版社．

[4] 宋晓璐、王林，2016．中成药说明书交际翻译[J]．中国中西医结合杂志，36（6）：757–759.

[5] 沈晓华，2020．交际翻译策略视角下的《金匮要略》英译研究——以罗希文译本为例[J]．中国中西医结合杂志，40（1）：116–120.

[6] 原虹，2003．论语义翻译和交际翻译[J]．中国科技翻译，16（2）：1–2.

[7] 曲倩倩，2019．交际翻译视角下中医典籍书名翻译探讨[J]．中国中西医结合杂志，39（7）：878–880.

[8] 付甜甜、刘珊，2022．四字格中医脏腑病机术语的词法结构及英译分析[J]．中国中医药现代远程教育（1）：137–139.

[9] 北京大学第一医院中西医结合研究所，2022．WHO西太平洋地区传统医学名词术语国际标准[M]．北京大学医学出版社．

[10] 王尔亮、晋永、段英帅等，2010．从"三字格"中医术语翻译看中医术语的等效翻译[J]．现代中医药（4）：96–99.

[11] Karl Buhler. *Theory of Language: The Representational Function of Language* [M]. John Benjamins Publishing Company, 2011.

[12] Peter Newmark. *Approaches to translation* [M]. Shanghai: Shanghai Foreign Language Education Press, 2001.

[13] World Health Organization. *WHO international standard terminologies on traditional Chinese medicine* [M]. 2022.

A Feasibility Study on the Translation of TCM Terminology into English

Hubei University of Chinese Medicine   YANG Hanya, LIU Jin

Abstract: The lexicon and conceptual framework of Traditional Chinese Medicine (TCM) are deeply rooted in Chinese cultural heritage, with terminologies composed of four-character, three-character, and two-character phrases forming an integral part of the TCM linguistic architecture. These terms not only encapsulate the quintessence of TCM theories but also bear profound cultural significance. In the endeavor to translate TCM terminology into English, it is imperative to achieve precise comprehension and rendition of these terms, ensuring both their scholarly precision and broad accessibility. Among Newmark's translation paradigms, semantic translation and communicative translation stand out as pivotal and distinctive elements. This paper, guided by the principles of semantic and communicative translation, elucidates and examines their application in the translation of TCM terminology, seeking to offer a novel perspective for the English translation of TCM terms and to expand the scope of research in this field.

Keywords: Translation of Traditional Chinese Medicine (TCM); Semantic Translation; Communicative Translation; TCM Terminology

中医翻译过程中的不可译现象研究[①]
——以"鬼门"一词为例

江西中医药大学 胡亚柳[②] 彭咏梅[③] 王 涵[④]

【摘 要】中医是中华文化的重要组成部分,集结了千百年来古人丰富的临床实践经验,现在仍为中国人民乃至世界人民做贡献。自改革开放以来,中医逐渐走上世界的舞台,中医药的国际传播发展事业蒸蒸日上。但由于中西方的文化差异以及中医学的特殊文化背景、历史演变、思维方式、哲学观念、医学理论等方面的因素产生了中医翻译不可译现象。中医翻译不可译是指中医学领域中存在的一些概念、术语、理论等无法完全准确地翻译成其他语言的现象。本文借用文本研究分析的方法,以"鬼门"一词为例进行研究,通过分析"鬼门"一词中医学的内涵和西方的内涵,进而探讨中医可译的方法和途径。

【关键词】不可译性;中医翻译;鬼门;文化

一、引言

中医历史悠久,是古人经过数千年临床实践及经验总结创造出的文化瑰宝,是中华优秀传统文化的组成部分,为中华民族的健康事业乃至世界人民的健康事业做

[①] 课题基金:(1)江西省教育厅科技项目"数字化视角下中医翻译和中医传播多模态数据库的构建与应用研究"(项目编号:GJJ2200194);(2)江西省教育厅教改项目"讲好中医故事的中医翻译多模态教学实证研究"(项目编号:JXJG-22-12-16)。
[②] 胡亚柳(1996—),硕士研究生,研究方向为语料库语言学和中医翻译。邮箱:1005512116@qq.com。
[③] 彭咏梅(1980—),博士、副教授、硕士生导师,研究方向为语料库语言学和中医翻译,本文通讯作者。邮箱:1752972324@qq.com。
[④] 王涵(2001—),硕士研究生,研究方向为语料库语言学和中医翻译。邮箱:1983183589@qq.com。

出巨大贡献。在改革开放后，中医药的英译及国际传播呈现欣欣向荣的发展势头，不少专家学者潜心研究中医英语翻译，为中医走向世界铺垫了道路。然而，由于中医具有独一无二的特色，加之中西文化的巨大差异，使得中医翻译难度较大。因此，在翻译过程中，中医词汇的不对应性使得中医翻译有时候呈现"百花齐放"的状态。也就是说，中医翻译存在一定的不可译性。中医翻译的不可译指中医特有的概念、术语、理论和实践方法在翻译过程中难以完全准确地用另一种语言表达的现象。这是因为中医学术思想和理论体系的形成，经历了长期的历史积淀和文化沉淀，与西方医学有很大的不同。部分中医术语无法找到完全对应的外语词汇，或者其外语译名无法表达其内涵和特殊含义。中医的理论、观念、方法与西方医学的不同，无法通过单纯的翻译来准确地表达。中医学的一些概念或理论缺乏现代科学支持或验证，难以在西方医学的框架下得到准确翻译。中医翻译不可译的现象，在跨语言交流和中医传播中需要特别注意。在进行中医翻译时，需要考虑到不同文化背景和语言之间的差异，以及确保所翻译的内容准确彰显中医学的精髓和特色。

二、不可译相关研究

（一）中医翻译不可译相关研究

中医翻译不可译是指中医学领域中因中医学的特殊文化背景、历史演变、思维方式、哲学观念、医学理论等方面的因素导致一些概念、术语、理论等无法完全准确地翻译成其他语言的现象。中医的理论、观念、方法与西方医学的不同，无法通过单纯的翻译实现准确的表达。同时中医学的一些概念或理论缺乏现代科学支持或验证，所以西方医学中没有对应的概念或词汇。

目前关于中医翻译不可译研究有很多。宫颖（2021）从新冠肺炎疫情期间中医诊疗发挥作用入手，同时也从中医基本概念、中医临床诊断、中药学以及方剂术语，发掘和整理中医文化价值，寻求源文化的翻译策略，同时提出在文化不可译的视域下，译者应该充分把握主体，保持译语简洁，传递源语中的中医文化。王珊珊（2019）分别从语言和文化两个层面中的音韵、句法、修辞、方剂名、病症名、药名诗翻译几个方面举例探讨。分析了中医翻译中的不可译现象，探讨中医翻译的途径和方法。郭雅红（2016）从跨文化的角度，通过详细阐述中医术语的含义，充分分析译文，指出中医术语因语言文化差异，其可译性是有限度的，甚至存在不可译性。通过对具体术语翻译的研究，该文提出解决中医术语不可译问题应遵循意译和音译的原则，以及归化和异化的翻译方法，旨在引起更多学者对可译性限度的研究与探讨。谢舒婷（2016）从翻译美学角度谈论中医翻译的不可译。中医古籍作为中国传统文化的瑰宝，其语言具有音韵美、修辞美、简洁美以及文化美的美学特点。然而，由于中医翻译不可译的存在，不可避免的是在语言交际过程中这些美学特点会有所流失。

（二）其他不可译相关研究

翻译中的可译与不可译是翻译中一对矛盾的问题，从结构主义、功能对等理论、跨文化视角等方面着手，当然也有学者从目的论角度加以分析。目前关于翻译不可译相关研究也有不少。王春旭（2019）从文化差异角度入手讨论了汉语与英语翻译中的"不可译"现象，对这一现象进行分析的同时也提出了应对方法。邓俊文（2021）以中国传统翻译理论发展时间为线索，探索了中国传统译论对不可译成因的认识。刘书臻（2022）以由美国诗人桑德堡所作的诗歌《芝加哥》的翻译进行探析，译者在翻译的过程中，分析原文的同时把握作品时代背景，来探讨翻译中的可译性与不可译性，旨在通过分析，对翻译产生积极的影响。梁欢（2022）以诗歌翻译中的"可译"和"不可译"入手，结合"三美论"，从音、形、意出发找出诗歌翻译的重点、难点，找到不可译的原因，并提出"三美论"有助于降低诗歌翻译的不可译。魏精良、仇伟（2019）从目的论的角度入手，研究英汉翻译中的不可译，英汉两种语言不仅在语言层面会出现不可译的现象，在文化层面（如称谓语和商标语等）也会出现不可译的问题。翻译不仅仅体现了简单的语言的转换，同时也是文化交流以及传播的重要途径之一。在翻译过程中译者应结合实际进行翻译，尽量减少不可译的现象出现。

三、"鬼门"一词的理解

（一）中医术语"鬼门"概述

中医术语"鬼门"不同于单纯字面之意，该术语主要有两个出处：一是出自《素问·汤液醪醴论》篇中的"开鬼门，洁净府"；二是一种针灸治疗方法——"鬼门十三针"。二者虽然同用"鬼门"一词，含义却大不相同。目前国内关于"鬼门"一词的研究是从中医翻译概念整合理论出发（如李辰蝶、吴莲英，2017），其余的均是从中医学角度入手。

（1）"开鬼门，洁净府"中"鬼门"的含义

在《黄帝内经》谈论治疗水肿的疾病篇中，王冰注云："开鬼门……洁净府。"理解为发汗利小便，鬼门释为玄府，即汗孔。"开鬼门，洁净府"，即宣肺透表，这种方法可以使肺气得宣，营卫相和，以求"上焦得通，濈然汗出"。对肺会起作用，借此达到发汗利小便的效果，从而消除水肿，真武汤可以作为主要的方子，在此基础上可进行加减，若是肺部热象明显，可以配伍麻黄杏仁甘草汤。各位学者对于这里"鬼门"一词的解释仍旧有歧义。那么翻译的过程中就需要具体情况具体分析，根据不同的情景进行翻译。

（2）"鬼门十三针"中"鬼门"的含义

鬼门十三针是治疗癫、狂、痫等精神情志病经常用的方法，针灸学指出鬼门十三针是由十三鬼穴命名的。痰气互结会引起癫病，表现为心情抑郁、表情冷淡、沉默痴呆、喃喃自语。痰火互结会引起狂病，起病骤急，突发狂乱无知，毁人伤物，哭笑无常，头痛失眠。痫病因气机逆乱、元神失控导致猝然昏倒，不省人事，口中怪叫，口吐白沫。由以上可以看出，无论是癫证、狂证，还是痫证等其他的情志病都会有行为异常。《千金翼方》云："凡百邪之病示……表癫邪之端而见其病。"遂记载"百邪所病者，针有十三穴"。由于当时那个年代严重缺乏医学知识，古人无法深究以及解释发病迅速、行为异常的精神情志疾病的真正病因，便认为是有鬼神作祟，这为其蒙上了神秘以及迷信的色彩，因此直接称此类疾病为邪病。当时民间见到这类病发作的病人都认为是"撞邪"或者是"沾了什么不干净的东西"。因此，治疗此病的穴位称为"鬼穴"。通过针刺鬼穴治疗这类病人，"中邪"或者"撞邪"的症状会消失，"不干净的东西"也会离开人体，而这套针法则被称为"鬼门十三针"。

（二）西方关于"鬼门"一词的理解

西方并没有传统的"鬼门"概念，但是在一些文化和宗教中，有类似的概念或者地方。在基督教中，人死后的灵魂会被判定去向天堂或地狱。天堂是永远的福乐之地，而地狱则是永远的惩罚之地。因此，地狱也可以被认为是一种"鬼门"。在希腊神话中，人死后灵魂会被送到冥界，在那里会经过审判，然后被分配到合适的领域。冥界也可以被看作一种"鬼门"。在某些文化中，人们认为死亡是进入另一个世界的过程，这种世界可能是幸福的乐园，也可能是可怕的恐怖之地。这些地方

也可以被视为"鬼门"。由此可见"鬼门"在西方并没有一个具体的定义，但可以被理解为一种与死亡相关的领域或者概念。

（三）"鬼门"英译探析

通过查阅对比，不同词典对"鬼门"有不同的翻译。《实用汉英中医词典》将其翻译为"Gate of the soul"；《英汉·汉英中医词典》将其翻译为"Ghost gate（pore）"；《新汉英中医学词典》将其翻译为"Sweat pore"。"鬼门十三针"中"鬼门"的含义与鬼的基本含义是一致的，可以理解为人死后的魂。那这里的"鬼门"就会带有一些迷信色彩，与英语中"ghost"十分相似。在《牛津高阶英汉双解词典》中对"ghost"的英文解释为"the spirit of dead person that a living person believes they can see or hear"，意思是活着的人可以看见或听见的人死后的灵魂。《牛津高阶英汉双解词典》中将"鬼门"翻译为"Gates of Hell"，意为"地狱之门"。这种翻译方式强调"鬼门"所在的地点是地狱或者与地狱有关联。还有其他几本字典关于"鬼门"的翻译。其中《汉英词典》将"鬼门"直译为"Ghost Gate"，这种翻译方式比较直观，能够传达"鬼门"指代"阴间入口"的含义。《新世纪汉英大词典》将"鬼门"翻译为"Ghost Gate"，这种翻译方式强调"鬼门"是通向阴间的入口。《朗文当代英语词典》则将"鬼门"翻译为"Entrance to the Underworld"。这种翻译方式也强调"鬼门"是通向阴间的入口。从这些字典对"鬼门"一词的翻译可以看出，"Sweat pore"和"Ghost gate"更加贴合中医文化，反而"Gates of Hell"或者"Netherworld Portal"更加贴合西方的文化。因此，在翻译"鬼门"时，还应考虑具体的语境和目标读者的文化背景，注重文化的差异以及受众者的接受度和包容度，以确保翻译的准确性和易读性。当然随着中医逐步走上国际大舞台，我们要注重文化自信，在保证中医文化"真"的同时考虑文化差异，将"不可译"转化为"可译"。

四、结语

通过对"鬼门"一词不可译现象进行探讨，可以发现中医翻译不可译现象客观存在，而且比较普遍。中医翻译不可译，可以总结为以下几个方面的原因。首先，中医概念具有语境依赖性的特点。中医学术思想和理论体系中的许多概念，如"气""血""阴阳"等，具有强烈的语境依赖性，难以直接用另一种语言准确表达。

因此，研究者通常会从中医概念的内涵、外延、语义等多个方面入手，探讨中医概念在翻译中的不可译及其解决方法。其次，中医特有的思维模式也是一个重要原因。中医学术思想和理论体系具有独特的思维模式和方法，如"辨证施治""以治未病"等，这些概念在西方医学中很难找到对应的概念，翻译时需要进行解释说明。研究者通常会从中西医学的哲学、思维方式等方面入手，探讨中医思维模式在翻译中的不可译及其解决方法。最后，实践技术的文化差异也是中医翻译不可译的影响因素。中医实践技术和方法在不同的文化背景下有着不同的名称和应用方式，如针灸、中药疗法等，其具体的操作和效果在不同的文化环境下也会有所不同。因此，研究者通常会从中西医学的实践技术和方法、文化差异等方面入手，探讨中医实践技术在翻译中的不可译及其解决方法。

本文以"鬼门"一词的翻译为例，浅谈中医翻译不可译，发现这是一个复杂的问题，需要从多个角度进行分析和探讨，才能找到合适的翻译策略。当今趋势，全球多元化文化互相交融，疫情期间中医药在中国乃至世界发挥了重大作用，一定程度上推动了中医药在国内外的发展，使中医文化在不同文化中的被包容度和接受度得到极大提高，可译与不可译具有相对性，"不可译"将无限趋向于"可译"。在推动中医药与国际接轨进程中，中医译者应当在保存中医文化之"真"、中医文化之"美"的同时考虑受众者的文化差异、接受程度以及包容程度。

【参考文献】

[1] 宫颖，2021．文化不可译性视阈下中医临床诊疗的英译策略 [J]．山西卫生健康职业学院学报，31（05）：128–130.

[2] 王珊珊、吴青，2022．中医翻译中的不可译现象刍议 [J]．亚太传统医药，18（07）：189–192.

[3] 郭雅红，2016．语言文化差异对不可译的影响 [D]．福建师范大学．

[4] 谢舒婷，2016．翻译美学视角下的中医翻译不可译性研究 [J]．海外英语（10）：3–4.

[5] 王春旭，2019．从文化差异视角看中西方翻译中的不可译性 [J]．现代交际，No. 509（15）：87–88.

[6] 邓俊文，2021．中国传统译论对不可译性的成因认识研究 [J]．散文百家（理论）(08)：91–92.

[7] 刘书臻，2022．探析翻译中的可译性与不可译性——以《芝加哥》的翻译为例 [J]．时代报告（奔流），No. 439（05）：19–22.

[8] 梁欢，2022．浅谈诗歌翻译中的"可译性"和"不可译性" [C]// 四川西部文献编译研究中心．外语教育与翻译发展创新研究（11）．[出版者不详]，2022：4.

[9] 魏精良、仇伟, 2019. 目的论观照下的英汉翻译不可译研究 [J]. 牡丹江教育学院学报, No. 206(11): 11–13+76.

[10] 陈媛、黄忠廉, 2021. 李照国中医外译理念研究 [J]. 中国中西医结合杂志 41(01): 112–115.

[11] 李辰蝶、吴莲英, 2017. 概念整合理论下的中医术语翻译——以"鬼门"为例 [J]. 大众科技 19(02): 106–108.

[12] 张振卿、刘新军、秦淼, 2007. "鬼门"与"魄门"注解小析 [J]. 上海：中医文献杂志.

[13] 张奇文, 2001. 实用汉英中医词典 [M]. 济南：山东科学技术出版社, 333.

Discussion of untranslatable phenomena in TCM translation
—Taking "Ghost gate" as an example

Jiangxi University of Chinese Medicine   Hu Yaliu, PENG Yongmei, WANG Han

Abstract: Traditional Chinese Medicine (TCM) is an important part of Chinese culture, which has gathered the rich clinical experience of ancient people for thousands of years. Since the reform and opening up, TCM has gradually stepped onto the world stage, and the international communication and development of TCM has been flourishing. However, due to the cultural differences between China and the west, the special cultural background, historical evolution, mode of thinking, philosophical concepts, medical theories and other factors, the untranslatability of TCM translation occurs. Untranslatability in TCM translation refers to the phenomenon that some concepts, terms and theories in the field of TCM can not be translated into other languages completely and accurately. This article adopted the method of text research and analysis, taking the word "Ghost" as an example while analyzing the connotation of the word "Ghost" in Chinese medicine and western connotation, and then discussed the method and approach of translatability of traditional Chinese medicine.

Keywords: Untranslatability; Ghost Gate; TCM Translation; culture

翻译技术与本地化
TRANSLATION TECHNOLOGIES
AND LOCALIZATION

《黄帝内经·素问》汉法平行语料库的构建路径与方法

田知灵[①]　许　明[②]　潘晓颖[③]

【摘　要】本文重点探索《黄帝内经·素问》汉法平行双语料库的构建过程。《黄帝内经·素问》汉法平行语料库的构建需要经过语料预处理、语料降噪、语料对齐等步骤，在此过程中，本文解决了在构建双语平行语料库过程中遇到的 OCR 识别错误、古汉语句段切分问题及困难，总结了构建双语平行语料库的经验及规律，最终构建容量为 30 万字左右的汉法双语平行语料库；最后依托双语平行语料从词汇和句段层面深入分析了译本的可读性。

【关键词】《黄帝内经·素问》；语料库翻译学；平行语料库

一、引言

语料库语言学在世界范围内蓬勃发展，并在 20 世纪 80 年代进入中国。近十几年来，语料库已经成为语言学研究的热点，在教学、翻译、语法、语义、词典和词汇等方面发展迅速。语料库翻译学起源于英国学者蒙娜·贝克发表的题为"*Corpus linguistics and translation studies: implications and applications*"的论文（Mona Baker, 1993）。该文指出语料库可用于翻译研究实践中，揭示了语料库与翻译研究结合的

[①] 田知灵，北京语言大学高级翻译学院硕士研究生，研究方向为跨学科翻译研究，邮箱：1051861412@qq.com。
[②] 许明（1979—　），北京语言大学教授、博士生导师。研究方向为翻译跨学科研究、口笔译认知过程、术语学等。邮箱：22415591@qq.com，本文通讯作者。
[③] 潘晓颖，社会科学文献出版社数字分社编辑，研究方向为外国语言学及应用语言学，邮箱：pxy@ssap.cn，本文通讯作者。

理论价值与应用价值（王帅，2014：29–32）。当前，翻译学研究中的一个关键方向是基于语料库的方法，主要涉及利用双语平行语料库进行相应的研究。语料库已成为翻译学领域中一个重要的研究手段，它不仅关注语料库翻译研究的理论与方法，还探讨了语料库技术在机器翻译系统中的运用，可以说语料库翻译学的发展为双语平行语料库的建立奠定了基础。

从国内研究现状来看，双语平行语料库研究受到越来越大的重视，在建库意义、语料采集、标注、应用等方面均有详细阐述。在语料库翻译学的发展过程中，许多学者以及企业出于学术研究或其他目的建立了众多平行语料库、类比语料库，但在专门用于中医翻译的中医双语平行语料库方面的研究相对滞后贫乏（蒋亦文，2023：19–23）。目前，就语料库的语料类型来说，文学类文本较多，科技、经济、法律等文本类型较少，如北京外国语大学的王克非教授等学者已开始建立的文学翻译相关的平行语料库。而研究方向也多以译者风格、翻译策略为主，鲜有专门用于中医翻译的双语平行语料库，如朱珊（2021）基于自建语料库，分别从词汇、句法和语篇三个层面分析了《狂人日记》两个版本的译者翻译风格，吴光亭、张涛（2020）进行了基于英汉双语平行语料库的模糊限制语汉译策略研究。

笔者以"中医语料库"为关键词在中国知网上进行检索，主要主题限定为"语料库"以及"基于语料库的"，从检索结果来看，2010年至今的相关学术期刊论文有79篇，学位论文仅有5篇。其中代表性的有南京中医药大学施蕴中（2009）的》《黄帝内经》汉英语料库建设研究，作者在文中指出了《黄帝内经》汉英语料库建设的意义和必要性，并对《黄帝内经》汉英语料库建库提出了设想。另外还有陈滟、施蕴中（2005）提出的中医英语汉英口语语料库的建设，但这两个汉英语料库目前只是将汉英语料汇总，都没有做到平行对齐。在中药方面目前则并未出现专门的语料库，只有中国药科大学的药学英语语料库中含有一小部分内容。

综上所述，基于古汉语的汉英、汉法等多语言语料库的建设是一项长期任务，需要在不断摸索中逐渐完善，也需要中医、翻译、计算机技术等多学科的交融合作。本文将重点探究基于《黄帝内经·素问》和古汉语的汉法双语平行语料库的构建。

二、研究设计

（一）研究方法

本研究主要采取语料库研究法。通过语料库研究法，确定建库的方式方法和原则，明确建库步骤，包括语料获取、语料预处理、语料降噪、语料的校对与对齐等。同时结合实践研究法，通过实际建库操作，解决在建库过程中遇到的一系列困难，总结建库的经验及规律。

（二）研究问题

本研究拟解决的关键性问题：
（1）汉法双语平行语料库的构建遵循怎样的流程？
（2）以古汉语为基础的双语平行语料库的构建会遇到怎样的问题和困难？如何解决这些问题？
（3）依托双语平行语料，如何对比分析译本的可读性？

（三）研究步骤

在构建双语平行语料库之前需要明确建立语料库的目的与需求，本文中的汉法平行语料库的目的是实现从古文到法语译文的句级对应，因此不需要进行分词标注。在构建过程中首先进行语料选取，在获取原文与译文语料的基础上进行预处理，并通过 OCR 文字识别将语料转化为可编辑的 DOC 格式，通过文本处理软件 EmEditor 等对语料进行降噪，并使用对齐软件 ABBYY Aligner 以及 Excel 等对汉法双语语料进行句子层级的对齐。接下来将校对后的对齐语料导出并存储，方便后续检索与分析。最后使用语料库工具 LancsBox 分别对导出的两个译本的平行语料进行对比分析。

（四）语料选取

（1）原文语料
《黄帝内经》是中国最早的医学经典著作，也是中医典籍的核心代表。《内经》分为《素问》和《灵枢》两部分，全面论述了中医的基本理论与学术思想，为中医的发展奠定了建设性的基础。其中《黄帝内经·素问》融合了中国古代哲学思想，道家、阴阳家、儒家、墨家以及先秦诸子的哲学思想在书中均有体现（程雅君、刘春燕，2021：56–60）。因此本文选取《黄帝内经·素问》原文为原始语料，全文共计 81 篇，其中"刺法论"篇第七十二和"本病论"篇第七十三现已缺失。

（2）译文语料
随着中华文化的传播，越来越多的国家意识到中医的功效与魅力。迄今，《黄帝内经》拥有 7 个法语译本，笔者分别选取了汉学家兼医生雅克·安德烈·拉维耶（Jacques-André Lavier）以及法国华裔陈耀华的译本作为译文语料。拉维耶曾是早年法国传统中医的积极传播者和坚定倡导者，其深厚的中医理论与独特的教育模式对后世法国乃至整个欧洲中医的发展产生了深远的影响。拉维耶在中医领域的研究涵盖翻译研究与学术理论研究两大方面，这两大研究领域的成果均对中医在法国及欧洲的普及与发展起到了关键的推动作用。他对中医的翻译研究结合了甲骨文，通过解读古汉字的象形意义来阐释中医理论，其译本结合了其翻译与中医的综合经验，致力于在西方还原传统的中医名词术语（谢羽璐等，2020：112–117）。出生在法国的华裔陈耀华进行了系统的中医学习，具有丰富的针灸和中医治疗的临床经验，他的《黄帝内经》法译本最受欢迎，其译本注重再现中国传统文化，最大限度地向西方阐释中医思想与理论。

表 1　译本介绍

出版作者（译者）	Jacques-André Lavier	You-Wa Chen
出版日期	1990	2013
出版社	Édition Pardès	Éditions You Feng
出版编号（ISBN）	0992-5848	978-2-84279-571-9

三、双语平行语料库构建

平行语料库，也称 parallel corpora 或 parallele txts，是由原语文本及其平行对应的译语文本构成的双语语料库，其双语对应程度有词级、句级和段级几种（王克非，2004：27–32）。由于本语料库的研究目的之一为中医典籍翻译研究，因此采用句级对齐的形式。

（一）语料预处理

本研究获取的原文语料为 PDF 格式，译文语料为纸质文本，因此需要使用 OCR 文字识别软件将这两者转化为可编辑的 DOC 格式文本。PDF 格式和纸质文本扫描的处理工程量大，在此过程中，笔者主要以手工进行 OCR 识别录入为主。

在语料预处理过程中，笔者选择白描作为预处理工具，其优点有支持多语种识别、准确率高、速度快以及校对方便等。

在处理原文语料时，因原文中的文字为古汉语，在 PDF 格式转 DOC 格式的过程中出现了一些无法识别的生僻字，如膩、炲、蒸、睭、䐔、膆等，笔者通过《中华字海》在线版以及《康熙字典》在线版进行查找，并在原文中补充修改。值得注意的是，"月刍"一字并未在这两个在线字典中查询到，但根据《中华字海》在线版的解释，原文语料中的"月刍"一字是"腐"字的类推简化字，因此笔者选择在原文语料中保留"月刍"这一形式，并用括号标注。

OCR 文字识别软件在处理译文语料时出现的问题主要包括以下几类。

（1）窜行问题：窜行问题是指在识别过程中出现句段识别错误的问题，体现在句段上下颠倒或混乱。

（2）换行问题：即前后句子粘连的问题，需要断行的两个句子粘连在一起，没有完全匹配译本格式，需要进行手动断行。

（3）法语特殊字符问题：法语中带有音符的字母，如 î、ï，或 œ 无法被有效识别。

（4）标点符号问题：标点符号问题是在识别过程中出现的最常见的问题。法语中标点符号的使用规则与中文不同，法语中的分号、问号、感叹号等前后都有空格，并且两种语言的标点符号还存在全角、半角的区别。

因译本图片部分遮挡或图片不清晰，识别完成后拉维耶版的译本中第 42、43、47 篇以及第 81 篇有部分内容缺失，陈耀华的译本中第 35 章部分内容缺失，笔者将对照原文，部分删除，以方便后期对齐。同时在识别过程中，笔者发现陈耀华的译本中有许多帮助读者理解以及扩充知识的人物介绍图、五行结构图、穴位图等图绘，另还有穴位标示图，因原文中没有与之相对照的信息，在建库过程中只能舍弃。

语料预处理结束之后，分别形成原文与译文两个对照版的 DOC 格式文档：原文 108 981 字，拉维耶版译文 90 344 词，陈耀华版译文 100 567 词。

（二）语料降噪

完成语料的预处理工作后，需要对文本进行清洁降噪，即去除文本内的多余内容。语料降噪阶段的主要工作为集中解决语料预处理阶段出现的问题，在此过程中笔者使用了 EmEditor 文本编辑器。EmEditor 是一款用户友好的文字编辑工具，运作轻巧、功能完备，同时支持中文。通过其转换和查找替换功能，可以快速处理标点符号及空格问题。笔者已经在 OCR 文字识别过程中处理了原文中的生僻字问题以及译文中的法语特殊字符、换行以及窜行等问题，因此降噪阶段着重处理标点符号及空格问题并加以复查,语料降噪工作与校对工作统一进行。

(三) 语料对齐

人工对齐双语翻译语料,虽然准确率较高,但费时费力。目前,计算机辅助翻译已经在翻译领域应用,借助语料对齐工具,能够最大化实现对齐自动化,大大提高了对齐效率,节省了译者的时间。虽然目前自动化语料对齐工具的准确率有待提升,仍需要人工校对,但这种人机结合的工作模式仍高于纯人工对齐的效率。

ABBYY Aligner 2.0 是一款专业实用的双语对齐工具,其界面直观、简单易用,对齐精确度和质量较高。与其他同类软件相比,ABBYY Aligner 2.0 可以选定单元格进行批量对齐,同时支持 24 种语言的对齐语料导出与检索。因此经过实证对比,笔者选择使用 ABBYY Aligner 2.0 这一工具来对齐中法双语语料。

鉴于原文文本为古汉语,ABBYY Aligner 2.0 的对齐率较低,还需要手动进行校对。整个对齐过程包括:初步导入、逐行人工对齐与校对。

初步导入:首先选择原文本和目标文本的语言并且导入降噪后的文本,之后一键对齐文本,经过自动化的切分会得到初步对齐后的语料。

逐行人工对齐与校对:鉴于文言文的特殊性,对齐过程中首先要注意语义的切分,需要根据内容进行对应。人工对齐过程中笔者发现点击软件的"操作""从当前行对齐"可以大大提高对齐效率。

拉维耶版译本对齐前后的语料对比如图 1、图 2 所示。

1		1.
2		Vérité sur les anciens¶
3		Il était autrefois un Empereur nommé Houang Ti ↵ Oui, à sa naissance, fut doté d'une intelligence ↵ Surnaturelle.¶
4	上古天真论篇第一¶	
5		Nouveau-né, il parlait déjà ;¶
6	昔在黄帝,¶	
7	生而神灵,¶	Petit garçon, il avait un esprit vif et pénétrant ; ↵ Adulte, il fut toujours généreux et compréhensif. ↵
8	弱而能言,¶	
9	幼而徇齐,¶	
10	长而敦敏,¶	
11	成而登天。¶	Sa vie accomplie, il accéda au Ciel à sa mort. ↵
12	乃问于天师曰:¶	Un jour, il interrogea le Maître Taoïste Tch'i Pai ↵
13		En ces termes :¶
14	余闻上古之人,¶	J'ai entendu dire que les hommes de jadis¶
15	春秋皆度百岁,¶	Vivaient jusqu'à l'âge de cent ans, ↵ Restant toujours actifs, ignorant la sénescence. ↵
16	而动作不衰;¶	
17	今时之人,¶	Or, les hommes d'aujourd'hui ↵
18	年半百而动作皆衰者,¶	Sont des vieillards à cinquante ans.¶
19	时世异耶?人将失之耶?¶	Les générations actuelles seraient-elles différentes¶
20		Des anciennes ?¶

图 1 拉维耶版译文语料未对齐界面(部分)

118

1	上古天真论篇第一¶	1. Vérité sur les anciens¶
2	昔在黄帝，¶	Il était autrefois un Empereur nommé Houang Ti¶
3	生而神灵，¶	Oui, à sa naissance, fut doté d'une intelligenceSurnaturelle.¶
4	弱而能言，¶	Nouveau-né, il parlait déjà ;¶
5	幼而徇齐，¶	Petit garçon, il avait un esprit vif et pénétrant ; ¶
6	长而敦敏，¶	Adulte, il fut toujours généreux et compréhensif. ¶
7	成而登天。¶	Sa vie accomplie, il accéda au Ciel à sa mort. ¶
8	乃问于天师曰：¶	Un jour, il interrogea le Maître Taoïste Tch'i Pai ¶ En ces termes ¶
9	余闻上古之人，¶	J'ai entendu dire que les hommes de jadis¶
10	春秋皆度百岁，¶	Vivaient jusqu'à l'âge de cent ans, ¶
11	而动作不衰，¶	Restant toujours actifs, ignorant la sénescence. ¶
12	今时之人，¶	Or, les hommes d'aujourd'hui ¶
13	年半百而动作皆衰者，¶	Sont des vieillards à cinquante ans.¶
14	时世异耶？	Les générations actuelles seraient-elles différentes¶ Des anciennes ? ¶
15	人将失之耶？¶	Ou alors le genre humain a-t-il perdu quelque chose ? ¶
16	岐伯对曰：¶	Tch'i Pai répondit :¶
17	上古之人，¶	Les hommes de jadis¶
18	其知道者，¶	Etaient des sages qui obéissaient au Tao.¶
19	法于阴阳，¶ 和于术数，¶	La loi universelle du Yin-Yang, ¶ Seule règle de vie possible.¶
20	食饮有节，¶	Ils buvaient et mangeaient modérément,¶

图 2 拉维耶版译文语料对齐后界面（部分）

笔者将对齐过程中遇到的问题与难点总结如下。

（1）理解与翻译：在语料平行对齐的过程中，原文语料为文言文，文字表达通常比较简练。拉维耶版的译本力求达到原文的凝练，而陈耀华的译本则考虑到了中法文化层面的理解差异，在译本中多有补充增译。因此陈耀华的译本在对齐时更为困难。

（2）语句切分与标点符号：语句切分的处理贯穿了语料对齐的整个过程。原文语料的文言文文本多以逗号作为分割，拉维耶版的对应译文在结构与形式上忠于原文，行文呈现诗歌化。而陈耀华版的对应译文多有对原文的整合和补充，句段更长，因此语句切分耗费了大量的时间精力。

（3）译文与原文不完全对应：译文与原文不完全对应的现象出现频率较高。前期工作中出现的误差、译文段落错位和缺失、对齐软件不能精准识别和切分等都可能导致译文与原文不完全对应的情况。出现这种情况可在人工校对后，手动对齐明显不对应的部分，再使用"从当前行对齐"的自动对齐功能。再者可以结合纸质版语料手动删除、拆分或录入语句。

（四）语料导出与检索

ABBYY Aligner 2.0 对齐导出语料可选择两种格式：双语 RTF 格式、TMX 格式，为方便检索与存储，笔者分别导出了这两种格式的对齐语料。为方便后续的检索，笔者将这两个对齐后的语料转换为 Excel 格式导出保存。

导出后的拉维耶版译文双语平行语料共 491 页，共 34 714 行，库容量为

184 521，其中非中文单词有 91 513 个。陈耀华版译文双语平行语料共 365 页，共 22 397 行，库容量为 187 982，其中非中文单词有 98 615 个。

四、双语平行语料分析

可读性，又称易读性，是指文本容易为读者所理解和阅读的程度（宋瑛明、孙田丰，2023：5–8）。语料库翻译学利用语料库技术的优势，通过对大量翻译语料或双语语料进行数据统计和定性分析，从个案到普遍，总结或论证翻译活动和翻译本质的规律性特征（胡开宝等，2018：29）。通过基于语料库的方法量化研究文本的可读性，凸显了语料库研究的实证性特征。下面笔者将从词汇和句段两个层面分别分析拉维耶和陈耀华两个译本的可读性。

（一）词汇层面

类符/形符比与平均词长：类符/形符比（Type-Token Ratio，TTR）和平均词长是两个分析文本词汇特性的重要指标，可以从不同的角度提供关于文本词汇复杂度和可读性的信息。将拉维耶和陈耀华版本的译文分别导入语料分析软件 LancsBox 可得到类符形符总数，通过计算得出表 2。

表 2 类符/形符比与平均词长

指标	拉维耶版译文	陈耀华版译文
形符	89 034	96 264
类符	7 452	8 336
类符/形符比/%	8.37	8.66
平均词长	5.75	6.04

表 2 可以看出，拉维耶版译文与陈耀华版译文的类符形符比分别为 8.37% 与 8.66%，说明在词汇丰富程度方面，前者不如后者，平均词长也低于后者。这些数据表明，陈耀华版译文的整体词汇丰富度和阅读难度要高于拉维耶版译文。

（二）句段层面

拉维耶版译文与陈耀华版译文在句子结构层次性方面也存在显著差异，如表 3、表 4 所示，原文语料中的文言文文本多以逗号分隔。拉维耶版的对应译文在结构与形式上忠于原文，行文呈现诗歌化，句段较短。而陈耀华版的对应译文多有对原文的整合和补充，句段更长。

表 3　拉维耶版译文对齐语料举例（部分）

上古之人，	Les hommes de jadis
其知道者，	Etaient des sages qui obéissaient au Tao,
法于阴阳， 和于术数，	La loi universelle du Yin-Yang, Seule règle de vie possible.
食饮有节，	Ils buvaient et mangeaient modérément,
起居有常，	Se couchaient et se levaient à des heures régulières,

表 4　陈耀华版译文对齐语料举例（部分）

上古之人，其知道者，	« Ceux qui savaient garder une bonne santé dans les temps anciens menaient quotidiennement leur vie en accord avec la nature.
法于阴阳，	Ils suivaient le principe du Yin et du Yang, en observant l'art de l'équilibre basé sur les interactions entre le Yin et le Yang.
和于术数，	Ils étaient capables de réguler leur vie dans l'harmonie en récupérant l'énergie et l'essence vitale, pratiquant la voie de la préservation de la santé.
食饮有节，	Leurs habitudes de la vie quotidienne consistaient par exemple à suivre des modèles réguliers comme celui de manger et de boire en quantités modérées et à heures fixes,
起居有常，	de pratiquer les activités journalières de manière régulière.

综上所述，词汇层面陈耀华版译文的整体词汇丰富度和阅读难度要高于拉维耶版译文，句段层面拉维耶版译文在形式上的可读性更高。因译者的身份和所处时代不同，可读性的差异与译者的文化背景、思维模式、翻译策略密不可分。

五、结语

讲好中国故事、传播中国文化是"一带一路"倡议的宏伟战略目标,而中医国际化是讲好中国故事的重要一环,也是重要的突破口之一。建立中医汉法平行语料库及术语库在促进中医文化的国际传播和跨文化理解方面发挥着双重作用。《黄帝内经》是中国最早的医学经典著作,也是中医典籍的核心代表,为中医的发展奠定了坚定的基础,因此《黄帝内经》无疑是中华医学文化的载体和结晶。

本文以《黄帝内经·素问》原文及雅克·安德烈·拉维耶和陈耀华的法语译本为语料,围绕汉法双语平行语料库和术语库建设而展开。实验过程中详细阐述了建库的实际过程,包括建设语料库的工具分类、建库的流程、建库过程中遇到的问题及困难、建库过程中的发现与总结等,最后从词汇和句子层面对对齐后的平行语料进行了简要分析。实验结束后得到拉维耶版和陈耀华版两个双语平行语料库,库容量分别为 184 521 词和 187 982 词。

实验过程中笔者发现语料库对齐工具仍高度依赖人工校对,建库过程中的大量表格、图片无法与汉语原文对应等问题,可见中医语料库的建设是一项长期而艰巨的任务,需要持续的探索和完善,更需要中医学、翻译学、计算机技术等多个学科之间的密切合作与融合。

【参考文献】

[1] 陈滟、施蕴中,2005. 语料库语言学和中医汉英口语语料库 [J]. 江西中医学院学报(05):69–71.

[2] 程雅君、刘春燕,2021.《黄帝内经素问》甄论:中国哲学视域的中医之道 [J]. 江海学刊(04):51–60.

[3] 胡开宝、朱一凡、李晓倩,2018. 语料库翻译学 [M]. 上海:上海交通大学出版社.

[4] 蒋亦文,2023. 中医典籍汉英平行语料库的构建与应用 [J]. 中国科技翻译,36(04):19–23.

[5] 李苹、施蕴中,2009. 语料库语言学和《黄帝内经》汉英语料库 [J]. 中国科技信息(03):259+261.

[6] 宋瑛明、孙田丰,2023. 基于语料库的《药》三个英译本的可读性研究 [J]. 海外英语(12):5–8.

[7] 王克非, 2004. 双语平行语料库在翻译教学上的用途 [J]. 外语电化教学（6）: 27–32.

[8] 王帅, 2014. 我国语料库翻译学发展综述 [J]. 中国编辑（06）: 29–32.

[9] 吴光亭、张涛, 2020. 基于英汉双语平行语料库的模糊限制语汉译策略研究 [J]. 外语学刊（01）: 102–108.

[10] 谢羽璐、戴翥、贺霆等, 2020. 西方中医医家腊味爱的学术思想及其影响 [J]. 中医药导报 26（06）: 112–117.

[11] 朱珊, 2021.《狂人日记》译者风格：一项基于语料库的研究 [J]. 外国语文, 37（05）: 119–128.

[12] BAKER M. Corpus linguistics and translation studies: Implications and applications [A]. Amsterdam and Philadelphia: John Benjamins, 1993.

Approach and Methods for Constructing Bilingual Parallel Corpus of *Neijing Suwen*

Beijing Language and Culture University   TIAN Zhiling, XU Ming

Social Sciences Academic Press (CHINA)   PAN Xiaoying

Abstract: This paper focuses on exploring the process of constructing Chinese-French parallel bilingual corpus of *Neijing Suwen*. The process follows the steps of corpus preprocessing, corpus noise reduction, corpus alignment, etc, during which we solved the problems and difficulties encountered in the process of constructing the bilingual parallel corpus such as the OCR recognition errors, the segmentation of Classical Chinese sentence. We sumed up the experience and rules of constructing the bilingual parallel corpus and constructed a Chinese-French bilingual parallel corpus with a capacity of about 300,000 words. In the end, we also analyzed the readability of the translated text at the lexical and segmental levels based on the bilingual parallel corpus.

Keywords: *Neijing Suwen*; corpus methodologies; parallel corpus

医古文隐喻英译策略及隐喻效度研究[①]
——以《黄帝内经·灵枢》三英译本为例

重庆邮电大学 王子鹏[②] 刘世英[③]

【摘　要】本研究以《黄帝内经·灵枢》为蓝本，选取李照国、文树德、吴连胜和吴奇的英译本为参照，借助 Weread 语料检索平台，通过自建小型汉英双语平行语料库，提取语义功能相同的典型句段进行归类分析，并对不同的译者风格做出对比。此外，本研究综合采用定性分析与定量分析相结合的方法，参照国际通用的机器翻译质量评价方法，对医古文的隐喻效度及其隐喻的英译策略展开研究，以期为新时代中华优秀传统科学技术文化"走出国门"提供几点有益的参考与启示。

【关键词】黄帝内经·灵枢；定量分析；机器翻译质量评价；隐喻效度

一、引言

《素问·示从容论》有云："夫圣人之治病，循法守度，援物比类，化之冥冥。"中医学的表达，是一种以"取象比类"为基本方法，植根于中国传统文化的原创思维（郑洪新、杨柱，2021：39）。《黄帝内经·灵枢》（以下简称《灵枢》）是《素问》的姊妹篇，作为中医药文化的滥觞，字里行间透露着"近者取诸身，远者取诸物"的智慧。换言之，在《内经》的时代，限于当时的科学技术水平和认知方法，远古

---

① 基金项目：本文为重庆市语言文字科研项目，"智能时代大语言模型与人工翻译的协同模式研究"（项目编号：No. YYK23203）的部分研究成果。
② 王子鹏（1995— ），重庆邮电大学外国语学院硕士研究生。研究方向为：中医药翻译、认知翻译学。邮箱：993615393@qq.com。
③ 刘世英（1973— ），博士、教授、硕士研究生导师。研究方向为：认知语言学、功能语言学、应用语言学、对比语言学等。邮箱：liusy@cqupt.edu.cn。

的先民需要参照具体的"物象",来表达抽象的医理。这便成就了以《内经》为代表的中华医古文"无譬,则不能言"的语言魅力(石勇,2021:32)。因此,在中华文化"走出去"的大背景之下,做好医古文隐喻的英译,也就成了中医药文化外宣行稳致远的必由之路。

自 1949 年爱尔萨·威斯(Ilza Veith)发表西方国家第一部较为系统的《内经》译著至今,海内外共产生了 24 个不同的《内经》英译本(卢凤姣,2021:80)。其中,德国医史学家文树德(Paul U. Unschuld)译本(以下简称"文本"),以及我国首位中医学翻译博士李照国译本(以下简称"李本"),作为包含《素问》与《灵枢》在内的系统全译本而言,在西方的图书馆藏书量较多、传播较广(殷丽,2017:55);另外,美籍华人中医世家吴氏父子的英译本(以下简称"吴本")曾荣获 1996 年美国拉斯维加斯第三届世界传统医学大会最高荣誉金奖,极具代表性(唐路等,2013:85)。吴本注重展现中医临床实用价值,广受读者好评。

为避免一家之言有失偏颇,本研究特选取本国专家译本(李本)、外国专家译本(文本)以及外籍华人专家译本(吴本)进行综合考量。三个版本的成书背景各有不同,译本各有千秋,对隐喻的处理各具特色。因此,上述三个译本尤其适合作为医古文隐喻英译策略对比的研究对象。

二、医古文隐喻研究综述

陈战等将《素问》隐喻按主要内容分为四个大类,并总结出不同译者的翻译风格及概念隐喻的英译策略方法(陈战,2022:3),该研究在分类方法上具有创新性,但其分析主要依赖于定性描述,主观性较强,缺乏定量数据的支持,可能无法充分反映不同译者翻译风格的普遍规律;石勇以概念隐喻理论(CMT)与中医学结合为研究起点,整合现代中医和认知科学的研究方法,通过中医思维中的隐喻探索中医创新与发展的思维模式,创造性地提出了"取象比类"的"鲜花原理",认为医古文本中广泛存在着某种"共性之象"(石勇,2021:174),甚至在前人基础上改进了主体与象之间的类比可及性公式,但可惜的是,这种独特的视角虽然对读者理解医古文的隐喻内涵颇有裨益,但却并未涉及相关的英译策略,定量分析工具也并未能提供有效的数据支持;贾春华创造性地将 CMT 与中国传统造字领域的形、事、意、声相结合,探讨了隐喻认知视阈下的中医思维特点(贾春华等,2022:3283),一定程度上增进了读者对于医古文隐喻的理解,然而,文章虽借鉴了萨丕尔·沃尔夫的"语言决定思维论",但总体还是从中国本土文学语言的视角出发,而并未从英汉语言对比的视角对医古文隐喻的英译策略进行分析；李盼从认知翻译学的视角出发，探寻了中医文献中的隐喻信息和文化内涵，认为应实现"和谐翻译"，助力讲好中医故事（李盼，2023：53），文章援引了一系列隐喻英译常见的讹误，但定性分析仅针对单独的字词短语，缺乏独立完整的句段，一定程度上脱离了语境，丧失了部分语义的完整性。

综上，本研究在前人对医古文隐喻研究的基础上，借鉴当今世界机器译文质量评估的定量方法，以《灵枢》的三个专家译本为案例，提取语义完整的典型句段，分析对比不同译者对于医古文隐喻的英译风格，力求在英汉语言对比中实现取长补短，助力中华传统科学技术文化正向、真实、全面地展现给世界。

三、隐喻效度分析

为了尽量形成客观中立、不偏不倚的研究结果，本研究拟引入定量分析方法来测定上述三个参考英译本的隐喻效度（Metaphorical Force, MF）。

（一）机器翻译质量评估参考

在机器翻译质量测评领域，黄书剑等人表示：BLEU、METEOR、TER等算法是当下主流的测评方式（王子鹏、刘世英，2024：702）。现以TER（Translation Edit Rate）算法（公式1）为例，说明以单词数为量化指标的测算法则。TER是由Snover等人提出的一种基于编辑距离模型的评价指标（Snover & Schuarts, 2006：225）。它通过统计机器译文修改为参考译文后的编辑次数来分析机器译文的质量。TER公式如下：

$$(1)\ \text{TER} = (S+I+D+Sh) / R$$

其中，S（Substitution）表示"替换操作单词数"；I（Insertion）表示"插入操作单词数"；D（Deletion）表示"删除操作单词数"；Sh（Shift）表示"移动操作单词数"；R（Reference）表示"参考译文单词数"。

简言之，该算法的计算逻辑为：将待测机器译文与参考译文进行对比，计算出相较于参考译文而言机器译文变动的单词数占参考译文总词数的比例。该数值越低，说明机器译文与参考译文的近似程度越高，机器译文的质量越好。

同理，李照国也曾应用"信息密度"理论（李照国等，1993：370）来判定医学文献译文质量的高低，即：

（2）信息密度 = 原文词的意义单位数 / 译文词的意义单位数

其中，信息密度指标分为三档，0.5、0.25 和 0.1。译文的信息密度应当不低于 0.5，低于 0.25 的译文应反复推敲，低于 0.1 的译文应推翻重译。

这类以单词数为量化指标的测评方法客观具体、易于把握，已被广泛应用于机器译文质量测评领域。因此，类似的方法也可延迁至隐喻效度的测定中来。

（二）算法逻辑

首先，本研究结合 Weread 语料检索平台与自建小型汉英平行语料库，将《灵枢》中的隐喻按内容划分为六大类（如图1）。从六个大类中的随机位置提取源文典型样本共计 52 例，从 3 个英译本中各整理出文本功能相同的 52 条平行文本，英译单元样本总量为 156。

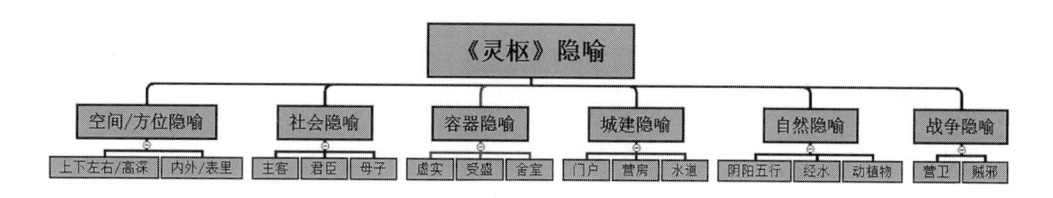

图 1　《灵枢》隐喻分类

其次，引入隐喻效度测算公式（3）（4），分别测算源文样本和参考译文样本的隐喻效度：

（3）$MF_O = L_S/L_O \times 100\%$

（4）$MF_T = L_S'/L_T \times 100\%$

其中，MF_O 表示源文本（Original Text）的隐喻效度；L_S 和 L_S' 分别表示源文与译文的语素长度（Length of Slots）；L_O（Length of Original Text）和 L_T（Length of Translation Text）分别表示源文样本长度及译文样本长度。

此处将文本功能相同的平行语料与源文的隐喻效度进行对比，根据经验规定可接受偏差 AA（Accepted Amplitude）=14.49%，若译文效度与源文效度差值在 ±14.49% 内，则判定译文效度为"守中"（$MF_T \approx MF_O$）；反之则为"过之"（$MF_T > MF_O$）或"不及"（$MF_T < MF_O$）。计算结果按四舍五入，精确到小数点后两位。

再次，取 MF_T 与 MF_O 差值的绝对值，输入计算机并绘制曲线，用以呈现译文与源文实际偏差（Actual AA）的波动幅度，判定译文隐喻效度的整体水平（AA_a 值越小，重现源文隐喻的水平越高），即：

$$(5) |AA_a| = |MF_T - MF_O|$$

最后，将上述所得数据进行分类统计，分别计算平均值，绘制图表，分析结果，得出结论。需要注意的是，由于《灵枢》样本量巨大，译本对比研究不能武断得出结论，说译本 A 比译本 B 隐喻效度高，译本质量更好，而应采取具体问题具体分析的方法，分门而论，如：从平均值来看，译本 A 的总体表现较好，但译本 A 在社会隐喻呈现方面略有所短，译本 B 在自然隐喻呈现方面略有所长。另外，为固定变量，保证研究结果客观公正，本研究一律不考虑译注、衍文等副文本的辅助功能。

（三）数据分析

通过系统整理统计 208 组样本数据，本研究发现：李本的 52 组样本中，$|AA_a|<14.49\%$ 的样本量为 34，合格率为 34/52×100%=65.38%。该译本的 $|AA_a|$ 算术平均值 $\bar{x}_1$=2.05%。其中，空间/方位隐喻、社会隐喻、容器隐喻、城建隐喻、自然隐喻、战争隐喻部分的平均值分别为 1.22%、6.76%、2.03%、1.47%、1.65%、3.16%。

文本的 52 组样本中，$|AA_a|<14.49\%$ 的样本量为 45，合格率为 45/52×100%=86.54%。该译本的 $|AA_a|$ 算术平均值 $\bar{x}_2$=1.91%。其中，上述六大隐喻的平均值分别为 6.59%、1.94%、3.53%、0.61%、0.59%、1.52%。

吴本的 52 组样本中，$|AA_a|<14.49\%$ 的样本量为 33，合格率为 33/52×100%=63.46%。该译本的 $|AA_a|$ 算术平均值 $\bar{x}_3$=3.72%。其中，上述六大隐喻的平均值分别为 9.64%、3.47%、4.93%、4.95%、3.08%、2.35%。

综合数据分析可以初步得出：文本合格率更高（86.54%），整体重现《灵枢》隐喻的水平更好，李本居中，吴本次之；文本平均波幅较小（1.91%），对隐喻的处理风格较为统一，李本居中，吴本次之；李本更善于重现空间（1.22%）和容器（2.03%）两类隐喻，文本则更善于处理其余四类隐喻（社会：1.94%；城建：0.61%；自然：0.59%；战争：1.52%）。

为了更直观地表现数据的整体趋势，反映《灵枢》三英译本的 MF 偏差值，本研究将 208 组数据以曲线图形式呈现（图 2）。

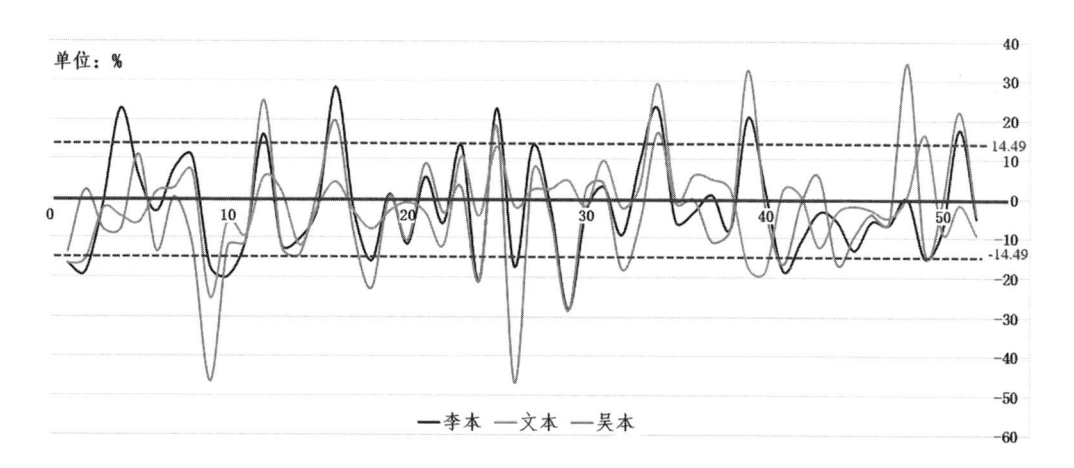

图 2 《灵枢》三英译本 MF 偏差曲线图

其中，横坐标为样本序号（1–52），表示三英译本 52 条样本的随机排列次序；纵坐标为偏差值 AA_a（单位：%），0 为基准偏差值，AA_a 值越接近 0，译文的隐喻重现程度越高，反之则越低；上下两条虚线为正负可接受偏差幅度（AA=±14.49%），两虚线区间内的部分表示合格，反之则不合格。

易知，吴本 MF 偏差值位于 AA 区间外的样本量最大（15 处），波动幅度较大，具有最高的波峰（–46.77%），与源文 MF 的平均偏差值最大（$\bar{x}_3$=3.72%）；文本 MF 偏差值位于 AA 区间外的样本量最小（7 处），沿 0 基准线的分布较密集，波动幅度较小，拥有最小的波峰（0），与源文 MF 的平均偏差值最小（$\bar{x}_2$=1.91%）；李本的 MF 综合表现位于吴本和文本之间。另外，还可以看出，三译本的总体水平大多位于 0 基准线以下（李本 33 处；文本 30 处；吴本 34 处），亦即译文的 MF 值总体小于源文，此处可以说明两点：三位译者不约而同、或多或少地对隐喻的语素（Slots）做了薄译处理（导致分子较小）；或对样本单元中的非 Slots 成分做了解释性的厚译处理（导致分母较大）。

四、隐喻英译策略分析

为了明晰《灵枢》三译本的 MF 数据反映出上述趋势特征的原因，本研究将结合三位译者的译文特点，从文字层面入手，精选典型样本，开展定性分析，解读上述定量分析的逻辑本末。

例1：

故曰上工平气，中工乱脉，下工绝气危生。(《灵枢·根结》)（空间/方位）(MF_O=18.75%)

李本：That is why it is said that excellent doctors regulate Qi, ordinary doctors disturb the Channels and unskillful doctors deplete Qi and threaten the life [of the patients].（MF_T=0）(李照国，2008：110)

文本：Hence it is said: The outstanding practitioner levels the qi. A mediocre practitioner generates chaos in the vessels. The **inferior** practitioner cuts [the flow of the] qi and jeopardizes life.（MF_T=3.33%）(Unschuld，2016：123)

吴本：The physician **of higher level** can keep the energies in balance, the physician **of medium level** can treat the patient according to the pulse condition, and the physician **of lower level** can only exhaust the energy and cause danger to the patient's life.（MF_T=20.93%）(吴连胜、吴奇，1997：531)

如上述，"上—下""表—里"等表述是医古文方位/空间隐喻的典型。"上""中""下"为源文方位/空间隐喻的 Slots，故 MF_O=3/16×100%=18.75%。李本将 Slots 分别做释译处理（上—excellent；中—ordinary；下—unskillful）。刘宓庆曾在"隐喻的翻译"一节中写道：要译得"既精准传神"，又要让目标语受众最大程度上感受源文"新鲜的原汁原味"（刘宓庆，2017：237）；英国著名学者泰特勒（Alexander Fraser Tytler）也曾在《论翻译的原则》（*Essay on the Principles of Translation*）一书中写道：好的译文，需要让"译文文字所属国家的人能明白地领悟、强烈地感受，正如读原作的人们所领悟、所感受的一样"（谢天振，2009：12）。"上""中""下"的释译处理虽然可以实现语义上的效能等同，但从审美角度来考虑，源文固有的 MF 似乎在译文中遗失殆尽，因此权且判定李本的方位/空间隐喻 MF_T=0；且看文本，方位/空间隐喻的 MF_T 值稍高，因其使用的"inferior"一词有"of lower rank"之义，可以将源文的"下"义迁移过来，而"outstanding"与"mediocre"则不具备这种迁移功能；再观吴本，在该样本中拥有最高的 MF_T 值，"higher""medium""lower"三个简单的单词恰好可以完美迁移源文的方位/空间隐喻 Slots，同时也对三个形容词做了解释性增译，如"of higher level"，最大限度实现了"精准""传神"且"原汁原味"。此外，本例还可以说明，尽管从整体的平均水平来看，吴本的 MF_T 值似乎不及另外两个译本，但是这种情况不会影响该专家译本在隐喻英译方面依然有许多可圈可点的出彩之处。

例 2：

审查卫气，为百病**母**。（《灵枢·禁服》）（社会／母子）（MF$_O$=12.50%）

李本：[You have to] examine [the changes of] the Weiqi（Defensive-Qi）as the basis for studying [the occurrence and pathogenesis of] various diseases.（MF$_T$=0）（李照国，2008：613）

文本：One examines the guard qi [because their failure is] **the mother** of all diseases.（MF$_T$=14.29%）（Unschuld，2016：467）

吴本：Examine the Wei-energy which can defend outside when the Yang energy is stable, and when the Yang is deficient, the Wei-energy will not be guarding outside and diseases will occur.（MF$_T$=0）（吴连胜、吴奇，1997：698）

本例主要讨论"母子"隐喻成分，暂不考虑"营卫"隐喻。首先，可以确定的是，李照国在处理医古文隐喻时，善于借用国际标准中西化了的中医术语，如在翻译《灵枢》中的众多针灸经穴时，以《WHO 国际针灸标准穴位》为参照，采用音译加注的方法，淡化了中医穴位名称的隐喻意义，而以技术传播为主要目的，如将"隐白穴"处理为"Yinbai（SP 1）"，其中，"SP"表示"Spleen"（以西医的实物脏器"脾"指代足太阴脾经），1 则表示该穴位为足太阴脾经的始穴。在本例中，李本同样将隐喻成分以西化术语来处理，将"百病母"（百病的起因、先导）翻译为"[the occurrence and pathogenesis of] various diseases"（诸多疾病的发生和病机），其中"pathogenesis"在狭义的西医语境中指"the way in which a disease develops"（病机），在广义上指"the origin, development, and resultant effects of a disease"（疾病的病因、转归及预后），因此可以很好地用于嵌入本例的 Slot，填补"母"在语义上造成的空缺，在传播的过程中"淡化"文化因素，将"意义"实现最大化，有利于提升技术传播的效率。然而，从 MF 的角度来看，这种翻译方式似乎将文化上的审美因素遗失殆尽，例如，中医针灸穴位共 360 处有余，为了方便认知每个穴位的位置特点、所属归经以及功效治则，古人以独特的隐喻为每个穴位赋予了生动的文化属性，如太仓、涌泉、合谷、百虫窝、足三里、阳溪、风府等等，高明的中医师在学习生涯中也会自觉结合医史、词源、哲学等领域的知识来精进自身的医术水平。正如英国著名中医翻译理论与实践家魏迺杰（Nigel Wiseman）所言——翻译中医典籍时使用"西医化翻译……容易将现代医学概念投射到古代去，掩盖古代作者原来的思想"（程颜、张洋，2021：59）。如若在英译过程中将这些内容悉数处理为"Acronym"的形式，那么医学生在学习的过程中就很难找到兴趣，且无法从词源视角出发，去深究每个穴位背后的深层逻辑，数百个穴位也只会退化为中医辞书中一个个仅供查阅的枯燥符号，不利于中医药文化的高质量传播。

再观文本，保留了源文的风韵，将"母"直译为"the mother"。这种处理方式有一定的风险，一方面很考验译者的双语功底，另一方面容易在两种不同的文化背景下造成望文生义的讹误，例如忠实于原意的隐喻形象可能会"在目的语中格格不入"（刘宓庆：2017）。然而，回到本例，如果目的语文化中恰好有近似的地道表达，且译者也深谙这种表达，则大可放心直译，最大限度保留源文的风貌。例如，在约定俗成的英语语境下，"Failure is the mother of success"是全世界人民共通的认知意象，其中"mother"的语义早已超越了原本的字面意义，而引申出事物发生时间顺序上的"先"义或事物发生的"因"义。另外，可以直观地发现，相较于李本和吴本，文本在"入国问俗"的传播原则下，控制了译文的长度，更有利于保持医古文"简"的形式属性。再者，如若《灵枢》之中涉及的所有隐喻成分都如本例中吴本这般译法，从 8 个汉字译出 30 个英文单词，那么中医典籍的译本都将变得又厚又重，"才能涵盖所有语言符号的外在特质和内涵意义"（程颜、张洋，2021：93），这同样不利于中医典籍在目的语读者群体中的推广传播。

例 3：

岐伯曰："春夏先治其**标**，后治其**本**；秋冬先治其**本**，后治其**标**。"（《灵枢·师传》）（自然/动植物—阴性隐喻）（MF_O=17.39%）

李本：Qibo answered, "In spring and summer, treatment [should concentrate on] **the Branch (secondary aspect)** first and then on **the Root (primary aspect)**; in autumn and winter, treatment [should concentrate on] **the Root (primary aspect)** first and then on **the Branch (secondary aspect)**."（MF_T=38.10%）（李照国，2008：453）

文本：Qi Bo: In spring and summer one first cures **the tip**, and afterwards cures **the root**. In autumn and winter one first cures **the root**, and afterwards cures **the tip**.（MF_T=26.67%）（Unschuld, 2016: 345）

吴本：Qibo answered: "In spring and summer, treat **the branch which is outside** first, and then, treat **the root which is inside**; in autumn and winter, treat **the root which is inside** first and then, treat **the branch which is outside**."（MF_T=50.00%）（吴连胜、吴奇，1997：642）

虽然文本素以简洁、忠实的风格著称，但有时译文过于简洁，也容易造成过犹不及的负面作用，让读者产生不知所云之感，如"cures the tip"似乎是在讲为树疗疾而非为人治病。《内经》常用"标"（树枝）与"本"（树根）来隐喻疾病的表证与病因，甚至后世的俗语"标本兼治"亦是来源于此。但反观英语文化，其中并没有以树木隐喻疾病的先例，因此"标""本"属于目标语文化中典型的文化缺省。换言之，虽然文本完美保留了源文的"能指"，但这种"能指"在译文中缺少必要的"所指"，就会给目标语读者造成不必要的认知障碍。退一步讲，本例中文本的译法，如果辅以脚注，似乎不失为一种经典的译法，初唐名医杨上善有云："春夏之时，万物之气，上升在标；秋冬之时，万物之气，下流在本。候病所在，以行疗法，故春夏取标，秋冬取本也。"（郭蔼春，2022：366）如果在脚注中佐以此句，似乎可以成功让读者明白"标"与"本"的阴性隐喻内涵，但如上述，如若为了释义一句30个字符的源文，而不惜调用50个字符的脚注，造成脚注的篇幅甚至远超正文的情况，让本就厚重的典籍更增添了许多阅读的压力，不免会有南辕北辙之嫌。

再看李本与吴本，虽跨越了时空，但二者不约而同地使用了"直译＋释义"的策略，足以说明在遇到文化缺省类的隐喻时，直译加注不失为既保留源文风貌，又便于读者阅读的良策。如李本增译"primary aspect"与"secondary aspect"来描述问题的主要方面与次要方面；而吴本虽无直接性的解释，但增译"inside"与"outside"似乎也能让读者结合上下文理解到"标""本"系疾病的"外因"与"内因"，可谓中规中矩。

五、结语

微观而言，关于MF的定量分析法既有助于隐喻英译研究，也对译者或译本风格分析颇有裨益。如上述，对《灵枢》三英译本的定量分析一方面以较为客观的数据反映了不同译者对隐喻处理的差异；另一方面，数据结果也印证了前文的论述，即文本善于保留源文的文化因素，这在数据中得到印证：文本AA_a的合格率达到了惊人的86.54%，远超出另外两译本。而吴本重实践、轻理论、重技术、轻文化的译文特色也在数据分析中得到了佐证：其译本相较于源文的AA_a值较大，重现源文隐喻的合格率较低。需要注意的是，本研究依然存在三点问题亟待深入探讨。如依照本研究的结论，文本对于隐喻的英译质量优于其余两译本。然而，译者在做具体的医古文翻译实践时，要意识到译无定法，仍需做到具体问题具体分析。文本的多数译例虽值得参考，但仍有小部分内容需要进行批判性思考，如例3的忠实直译若完全脱离脚注，会让读者有文化休克之感，若大篇幅增添脚注，也只是折中之举。换言之，一味追求保留源文的文化内涵，不免会牺牲一定的读者友好度。因此，如何既保留源文隐喻的原汁原味又能确保一定的目标语读者友好度，是本研究及后来学者仍需深入探讨的方向。在语料库方面，如果语料样本总量不够大，得出的结论则会呈现出片面的、有失客观的属性。语料库作为数据精度的保障（语料样本容量越大，越能反映真实情况），本研究期待建立容量更大且内容更为全面的医古文双语平行语料库，以助力隐喻语料的归类与分析研究。最后，在数据方面，如能辅以大语言模型（LLM）如 ChatGPT 或自动化编程软件如 Python 等，将算法植入其中，将大幅减少人为失误的概率，提升数据采集分析的效率。

宏观来看，正如文树德所言，现代科技并不是整理传统医学唯一的出路，要尊重中医的文化特色，"不要走最终把传统医学改造成西洋医学的道路"（程颜、张洋，2021：56）。在新时代，世界人民对于中医药技术文化的青睐将不再局限于技术应用层面，他们对中医药的兴趣将更多地转移至中医的哲学内涵与思维方式上来，并尝试从文化的源头上来理解中医、学习中医、应用中医。因此，在讲好中国故事的新时代背景下，中华传统医学文化及其技术的对外传播，应逐渐从追求范围与速率，深化至追求深度与质量，如此，方能为中医药技术文化真实又立体的传播奠下深厚的文化基础，助力铺就新时代的"中医西渐"之路。

【参考文献】

[1] 陈战，2022．《黄帝内经》素问隐喻英译对比研究 [M]．北京：中国中医药出版社．

[2] 程颜，张洋，2021．传播学视阈下中医典籍翻译研究 [M]．北京：中国中医药出版社．

[3] 郭蔼春，2022．黄帝内经灵枢白话解（第 2 版）[M]．北京：中国中医药出版社．

[4] 贾春华等，2022．隐喻认知视域下的中医思维研究 [J]．世界中医药（23）：3283–3288．

[5] 李盼，2023．认知翻译学视角下看译者如何讲好中医故事 [J]．文化创新比较研究（20）：50–53．

[6] 李照国，2008．大中华文库汉英对照黄帝内经·灵枢 [M]．西安：世界图书出版公司．

[7] 李照国等，1993．中医基本理论名词术语英译探讨（五）[J]．中国中西医结合杂志（06）：370–373．

[8] 刘宓庆，2017．翻译基础 [M]．上海：华东师范大学出版社．

[9] 卢凤姣，2022．《黄帝内经·素问》威斯译本的译者主体性分析研究 [D]．北京中医药大学硕士研究生毕业论文：80．

[10] 石勇，2021．中医隐喻研究［M］．北京：中国社会科学出版社．

[11] 唐路等，2013．从吴连胜《黄帝内经》英译看中医医古文翻译［J］．浙江中医药大学学报（1）：85–86．

[12] 王子鹏、刘世英，2024．当 ChatGPT 4.0 遇上医古文——以《黄帝内经·素问》英译为例［A］．第 28 届全球华人计算机教育应用大会会刊：698–705．

[13] 吴连胜、吴奇，1997．黄帝内经（汉英对照）［M］．北京：中国科学技术出版社．

[14] 谢天振，2009．中西翻译简史［M］．北京：外语教学与研究出版社．

[15] 杨渝、陈晓，2020．《黄帝内经》英译文本分类述评（1925—2019）［J］．中医药文化（3）：41–43．

[16] 殷丽，2017．《黄帝内经》海外译介模式研究与中医药文化"走出去"［J］．解放军外国语学院学报（6）：53–61．

[17] 郑洪新、杨柱，2021．中医基础理论［M］．北京：中国中医药出版社．

[18] Snover. M., Dorr. B, & Schuarts. R. *A Study of Translation Edit Rate with Targeted Human Annotation* [A]. Technical Papers: Proceedings of the 7th Conference of the Association for Machine Translation in the Americans Cambridge. 2006: 223-231.

[19] Unschuld, P. U. *Huang Di Nei Jing Ling Shu: The Ancient Classic on Needle Therapy* [M]. Berkeley: University of California Press. 2016.

Chinese-English Translation Strategy and Metaphorical Force in Traditional Chinese Medicine Texts: A Case Study of the Three English Versions of *"Huangdi Neijing Ling Shu"*

Chongqing University of Posts and Telecommunications   *WANG Zipeng, LIU Shiying*

Abstract: This study takes *"Huangdi Neijing Ling Shu"* as the primary text and examines the English translations by Li Zhaoguo, Paul Unschuld, and Wu Liansheng and Wu Qi. Utilizing the Weread corpus retrieval platform, we constructed a small bilingual Chinese-English parallel corpus to extract and categorize typical sentences with similar semantic functions for comparative analysis of the translators' styles. Furthermore, this study employs a mixed-method approach combining qualitative and quantitative analysis. We take the machine translation quality assessment methods internationally used as reference to explore the metaphorical force in traditional Chinese medicine texts and their English translation strategies. The aim is to provide valuable insights and references for promoting the fine traditional scientific and cultural heritage of China on the international stage.

Keywords: *Huangdi Neijing Ling Shu*; quantitative analysis; machine translation quality assessment; metaphorical force

人工智能辅助外宣翻译有效性研究
——以 ChatGPT 为例

天津大学　沈伊晗[①]

【摘　要】 外宣翻译不仅是一种语言转换的技术活动，更是一项涉及政治、经济、文化、社会等多层面的战略性工作。高质量的外宣翻译对于维护国家利益、推动国际合作具有不可替代的作用。随着生成式人工智能的高速发展，其运用在外宣翻译中的效果有待研究。本研究选取《理解当代中国》的部分内容作为源文本，分析对比了 10 名翻译专业在读硕士研究生的译文与 ChatGPT 生成的译文，探索以 ChatGPT 为首的人工智能辅助外宣翻译的有效性。结果显示 ChatGPT 在词汇多样性、句法丰富性上表现出色，学生译者在文化理解、意识形态方面更胜一筹。研究可为外宣翻译工作提供参考，以提升国家对外宣传效果，同时为高校翻译专业教学提供一定建议。

【关键词】 外宣翻译；人工智能；ChatGPT

一、引言

由于中国国际地位的变化，开放程度的逐渐扩大，讲好中国故事成为时代需求，翻译工作已经成为文化交流和知识传播的关键环节。随着 2022 年 11 月 OpenAI 正式推出 ChatGPT，生成式人工智能的崛起宣布了翻译工作进入一个全新的发展阶段。尽管 ChatGPT 在科技翻译、法律翻译等领域中表现优异（王克非，2024），但作为人工智能，ChatGPT 缺乏理解能力及译者主体性，在文本的文化背景、意识形态背

---

① 沈伊晗，天津大学外国语学院硕士研究生，研究方向为翻译理论与实践，邮箱：shenyihan_1@tju.edu.cn。

景等方面理解不足，在文学领域、外宣翻译中依然表现不佳。

外宣翻译，作为新形势下对外宣传工作中的重要角色，不仅需要考虑语言问题，还需要考虑文化背景、政治语境等复杂要素。在新时代的背景下，我们不仅要探讨如何积极响应新技术的发展，更好地满足国家战略需求，同时也需要深入探究新技术的不足之处，以期待能更好地利用新技术为翻译服务。

回顾现有文献，ChatGPT 应用于外宣翻译的研究仍处于起步阶段。因此，本研究以《理解当代中国》中的部分内容为源文本，收集了 10 名 MTI 在读研究生的翻译实例，使用 ChatGPT 4.0 生成译文，基于专业翻译教师的评审结果，将学生译者的译文与 ChatGPT 生成的译文进行对比，分析双方译文中存在的优势和局限性。本研究旨在探究 ChatGPT 类生成式人工智能在外宣文本的翻译中的潜力与不足，以期为将新技术应用于外宣翻译工作提供建议与启示。

二、研究现状

目前，基于大语言模型的生成式人工智能迅猛发展，成为翻译领域热议的焦点，为翻译及语言服务行业带来了深远的影响，其中最有代表性的莫过于 2022 年底由 OpenAI 推出的 ChatGPT，其在对话生成、持续优化、上下文记忆和创造性等方面展现出显著优势，为传统翻译行业带来了新的挑战，也将引领翻译技术未来发展方向（王华树，2023）。已经有不少学者对 ChatGPT 在翻译实践中的表现展开了研究。例如，于蕾（2024）分析得出，ChatGPT 翻译的词汇和短语比人工翻译更加多样，相较于 DeepL，在句法复杂度方面，也展现出强大潜力。耿建、胡芳（2023）发现 ChatGPT 在汉译英润色、校对工作中表现良好，但在英译汉的译后编辑任务中表现不佳。

现有研究虽然指出 ChatGPT 等人工智能在翻译实践中展现出的巨大潜力，但同时也指出，ChatGPT 在一些特定领域依然存在不足之处。王克非（2024）比较了 ChatGPT、文心一言两种人工智能的翻译实例及人工翻译实例的质量，指出人工智能在应用型翻译上具有优势，但在学术类翻译及文学翻译上依然有所欠缺。张慧玲（2023）分析了 ChatGPT 产出译文的方式，指出生成式人工智能缺乏理解能力，"并不会考虑到体认翻译学的三大核心内容：'现实、认知、语言'"。

上述研究分析了 ChatGPT 应用在翻译中的优势和不足，但目前关注 ChatGPT 在外宣翻译上的运用的研究并不多。外宣翻译，一般指"外宣资料或外宣文献的翻译，包括新闻外宣、政治外宣和文化外宣资料的翻译"（胡开宝，2023）。外宣翻译兼具"宣"和"译"的特点，一方面会受到传播效果、受众背景等影响宣传的因素的制约，另一方面在翻译策略和方法的选择上与其他类型的文本相比，既具有共性，也因其特殊之处具有个性（曾剑平，2018）。学界目前对 ChatGPT 在外宣文本翻译中的表现的研究尚在早期阶段。文旭、田亚灵（2023）比较了 Google 翻译、有道翻译、DeepL 翻译和 ChatGPT 翻译政治文本的表现，并指出 ChatGPT 在隐转喻识别、句子结构、文化敏感度、词语准确性四个方面的表现均优于其他翻译工具，但在意识形态、文化差异、准确性上仍然存在不足。

三、研究设计

（一）研究问题

本研究将从词法、句法、语篇三部分对学生译者和 ChatGPT 外宣翻译的结果开展实例分析，对内容进行具体研究，拟回答以下三个问题。

第一，ChatGPT 翻译外宣文本有哪些可取之处与不足之处？
第二，学生译者在外宣翻译时有哪些长处与短处？
第三，ChatGPT 与学生译者的翻译过程有何区别？

（二）源文本选择

本研究中的源文本选自《理解当代中国》一书中的第一章与第二章。"理解当代中国"系列教材的课文选自《习近平谈治国理政》《中共中央关于党的百年奋斗重大成就和历史经验的决议》，以及习近平总书记《在庆祝中国共产党成立 100 周年大会上的讲话》等权威文献（译文），具有典型的中国时政文献话语特征，符合外宣文本的要求。

通过对源文本的文本特征展开的定性研究，发现其具有以下几项主要特征。
第一，政治术语、范畴词等特定语境词汇使用普遍，专业性较强。
第二，无主句、流水句等句式使用频繁，需要句式转换。
第三，善用比喻、对偶等修辞，且多引经据典，语言工整优美。

（三）实验设计

本研究邀请了 10 名翻译专业在读硕士研究生翻译了实验文本，实验分为以下三部分。

第一，背景调查。10 名翻译硕士在读研究生来自同一所高校，入学年份相同，所选课程一致，本科均为国内各高校英语专业，对于翻译的学习水平较为一致，对外宣文本的了解水平一致，无职业翻译背景。

第二，翻译过程。该翻译为课程作业的一部分，要求学生在翻译时独立完成，可以借助网络资源获取背景知识，搜索词汇、语法等，但不可使用 ChatGPT。

第三，回溯性访谈。采访学生译者译前、译中所做的准备，译后所做的工作，在翻译时遇到的问题以及词汇及句式选用的原因与思路。

四、结果及讨论

（一）词汇层面

(1) 政治术语

源文本包含了大量政治术语，对翻译的精确度提出了很高要求。学生译者的相关知识储备不够充足，对某些术语熟悉度不够，在翻译过程中需要大量查询时间，明显降低翻译效率。而 ChatGPT 依赖于大数据训练，对有着官方译文和双语文本的政治术语的翻译准确度较高，如例 1。

例 1：

源文本：党章规定"四个服从"，最根本的是全党各个组织和全体党员服从党的全国代表大会和中央委员会。

学生译文：The fundamental requirement of the Party Constitution's "Four Principles of Deference" is that all Party organizations and Party members submit to the National Congress and Central Committee of the Party.

ChatGPT 译文：According to the Party Constitution's "Four Principles of Deference," it is essential that all party organizations and all Party members submit to the National Congress and the Central Committee of the Party.

在例 1 的源文本中，"四个服从"属于党章中的专业政治术语，已经有了官方的双语翻译。ChatGPT 对该术语所生成的译文质量准确度很高，不需要人工参与译后编辑。而根据学生译者的回溯性访谈，在翻译过程中遇到该术语时，他需要参考平行文本，查询中国特色话语对外翻译标准化术语库、中国日报点津网、术语在线等资料，花费大量时间确认术语的正确性。

(2) 特定语境中的词汇

外宣翻译中需要考虑特殊语境对于部分词汇翻译的影响。学生译者对目标语言不熟悉，有可能在词汇的选用上出错，难以准确表达源文本需要传达的意图，而ChatGPT 在这方面展现出了更好的表现，如例 2。

例 2：

源文本：执行党中央决策部署不讲条件、不打折扣、不搞变通。

学生译文：We will implement the decisions and arrangements of the CPC Central Committee without any conditionality, compromise or flexibility.

ChatGPT 译文：Execution of the Party Central Committee's decisions should be unconditional, without compromise or deviation.

学生在"不搞变通"的翻译上选择了"flexibility"，该英文词汇用于褒义语境的情况偏多，意为"灵活性"，但"搞变通"中的"变通"需要偏贬义的词汇。学生在回溯性访谈中提到在选词时搜索释义和例句后，仍然无法准确把握一些单词的用法，而 ChatGPT 的训练数据为英语，不存在对于词汇的理解偏差，能够得到较为准确的翻译。

(3) 范畴词

汉语的外宣文本中会出现大量的范畴词，例如经济"领域"，外交"工作"，等等，这些词汇常用于具体词语的后面，用于分类总括，并不表达实际所指意义。学生译者往往会正确处理，在汉译英中将其省略，但 ChatGPT 会出现无法正确识别范畴词的情况，以至于出现歧义，如例 3。

例 3：

源文本：在坚持党的领导这个重大原则问题上……

学生译文：In maintaining the fundamental principle of upholding the Party's leadership…

ChatGPT 译文：On the issue of adhering to the fundamental principle of the Party's leadership…

在该句中,"问题"为范畴词,并无实际含义,其对应的英文单词"problem"和"issue"都含有贬义,ChatGPT 选择直译为"issue"容易引发贬义联想,但学生译者采用介词"in"引导这一介词短语,强调了坚持党的领导这一过程,符合上下文语境。

(二)句段层面

(1) 汉语无主句的处理

无主句是现代汉语中的一种句型,是非主谓句的一种,是指根本没有主语的句子。这种句子的作用在于描述动作、变化等情况,而不在于叙述"谁"或者"什么"进行这一动作或发生这个变化。这种类型的句子在汉语的外宣文本中随处可见。然而,英语中无主句的用法较为罕见,在汉译英的过程中,必须补充适合的主语,才能使句子完整。学生在翻译外宣文本无主句时,一般都会添补主语"我"或"我们",而 ChatGPT 会选择翻译成被动句,使用形式主语,如例 4。

> 例 4:
> 源文本:必须旗帜鲜明、立场坚定。
> 学生译文:We must take a clear-cut stand and be firm.
> ChatGPT 译文:It must be done resolutely and unequivocally.

例 4 的源文本是一个标准的无主句,在汉译英时应补充主语或改变句型,使句子结构符合英文习惯。学生译者在本例中补充了"we"作为句子主语,但该主语多出现于领导人讲话,用于拉近与听众间的距离,不适于用在该文本中。ChatGPT 在此处选择了将无主句改成被动语态,不仅贴近了目标语读者,更突出了外宣文本的严肃性。

(2) 句子结构的重组

汉语往往以神统形,看重语言的意合,句子成分之间联系比较松散。而英语以形统神,看重语言的形合,句子成分结构紧密、主谓突出、层次分明。在汉译英中,结构松散的句子往往会成为学生译者最为头疼的困难之一。而 ChatGPT 在句子结构上会更加多变。如例 5。

> 例 5:
> 源文本:决不能羞羞答答、语焉不详,决不能遮遮掩掩、搞自我麻痹。

学生译文：We must never be shy or vague, never cover up or engage in self-paralysis.

ChatGPT 译文：It must be done without hesitation or ambiguity. There should be no attempts to conceal or engage in self-deception.

在例5中，源文本的前后分句使用了对仗的句式，又包括四个四字词，在翻译时难免造成困扰。学生译者选择使用与中文同样的结构，用两个"never"来表示"决不能"，过于直白。ChatGPT选择了更加灵活的策略，将其转换为两个句子。学生译者在翻译时容易反复出现同样的结构，而ChatGPT会进行适当的变化，增加了译本的可读性，也可以使翻译结果更加贴切和恰当。

（三）语篇层面

（1）古诗文的翻译

汉语中的古诗文在形式与意义上具备一定的艺术性，在外宣文本中被广泛使用，既能表达政治观点，也能凸显中华文化的博大精深。学生译者在理解源文本中的古诗文表述上一般没有问题，在经过训练后，可以使用意象替换、添加释义、删除比喻等多样的处理方法，获得准确且优美的译文。而ChatGPT则无法"信、达、雅"地处理修辞翻译，有时还会出现识别不出修辞或错误识别的问题，如例6。

例6：
源文本：全面深化改革和全面依法治国是为鸟之两翼，车之双轮。
学生译文：Comprehensive deepening of reform and comprehensive law-based governance is as wings are to a bird.
ChatGPT 译文：Comprehensive deepening of reform and comprehensive law-based governance is the two wings of a bird and the dual wheels of a car.

例6的源文本中"鸟之两翼，车之双轮"是一种对仗的表述，把同类概念的词语放在相对应的位置上，显得句子更为整齐，语气更为铿锵有力。对仗更多起到形式上的审美作用，使语句更具韵味，增加词语表现力，但意义上存在重复，因此不必全部译出，保留单一意象即可。学生译者采用省略的译法，仅翻译了前半部分，在准确传达源文本含义的同时维持了句子的简洁。而ChatGPT作为人工智能，并不具有理解能力，因此选择将前后句均译出，稍显冗余。

(2) 语义补偿

在翻译过程中，由于不同语言之间存在结构、语法、习惯用法等方面的差异，直接逐字逐句地翻译往往难以准确传达原文的深层含义和独特韵味。这时就需要译者运用自己的语言功底和文化理解，对译文进行适当的语义补偿，使其更加贴近原文的意图和风格。在外宣文本中，翻译时常会遇到成语、典故、诗句等语言精练的表达，如果不加以说明，外国受众由于不同的文化背景会不知所云，从而影响外宣效果。在增补说明方面，ChatGPT 无法像人工译者一样具有灵活性。如例 7。

例 7：

源文本：任何时候任何情况下都要坚定中国特色社会主义道路自信、理论自信、制度自信、文化自信，真正做到"千磨万击还坚劲，任尔东西南北风"。

学生译文：We must be as tenacious as bamboo, as described by Zheng Xie: "In the face of all blows, not bending low, it still stands fast. Whether from east, west, south, or north the wind doth blast."

ChatGPT 译文："Repeated sharpening makes the blade ever keener, facing all winds from the four directions."

源文本的诗句虽然并未明说，但了解中国文化的读者自然能明白该诗句是在描述竹子坚韧不屈的特点。对于目标语言的使用者来说，这点可能会造成理解困难。在翻译该句时，学生加上了诗句作者的信息，同时补充了诗句描述的对象是竹子及其特点，通过恰当的语义补偿，可以使译文更加忠实、生动、易于理解，更好地表现了原文的精髓和魅力。ChatGPT 不具备人工译者具备的语言功底、敏锐的文化洞察力和丰富的翻译经验，直接对诗句进行翻译，有可能会造成目标读者的理解困难。

(3) 文化理解

ChatGPT 与人工译者在文化理解方面具有明显的差异，外宣文本经常会出现带有传统文化元素的表达，ChatGPT 对于部分文化负载词可以处理，但有些翻译稍显单薄，而学生译者在翻译时会经过语内翻译和语际翻译两个过程，可以将其丰富内涵传达出来，达到跨文化交际的效果，如下文例 8。

例 8：

源文本：自强不息、厚德载物的思想，支撑着中华民族生生不息、薪火相传。

学生译文：The ideas of self-improvement and embracing the world through virtue have supported the Chinese nation's unceasing self-regeneration.

ChatGPT 译文：The idea of self-improvement and virtuous conduct supports the Chinese nation in its perpetuation and passing on of traditions.

该句中的"厚德载物"最早出自先秦《易经》，指有德行的君子以深厚的德行来容载世间的万物，在此处作为中华民族精神，应意译进行解释，ChatGPT 仅译出了"品行高尚"。"薪火相传"出自《庄子》，指传承绵延不尽，与生生不息同义，指中华民族的生长、发展。ChatGPT 选用了两个词，"perpetuation"代表着永存不朽，明显不如"self-regeneration"更能体现原义，且"passing on of traditions"的使用以传承传统来代表中华民族精神发展，过于局限和片面。

（四）意识形态

外宣文本的翻译不仅仅是语言的转换，更是一种文化交流和意识形态沟通的过程，往往涉及国家形象、政策宣传等内容，直接关联到国家的政治立场和外交关系。准确的意识形态表达有助于维护国家利益和国际形象。ChatGPT 是基于数据训练的大语言模型，它的预训练语料库以西方价值观为主，在翻译外宣文本时容易出现意识形态问题，甚至出现幻觉（Hallucination）现象，制造虚假信息，会给外宣翻译工作造成十足的困扰。而学生译者通常具有更加敏感的政治意识。如下文例 9。

例 9：
源文本：坚持算大账、算长远账，不打小算盘、不搞小聪明，自觉防止和反对个人主义。
学生译文：…oppose self-centered behavior
ChatGPT 译文：…oppose individualism

该例译文的差异出现在"个人主义"的词汇选择上。在源文本的中文语境下，"个人主义"为贬义，指的是"一切从个人利益出发，把个人利益放在集体利益之上，只顾自己不顾别人的错误思想"，因此，学生选择了"self-centered behavior"来传达源文本的批判思想。而在当代西方社会中，"个人主义"含有自由、人权的意味，词性偏褒义，ChatGPT 因此将"个人主义"译为"individualism"，意为"the belief that individual people in society should have the right to make their own decisions"，不符合源文本的意识形态。

五、结语

尽管 ChatGPT 并非专门为翻译而设计，但其在自然语言处理领域的快速发展和技术进步使其成为一种强大的工具。与传统的机器翻译系统相比，ChatGPT 能够更好地理解上下文和语境，从而提供更连贯、自然的翻译结果。基于大规模数据集的训练使其能够处理各种语言之间的翻译任务，包括将中文外宣文本翻译成英文。

在翻译过程中，ChatGPT 能够迅速处理大量文本，为用户节省时间和精力。对于一些简单且非专业性的翻译任务，ChatGPT 的翻译结果通常能够满足基本需求，确保信息的有效传达。它的翻译结果通常具有一定的准确性，能够帮助用户快速了解文本内容，对于日常交流或简单文档的翻译非常实用。

然而，对于涉及专业性较高或领域特定术语的翻译任务，比如外宣文本的翻译，ChatGPT 的局限性也变得明显。相较于人工译者，ChatGPT 在生成文本时主要依赖上下文和统计规律，难以真正理解文化背后的内涵和含义，尤其是在涉及文化差异较大的内容时，如古诗文、习语和俗语的翻译。

同时，意识形态问题对于 ChatGPT 仍是挑战，其缺乏对政治敏锐性的辨别能力，导致翻译结果出现偏差或误解。在这种情况下，仍然需要专业人员的干预和审查，以确保翻译结果的准确性和专业性。

综上所述，虽然 ChatGPT 在将中文外宣文本翻译成英文时能够提供快速、连贯和相对准确的翻译，但在专业性和文化理解方面存在一定局限。对于重要或专业性较高的翻译任务，仍建议寻求专业翻译人员的帮助，以确保翻译质量和准确性。ChatGPT 可以作为翻译过程中强有力的辅助工具，提高工作效率和翻译成果的质量。

【参考文献】

[1] 张健, 2016. 国际传播视阈下的外宣翻译特点探析 [J]. 西南政法大学学报（06）: 110–115.

[2] 王克非, 2024. 智能时代翻译之可为可不为 [J]. 外国语（上海外国语大学学报）（01）: 5–9+13.

[3] 陈芳，2023．外宣翻译过程中译者的适应与选择过程研究——评《外宣翻译译者主体性能力范畴化研究》[J]．新闻爱好者（02）：121–122.

[4] 胡开宝，2023．国家外宣翻译能力：构成、现状与未来 [J]．上海翻译（04）：1–7＋95.

[5] 文旭、田亚灵，2024．ChatGPT 应用于中国特色话语翻译的有效性研究 [J]．上海翻译（02）：27–34+94–95.

[6] 耿芳、胡健，2023．人工智能辅助译后编辑新方向——基于 ChatGPT 的翻译实例研究 [J]．中国外语（03）：41–47.

[7] 王金铨、牛永一，2023．计算机辅助翻译评价系统中的翻译质量评估 [J]．上海翻译（06）：52–57.

[8] 周忠良，2020．政治文献外译须兼顾准确性和接受度——外交部外语专家陈明明访谈录 [J]．中国翻译（4）：92–100.

[9] 王华树、谢亚，2023．ChatGPT 时代翻译技术发展及其启示 [J]．外国语言与文化（04）：80–89.

[10] 于蕾，2024．ChatGPT 翻译的词汇多样性和句法复杂度研究 [J]．外语教学与研究（02）：297–307+321.

[11] 张慧玲，2024．体认翻译学下对人工智能的翻译动态模式构建的探究——以 ChatGPT 为例 [J]．文化学刊（12）：191–194.

[12] 曾剑平，2018．外宣翻译的中国特色与话语融通 [J]．江西社会科学，38（10）：7.

Research on the Effectiveness of Artificial Intelligence Assisted Publicity-oriented Texts Translation
— Taking ChatGPT as an example

Tianjin University   SHEN Yihan

Abstract: Publicity-oriented text translation is not just a technical task of converting language, but also a strategic activity that involves various levels such as politics, economy, culture, and society. High-quality translation is crucial in safeguarding national interests and promoting international cooperation. With the rapid development of generative artificial intelligence, it is important to research its effectiveness in translating external communications. This study selected content from "Understanding Contemporary China" as the source text, analyzed and compared the translations of 10 master's students majoring in translation with ChatGPT translations, and explored the effectiveness of artificial intelligence-assisted publicity-oriented text translation led by ChatGPT. The results indicate that ChatGPT performs well in terms of vocabulary diversity and syntactic richness, while student translators excel in cultural understanding and ideology. This research can provide references for publicity-oriented translation work, improve the effectiveness of national foreign propaganda, and offer suggestions for teaching translation majors in universities.

Keywords: Publicity-oriented texts; Artificial intelligence; ChatGPT

翻译教学与实践
TRANSLATION TEACHING AND PRACTICE

技术赋能时代基于实践共同体的翻译教学探究

西北师范大学外国语学院　白丽梅[①]　胡文娟[②]

【摘　要】 本文通过探究实践共同体的内涵与特征，构建了技术赋能时代的翻译实践共同体实践模型。实践共同体由学习者、教师、行业专家和技术人员等成员构成（共同社区），围绕真实或虚拟的翻译任务，以提高学生翻译能力，培养学生翻译职业素养为目标（共同领域），在翻译实践中体验、探究、交流、协商、合作，相互介入，不断提升翻译能力，从而实现翻译技能迁移（共同实践），实现从翻译新手成长为成熟译者甚至专家的蜕变。技术赋能时代的翻译实践共同体具有实践性项目驱动、协作式问题探究、动态式身份建构等核心特征。基于实践共同体的翻译教学模式实现了"学生主体、教师指导、技术主导"的教学理念，真正推进翻译教学内涵式发展。

【关键词】 技术赋能；实践共同体；翻译教学；深度学习

一、引言

随着全球化的发展和信息技术的蓬勃发展，翻译行业和翻译人才培养正面临着前所未有的挑战和机遇。机器翻译、云端协作平台、ChatGPT等新技术的发展和应用，提高了翻译效率和质量，但也不断刷新着翻译活动的内涵和外延，给翻译教学、翻译学习和从业人员带来了不小的压力，给翻译行业带来了巨大变革。在这个技术

[①] 白丽梅，西北师范大学教授，研究方向为翻译教学、语用学及社会语言学。邮箱：329921879@qq.com。
[②] 胡文娟，西北师范大学外国语学院硕士研究生，研究方向为英语笔译。邮箱：18794790627@163.com。

赋能时代，作为一门偏重职业性和实践性的学科，传统的翻译教学模式已经无法满足多样化的翻译学习需求。翻译教学作为培养高级翻译人才的重要途径，需要不断进行教学探索和创新。因此，在翻译教学与现代化教育技术深度融合的背景下，如何协同翻译技术，将理论学习与实践能力培养相结合，促进学习者学习方式的优化与转型，实现智能化的翻译教学新模式，培养适应技术赋能时代需求的翻译人才是目前翻译教学的重要任务。

实践共同体理念作为一种新的教学模式，关注技术化、项目化和职业化等时代特征，强调师生在实践中参与、合作，培养学生的翻译实践能力和团队合作精神，实现情境、实践与翻译学习的联结，助力学习者从"边缘性参与者"发展为"充分参与者"，再到"核心实践者"，从而实现从"新手"到"专家"的蝶变（舒晓杨，2021）。基于技术赋能的实践共同体则是一种以教师、学生和技术为基础的教学新模式。在这种模式下，教师不再仅仅是知识的传授者，学生也不再仅仅是知识的接受者，而是积极的参与者，技术则是教学的重要工具和平台，成为翻译教学和实践中不可分割的部分。因此，将技术与实践共同体理念引入翻译课程教学，对加强语言服务人才的技术素养，整合优质翻译技术资源，推动翻译技术与翻译教学的融合发展，促进技术与人的和谐共生，培养高级翻译人才具有重要意义。高校必须抓住机遇，充分利用翻译技术，调整传统的思维模式，创新翻译人才培养模式，培养学生"人机耦合"翻译观，在实践中培养出适应时代需求的"懂语言+懂技术"的国际化翻译人才（丁大琴、刘慧，2022）。

二、实践共同体的内涵与特征

实践共同体指一个有着共同关注点的群体，在不断的发展过程中相互影响、相互作用，以加强彼此在领域内的知识与专业技能（Lave & Wenger, 1991）。Wenger（1998）提出实践共同体有三个维度：共同愿景、共同参与和共享资源。共同愿景是指经过实践共同体全体成员共同协商确定的共同目标，是共同体合作的基础，并在实践中得以发展。共同参与指共同体成员通过协商和互动达到相互分享和认同的目的，每位参与者都有自己特定的位置和身份，在互动中实现"旁观者"向"核心参与者"的角色转化。共享资源是共同体实践的源泉，指共同体成员共享、整合各自所拥有的信息、观点、知识等。Lave & Wenger（1991）认为，学习过程是一个新手通过与更有经验的成员互动而逐渐全面参与共同体活动的社会情境化过程，这一过程被称为"合法的边缘性参与"。在共同体工作情境中，一开始作为新手的学习者部分地、不充分地参与共同体活动，通过与同伴、专家的互动，逐步实现专业技能的发展。

Wenger 等人（2002）提出了新的实践共同体三要素：共同领域、共同社区和共同实践。共同领域（Domain）是把共同体成员聚在一起的原因和起点，即成员共同关注的专业内容。共同社区（Community）是与他人互动协作的社会结构，成员在共同社区里开展有规律、有组织的活动，相互影响，共同成长。共同实践（Practice）是分享、发展与保持特定知识的过程，共同体成员之间相互介入，共同参与。总之，实践共同体就是具有共享专业知识和共同事业热情的共同体成员（共同社区），围绕特定的学习主题或专业领域（共同领域），在参与实践的过程中探究体验、交流合作、资源共享、充分协商（共同实践），从而使共同体成员从旁观者、合法的边缘性参与者发展为积极参与者、核心参与者，成员在实践中不断促进自身专业发展，实现共同体成员间的共同进步（赵雯、李广利，2022）。实践共同体强调学习者在实践中的主体地位，强调在学习过程中的合作学习。学习者通过协商和分享各种资源而构成一个相互影响、相互促进的集体（张红波、徐福荫，2016）。共同体聚焦知识意义的社会建构和情境性，激发成员之间的经验交流和协商冲突，从而引发反思，实现深度学习（卢强，2013）。在翻译教学中，通过引入实践共同体理念，组织学生参与翻译实践，与专业人士进行充分互动、合作，对契合翻译专业教育发展内在要求，推进技术赋能时代翻译教学与行业需求有效对接，提升学生翻译实践能力具有重要意义。

三、技术赋能时代翻译实践共同体构建

根据欧洲翻译硕士联盟（2017）更新的 EMT 翻译能力框架，翻译能力由语言与文化能力、翻译能力、技术能力、个人与人际能力、服务提供能力五个模块组成。通过课堂教学，教师和行业专家可以将具体、静态的知识和翻译技能讲授给学生，部分翻译能力可以转换成具体的翻译知识和技能，但有的隐性翻译能力却无法通过讲授获得，只能在教师和行业人士创设的真实或虚拟情境中，通过实际参与翻译项目，相互协作，不断反思，才能提升翻译能力，并逐步实现"旁观者—边缘性参与者—积极参与者—核心参与者"的转变，以构建一个情境化的递进式翻译实践共同体教学模式（舒晓杨，2011、2021）。

技术赋能时代的翻译实践共同体是由学习者、教师、行业专家和技术人员等共同体成员构成的团队（共同社区），围绕真实或虚拟的翻译任务，以提高学生翻译

能力，培养学生翻译职业素养为目标（共同领域），在翻译实践中体验、探究、交流、协商、合作，相互介入（共同实践），不断提升翻译能力，从而实现翻译技能迁移，实现从翻译新手成长为成熟译者甚至专家的蜕变（如图1所示）。翻译实践共同体是技术赋能时代学习共同体在专业领域衍生出来的新形式，是为适应市场需求而形成的一个师、生、行业多方联动的共同立体网络（刘畅，2021）。

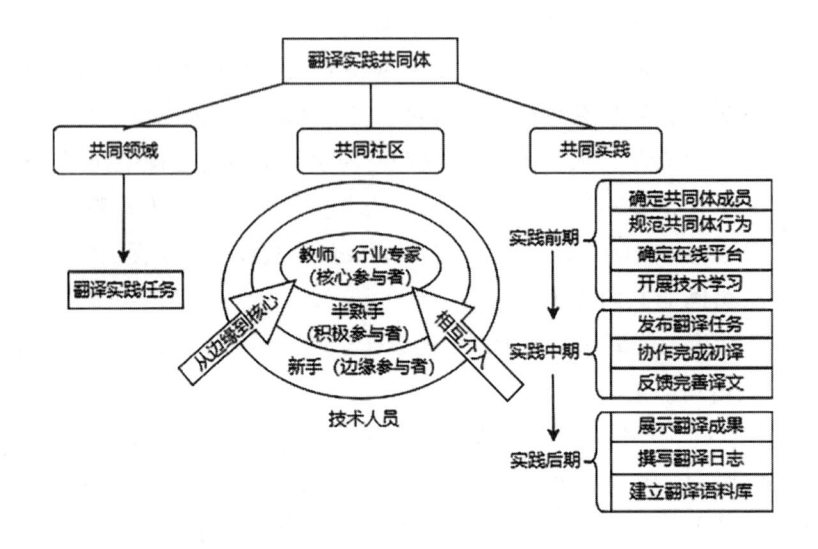

图1 技术赋能时代翻译实践共同体模型

（一）实践前期

1. 确定实践共同体成员

翻译学习者掌握职业翻译技能的最佳途径是在职业译者的指导下完成职业翻译项目。翻译实践共同体基于特定的翻译任务或项目，以参与翻译实践、解决翻译实践问题为目标，由学生、教师、行业专家、技术人员构成。首先由学生组建翻译小组，翻译小组兼顾学生的学习风格和翻译水平，按照"组内异质，组间同质"原则，每组5~6人，由能力强的同学或教师担任项目经理，其他同学负责资料查询、术语规范、初译、译审等工作。教师作为翻译实践共同体的策划者和助学者，负责开展翻译教学活动，组织线上线下翻译实践活动，将任务进行合理规划和分工，并给予合理的引导、帮助、反馈。来自翻译公司、出版社等具有丰富口笔译实践经验的行业专家，负责为学生提供翻译实践素材，分享实战经验，进行实践指导与译文反馈。另外，教师和行业专家作为助学者，要不定期向学生推送、分享典型翻译案例和素材，与学生共同探讨问题、研习、总结翻译技巧，使学生逐步将其内化为自身能力，在实践中不断提升翻译素养，实现师生共同成长。技术人员提供技术支持，如社交软件、在线教学平台（如雨课堂）的搭建，尤其是翻译技术支持。技术人员可以是专业的技术人员，也可以是共同体成员中具有较高技术素养的教师、行业专家乃至学生。共同体成员年龄、经历、技能背景不同，但拥有共同的兴趣和对"共同利益"的追求，通过成员协作，共同参与、探讨和反思翻译案例，通过传递和分享学习资源来完成知识积累，让翻译理论修养和实践技能得以提升。

2. 规范实践共同体行为

行为规范是共同体成员必须遵循的行为准则和共同体活动开展的前提条件。共同体成员共同协商，从资源管理、人员分工、任务协调、完成周期、评价方式等多个环节制定规则，明确不同成员的责任，确保翻译实践共同体任务的顺利进行。此外，各成员之间要彼此尊重，认真听取每一位成员的观点，既要包容同伴的看法与观点，也要具有独立的思辨能力和大胆质疑的批判精神。成员之间相互尊重，有利于促进学习者在共同体中的认同感和归属感，提高成员参与度（李志河等，2019）。

3. 确定在线沟通平台

确定在线教学平台，建立网络沟通平台是确保翻译实践任务顺利完成的重要保障。雨课堂为师生提供了较为完整、立体的数据支持，功能较为齐全，包括课前公告、课前提醒、上课签到、弹幕互动、在线答题、实时讨论、课程回放、数据统计等。课前教师通过雨课堂发布公告，上传插入视频，推送带有MOOC视频、习题、语音的课前预习课件，让学生了解课程内容，做好课前预习；课堂上结合讲授内容和课程进度提出拓展性问题、翻译练习，学生实时答题、弹幕互动，为实现师生互动提供完美解决方案。同时推荐学生学习由名校名师主讲的慕课。课后及时布置翻译作业，以督促学生巩固课堂学习成果。学生适时观看雨课堂的课程回放以做到查漏补缺，完善课堂笔记并及时完成练习。教师利用雨课堂教学平台，对翻译理论知识和技能进行讲解，强化学生翻译知识体系的内化以及翻译工具的运用。行业专家分享实训素材与案例，并在翻译实务、翻译技术、翻译工具及翻译管理等职业技能方面指导学生实践。此外，建立微信群或QQ群让学生进行互动讨论，教师为学生答疑解惑。通过在线教学平台和沟通平台可以打破时空限制，实现师生顺畅交流。

4. 开展翻译技术学习

作为技术赋能时代翻译教学和实践的主体，教师和学生都应该适应数字化生存环境，不仅要拥有传统的翻译能力，还应熟悉智能技术在翻译实践中的应用，具备娴熟的翻译技术能力。在翻译实践中急需培养学生的计算机基本技能、信息检索能力、CAT工具应用能力、翻译记忆库构建能力、术语处理能力、译后编辑能力等。技术赋能时代翻译技术的广泛应用变革了传统翻译实践模式，在技术驱动下，新技术、新问题不断涌现，翻译对象、主题、模式、环境和教育等发生了显著的技术转向，翻译范式发生了巨大改变（王华树、刘世界，2021）。翻译技术已经成为翻译实践不可或缺的部分，学习者必须为搭建专属于自己的机器翻译系统做好心理准备和技术准备。

  对于翻译学习者和语言服务从业者来说，术语管理对语言服务管理的改进和个人翻译质量和效率的提升具有重大意义。关注术语使用的准确性和恰当性极其重要，准确理解不同词语之间含义和用法的细微差别是一位优秀译者的必备素养。计算机辅助翻译（CAT）工具可以自动识别译文中重复的内容和术语，为术语转换、术语标注、术语提取等提供有益帮助，减少翻译过程中的重复劳动，提高术语翻译的一致性。虽然机器翻译的质量还有待提高，但可以作为翻译实践的参考和辅助工具。此外，巧妙应用语料库也可以解决翻译中的各种疑难问题。常见的语料采集工具 ABBYY FineReader、Teleport Ultra 等 OCR 识别软件可用于处理纸质材料、网页材料或其他不可编辑的材料；语料清洗软件 EmEditor、Notepad++ 等可以去除语料中的噪声，包括不符合规范的格式、符号、内容等。语料对齐工具 CAT 软件自带的 Trados 的对齐文档、memoQ 的 LiveDocs，和 ABBYY Aligner、Tmxmall 等独立工具提供了编辑、调整对齐结果的功能，可以极大提高语料对齐效率。常见的语料检索工具 AntConc、ParaConc 等具有平行文本预览功能、平行文本检索、检索行排序、词频统计、搭配提取等功能。搭配检索能够通过数据直观展示各种词条搭配、单词组合、近义词替换、常用词比较、词序查询等，帮助学习者快速选取最地道、最常用的表达，如 Netspeak 就是一款简单、高效、功能强大的单词搭配检索在线工具。除了人工审校外，也可以通过翻译质量保证（QA）工具对译文进行质量检查，帮助检查人工不易识别或容易忽视的问题，有效排除如标点、数字、空格等错误，有效节省时间，提高工作效率，确保译文质量。独立的质量保证工具有 ApSIC Xbench、ErrorSpy、Html QA 等；SDL Trados、Déjà Vu、Wordfast 等 CAT 工具也含有质量保证模块。

  在计算机辅助翻译工具学习过程中，可充分发挥共同体成员的主观能动性，要求每个小组学习 1～2 个工具，并向其他小组分享使用方法，切实增强学生的翻译技术素养、技术思维能力，促进信息技术与翻译实践的深度融合。翻译过程是译者自我思考和输出的过程，翻译工具只是起到辅助的作用，在利用工具节省时间和精力的同时，学习者更要明确译者在翻译过程中的核心和主体位置，努力借助工具呈现更为优质的译文。

（二）实践中期

1. 发布翻译任务

作为翻译学习的引导者和监督者，教师或行业专家围绕课程内容或现有翻译项目，共同设定基于工作过程或亲自参与过的真实翻译项目，在雨课堂定期发布翻译实践任务，通过实践提升解决翻译问题能力，提升学生在真实工作环境中的翻译能力。

2. 协作完成初译

翻译小组根据翻译任务，以翻译工作坊的形式开展协同翻译。首先查找平行文本，通过细读，把握文本的词汇、句法、语篇特征和写作风格，以产出与原文文本特征相匹配的译文。作为翻译学习的主体，学生一方面以个人为单位进行独立翻译，另一方面以翻译小组为单位，进行团队分工，分别承担查询资料、术语规范、初译、译审等工作，借助语料库、术语库、在线词典等网络共享技术和资源，解决文本理解或翻译处理中的难点，完成翻译任务。作为"客户"的行业专家和作为"项目经理"的教师共同把控翻译实践大方向，利用雨课堂和微信平台进行一对一、一对多和多方互动研讨，对文本类型、译语风格、语法措辞、翻译技巧、译文分歧等进行交流探讨，提供适时指导，解决学生在实践中遇到的疑难问题。学生经过润色、校对，完成初译。最后，借助质量保证工具对译文质量进行评估。

3. 反馈完善译文

翻译实践共同体成员在独立完成、互动讨论、同伴互查的基础上，合作完成翻译任务。各个翻译小组通过雨课堂提交译文，教师和行业专家对译文进行评价，提出反馈意见。学生通过反思，巩固翻译技能，修改完善译文，最终形成定稿。这一过程打破了"教师讲，学生听"的传统授课模式，为共同体成员共同参与翻译实践提供最大的可能和空间。师生关系也从过去的听从关系转变为对话与协作的关系。成员之间在观摩中积累学习，在实践中顺应学习，在合作中拓展学习，从而实现相互交流、信息共享，不断丰富、完善、提升翻译技能。

（三）实践后期

1. 展示翻译成果

各翻译小组指派代表通过 PPT 做成果展示，对文本分析、译前编辑、翻译过程、译后编辑、修订校对全过程进行陈述，重点阐述文本语体风格、翻译重点难点，以及解决重难点采用的具体翻译策略。共同体其他成员可以就译文发表意见，对疑难问题展开讨论。专业教师和行业专家组织和参与译文赏析及点评活动，并对实践成果进行评分，共同分析译文的优缺点，分析各组使用的翻译技巧和策略，指出翻译中出现的典型问题，并进行技巧总结和理论点拨。此外，通过雨课堂推送、传阅优秀译文，实现知识和实践性应用成果的共享。同时，教师和行业专家根据过程性评价结果，结合教学重点难点，布置相应的补充翻译任务，进一步巩固、内化学生的翻译能力，以达到深度学习的目的。

2. 撰写翻译日志

每个小组根据当次活动经历撰写翻译日志，对每一次翻译实践中遇到的问题、收获、感悟等做详细记录。对整个翻译过程进行复盘不仅能提高学生的团队意识、协作精神、责任意识和创新意识，也能大大提升学生独立思考和解决问题的能力。学生要想毕业以后马上融入职场，必须要提高职业能力，进行项目驱动式的翻译教学，让学生在真实的项目中习得更多真实的职业技能（陶友兰、刘敬国，2015），从而实现从显性翻译知识到隐性职业素养的转化。

3. 建立翻译语料库

最终成果全部形成电子档案袋，共享至雨课堂学习平台，使其转化为可用的教学、学习资源。通过共同建设并持续完善精彩译文的整理与收录，最终形成校本双语平行语料库，建成多元化的教学资源库。

四、技术赋能时代翻译实践共同体核心特征

（一）实践性项目驱动

翻译实践共同体在教师和行业导师的指导下，基于虚拟或真实的翻译项目，让学生在实践中体验项目人员分工、项目进度控制、项目管理规范、项目具体实施、项目实施评估等流程，熟悉从前期准备到初稿、一审、二审、统稿、定稿的全过程，从而提高学生的翻译能力和项目管理能力，有效促进学习者在批判理解、信息整合、构建反思、迁移运用、问题解决等方面的发展和内化，有效促进深度学习。通过完成与实践项目相关的课程内容，共同体成员在学习过程中直接应用所学知识，提高

实际操作能力。技术赋能时代的翻译行业需要熟练掌握各种翻译工具和技术。基于实践共同体的翻译教学强调学生的主体地位，学生有机会应用各种翻译工具和技术，实现技术对实践的赋能，从而提高翻译效率和质量。同时，学生也可以通过翻译实践，探索新的翻译技术和方法。

（二）协作式问题探究

协作式问题探究包括人际协作和人机协作。人际协作是学习者在参与、认同、协商的过程中，共同体成员之间相互施加影响，彼此成就。学习者以合法边缘参与者的身份进入实践共同体，借助教师、行业专家搭建的脚手架及丰富的学习资源、交流平台，实现个人认知的构建，获得参与实践共同体活动的能力。随着学习者在共同体中参与活动的程度逐步深入，在与其他个体进行互动和意义协商的过程中，知识体系不断完善，逐渐得到其他成员的认同，逐渐实现了人际层面的发展，在深度探究中解决问题、协作促学（李志河等，2019）。

人机协同技术是机器翻译技术中的另一个重要环节。人和机器在翻译过程中相互辅助、相互配合，协同模式灵活多变，可以根据翻译任务、需求、人力和时间等采取不同的实现方式，如译后编辑模式、协同翻译模式、混合翻译模式等。同时，学习者在实践过程中，可以熟练掌握 ABBYY FineReader、EmEditor、memoQ、ABBYY Aligner、ApSIC Xbench 等工具，软件技术应用能力能得到极大提升，在提高翻译效率的同时，确保译文质量。

（三）动态式身份建构

翻译实践也是一个身份建构的过程。实践共同体成员的身份是动态的，而非一成不变。一方面，部分学习者一开始可能只是观察、学习、模仿和练习，是旁观者或边缘参与者。在不断互动、协商的过程中，实践共同体为学习者提供充分的协商机会、丰富的资源和介入共同体的路径，从而实现知识建构和意义共享，由边缘参与逐步走向核心参与，成员在实践中相互学习、共享资源，不断增强从新手到熟手的身份感，从而促进自身专业发展，实现共同体成员间的共同进步。学习者在实践共同体中从参与、认同到协商的过程，标志着学习者的身份在个人层面、人际层面和共同体层面不断发展和认同，实践共同体由形成、发展逐渐达到成熟（李志河等，2019；赵雯、李广利，2022）。另一方面，教师也可以从"专家"转换为"学习者"身份，向行业专家或专业译者甚至学生请教；而学生也可能在某个方面从"学习者"转换为"专家"身份为共同体成员答疑解惑（舒晓杨，2021）。

五、结语

　　构建基于技术赋能的翻译实践共同体以"翻译技术"为切入点，促进智慧开放的教学改革，以"共同领域"为合作导向，达成共同发展的价值共识，以"共同社区"为合作形式，培育合作共赢的协作关系，以"共同实践"为合作手段，搭建翻译共同体交流平台。通过翻译实践共同体，学习者借助在线学习平台和人工智能辅助翻译工具，可以大大提高翻译效率和质量，同时学习者在协作互动中完成翻译实践，不但培养了实践能力和创新能力，也有效提高了共同体成员的交互水平和知识建构，从而达到深度学习的目的；另一方面，在实践共同体的教学模式下，教师需要不断学习新的技术和教学方法，以适应新的教学模式，对教师的专业发展大有裨益。基于实践共同体的翻译教学模式实现了"学生主体、教师指导、技术主导"的教学理念，为教师提供教学参考，帮助教师提高教学效果，培养有较高信息素养的翻译人才，真正推进翻译教学内涵式发展。

【参考文献】

　　[1] 丁大琴、刘慧，2022．基于人工智能新技术改革创新传统的翻译人才培养模式[J]．安徽理工大学学报（2）：99–103．

　　[2] 李志河等，2019．网络学习空间下混合式学习共同体活动机制构建[J]．中国电化教育（9）：104–111．

　　[3] 刘畅，2021．信息化教学环境下翻译学习共同体的探索与实践[J]．江苏高职教育（1）：71–77．

　　[4] 卢强，2013．学习共同体内涵重审：课程教学的视域[J]．远程教育杂志（3）：44–50．

　　[5] 舒晓杨，2011．合法的边缘性参与：网络环境下翻译新手提升翻译能力的新取向[J]．浙江外国语学院学报（6）：58–62．

　　[6] 舒晓杨，2021．AI环境下基于工作场所学习的递进式笔译教学工作坊实践探索[J]．外语电化教学（2）：65–72+10．

　　[7] 陶友兰、刘敬国，2015．以提高译者能力为中心的翻译硕士笔译教学综合模式新探[J]．外语教学理论与实践（4）：87–91+43．

　　[8] 王华树、刘世界，2022．人工智能时代机器翻译译后编辑能力探究[J]．中国科技翻译（4）：21–24．

[9] 王华树、刘世界，2021. 人工智能时代翻译技术转向研究 [J]. 外语教学（5）：87–92.

[10] 赵雯、李广利，2022. 大学英语课程群虚拟实践共同体建设研究 [J]. 外语界（4）：16–21.

[11] 张红波、徐福荫，2016. 基于社会网络视角的学习共同体构建与相关因素分析 [J]. 电化教育研究（10）：70–76.

[12] EMT Expert Group. European Master's in Translation — EMT Competence Framework [EB/OL]. (2017-12-31) [2020-03-06]. https://ec. europa. eu/info/sites/info/files/ emt_Competence_fwk_2017_en_web.pdf.

[13] Kiraly, D. *A Social Constructivist Approach to Translator Education: Empowerment from Theory to Practice* [M]. Manchester: St. Jerome, 2000.

[14] Lave, Jean & Wenger, Etienne. *Situated Learning: Legitimate Peripheral Participation* [M]. Cambridge University Press. 1991.

[15] Wenger, Etienne. *Community of Practice: Learning, Meaning and Identity* [M]. Cambridge University Press. 1998.

[16] Wenger, E. et al. *Cultivating Communities of Practice: A Guide to Managing Knowledge* [M]. Boston: Harvard Business Review Press. 2002.

Exploration of Translation Teaching in the Era of Technological Empowerment, Based on A Community of Practice

School of Foreign Languages, Northwest Normal University   BAI Limei and HU Wenjuan

Abstract: By exploring the connotation and characteristics of community of practice, this paper constructs a practice model of translation community of practice in the era of technology empowerment. The community of practice consists of learners, teachers, translators, technicians etc. (community). Centering on real or virtual translation tasks, the community aims to improve students' translation ability and cultivate their professionalism in translation (domain). In translation practice, the community experiences, explores, communicates, negotiates, cooperates, and engages with each other to continuously improve translation ability, so as to realize the transfer of translation skills (practice). In this way, learners can achieve the transformation from a novice learner to a mature translator or even an expert. The translation community of practice in the technology-empowered era is characterized by practical project-driven approaches, collaborative problem exploration, and dynamic identity construction. The translation teaching mode based on the community of practice realizes the teaching idea of "student-led, teacher-guided and technology-oriented", and truly promotes the connotative development of translation teaching.

Keywords: technology empowerment; community of practice; translation teaching; deep learning

齿轮类标准化文件翻译难点及应对方法[①]

全国齿轮标准化技术委员会 郑州机械研究所有限公司 郭情情[②]
江西师范大学 宜宾学院 闫 冰[③]

【摘　要】 本文以齿轮类标准化文件的翻译为研究对象,对标准化文件制定的流程、译者的群体特征、总体的文本和语言特点等进行总结,对标准化文件翻译的难点及应对方法进行归纳分析,得出在翻译标准化文件时,要特别注意情态动词的特殊含义、普通名词专业化及特定名词的规定译法、术语的唯一性与词组的多样化译法、行业内约定俗成的译法以及句子中会引起歧义的字词句的译法等,以期为今后与标准化文件翻译相关的实践和研究提供有益的参考。

【关键词】 标准化文件;翻译;国际话语体系;齿轮

一、引言

在"讲好中国故事,传播好中国声音"的倡导下,翻译界也开始积极探索构建国际话语权的新路径和新举措。近年来,翻译界在这一主题下的探索主要集中在两个方面,一是党政文本的翻译,二是文学文化的对外译介。但实际上,讲好中国故

[①] 基金项目:本文为宜宾市社科联项目"《诗经》中文化意象概念隐喻阐释翻译研究"(项目号:2021YBSKL32)与宜宾学院启航项目"《诗经》在英国的翻译,传播和影响"(项目号:2021QH042)的部分研究成果。
[②] 郭情情(1994—　),北京航空航天大学硕士、全国齿轮标准化技术委员会(SAC/TC52)、郑州机械研究所有限公司助理工程师,主要研究方向为翻译理论与实践,本文通讯作者。邮箱:qingqingguo0216@foxmail.com。
[③] 闫冰(1984—　),江西师范大学文学院博士后、宜宾学院国际教育学部讲师,主要研究方向为典籍翻译、应急语言服务。邮箱:ziyubingling1227@foxmail.com。

事，传播好中国声音，除了要宣介习近平新时代中国特色社会主义思想，讲好中国共产党治国理政的故事，展示中华优秀传统文化的精神标识和文化精髓之外，还提出要综合运用各种对外传播载体，尤其是多语化的国际传播产品，加强与国际智库和出版机构开展合作，注重海外落地和海外影响，提高对外传播效果，为解决人类问题贡献中国智慧和中国方案。[①]

标准化文件指的是为了在一定范围内获得最佳秩序而通过标准化活动，由公认机构批准并按照规定的程序经协商一致制定，为各种活动或其结果提供规则、指南或特性，供共同使用和重复使用的一种文件（GB/T 1.1—2020: 1–2）。从微观层面来讲，标准化文件为人们的生产和实践提供了规则和指导，与人们的生活息息相关；从宏观层面来讲，标准化文件常被作为各国在进行交易和贸易过程中的"契约性"要素文件，对制定国际规则和确立国际秩序有着十分重要的作用。在新形势下，标准化已上升为国家战略。标准化水平的高低，可以反映一个国家产业核心竞争力乃至综合实力的强弱（刘智洋等，2017: 57）。由此可见，标准化文件是新形势下"讲好中国故事，传播好中国声音"和"构建国际话语体系"的一种非常契合实际需要又与时俱进的对外传播载体和国际传播产品。

标准化文件与翻译密切相关。标准化文件的制定主要有两个渠道：一是自主研制；二是翻译采标国际标准，如 ISO、IEC、ITU 等国际组织制定的标准等。但是，由于标准化文件的内容专业性较强，其制定由特定的机构发起实施，文件本身的结构和用语也有特定的形式和规范，纯外语专业的人员对其翻译和制定的过程参与较少，与标准化文件翻译相关的研究也存在很大的空白。对此，本文将以与作为基础通用零部件的齿轮相关的标准化文件的翻译为研究对象，基于参与翻译、制定标准化文件的实践经验，对标准化文件制定的流程、翻译标准化文件的译者的群体特征、标准化文件的文本和语言特点等进行总结，从不同的方面对标准化文件翻译的难点进行分析，并给出对应的解决方法，以期为今后与标准化文件翻译相关的实践和研究提供有益的参考。

二、齿轮及齿轮类标准化文件的翻译

中国是一个制造大国。2021 年，中国制造业增加值占 GDP 的比重达到了

---

① 见求是网，2018 年 10 月 31 日《坚持讲好中国故事、传播好中国声音》。

27.4%，总量达到了 31.4 万亿元，连续 12 年位居世界首位。[①] 但中国的制造业却"大而不强"，从整体上看，中国的制造技术仍然缺乏科技创新的能力。为解决这一问题，我们一方面要加强与国际的交流和对接，以提升我国的制造技术和制造创新能力；另一方面，我们也要意识到中国在制造工艺和产品生产方面的优势，要积极推动我国的制造工艺和制造产品走向世界。齿轮作为加工制造领域的基础通用零部件，是我国制造业的一个缩影。本文选取齿轮类标准化文件的翻译为研究对象，一方面可以让外语专业的人员了解与工业及制造业相关的文本的翻译特点，另一方面也可以使与齿轮及机械制造业相关的人员了解在用英语表达相关术语或语句时应当注意的问题。

虽然翻译采标国际标准一直是我国制定标准化文件的一个重要来源，但当前我国对国际标准的翻译采标程度还远无法满足国家的实际需求，而我国的标准文件外文版的制定则更是处于起步阶段。中国标准化研究院标准信息研究所刘智洋研究员在报告中指出，截至 2022 年 6 月，我国的国家标准共 41 525 项，同步制定外文版的共 1304 项，占比仅 3%。而以 TC52 全国齿轮标准化技术委员会（以下简称"齿标委"）为例，本 TC 现行有效的国家标准和国家指导性技术文件中有超过 1/3 的文件是翻译采标国际标准；TC52 对口国际标准化组织 ISO 的 TC60 及其分技术委员会 SC1 和 SC2，当前齿标委对对口技术委员会及分技术委员会发布标准的采标率还不到 60%（截止到 2022 年 12 月）；标准外文版的同步制定从 2022 年才开始立项。而根据国标委联〔2021〕36 号通知，至"十四五"末（2025），国际标准转化率要达到 85% 以上，并积极推动国家标准等同步制定外文版（国标委联，2021：6）。可见，我国的标准化文件在与国际接轨方面还有很长的路要走，翻译在标准化文件领域还有很大的需求和发展空间。

三、标准化文件的制定和译者的群体特征

标准化文件的立项和后续流程的整体规划一般由相应的专业技术委员会按照国标委的要求统领负责。文件的起草人一般都是各起草单位的专业技术骨干、教授和高级工程师。标准化文件要求起草人精通专业技术，具有多年的专业研究或实践经验积累。如果是翻译采标标准或者标准需要同步制定外文版，还需对起草人的英语水平有一定的要求。虽然这类起草人专业技术和知识储备过硬，且由于常年阅读英

[①] 见中华人民共和国工业和信息化部 2022 年 3 月 10 日发布的文件。

文文献或者出国交流的原因，其英语在阅读理解和听说交流方面在大多数情况下不会出现什么问题。但是他们毕竟没有受过严谨、系统的语言文字训练，因此在有些情况下会出现对国际标准化文件中的原文理解不到位的情况，在将中国的标准翻译为外文时，常常会出现语言使用不规范、不严谨的情况。因此，从语言学习者或研究者的角度对标准化文件翻译中存在的问题加以阐述和分析，就十分有必要。

四、标准化文件的文本和语言特点

标准化文件，文本篇幅大小不一，总体来讲内容专业性较强，属于一种科技文本。标准化文件的语言，同其他很多类型的科技文本一样，具有显著的科技文本的特征，如专业词汇较多，英文中大量使用非谓语动词、被动语态和长句等。但相比其他类型的科技文本，标准化文件在语言的使用上，总体较为客观、简洁，表达更加准确、易懂，一般不使用模棱两可或容易产生歧义的词或句子。

五、标准化文件翻译的难点及应对方法

标准化文件的翻译难点主要有三个方面：一是专业内容的翻译；二是术语的唯一性；三是标准化文件在用词和表述方面的特定要求。具体可从以下五个方面来进行探讨。

（一）情态动词及其对应表述的特殊含义

标准化文件中的情态动词及其对应表述具有一些规定性的特殊含义，这一点在使用时要十分注意。比如，英文中的"shall"，我们查词典，可以译为"将要（将会）、必须（一定）、可以、应（应该）、就会"等，在翻译时我们可以根据具体表达的意思从中选取一个比较合适的译法。根据词典，"should"的释义我们可以从"应该（该）、可以、应该会（可能）、本当、竟然、假如（万一）"等中选取其一。对比以上列举的两个单词的词义，我们可以看出，虽说两个单词的词义并不完全相同，但两个单词在表意方面有很大的重合，在很多场景下是可以互换使用的，并没有什么天壤之别。但在标准化文件中，除极少数的特殊情况之外，情态动词

的译法是固定的,没有译者主体性的发挥空间。在标准化文件中,"shall"和"shall not"表达的是要求性条款,"should"和"should not"表达的是推荐性条款,"may"和"may not"表达的是允许性条款,"can"和"cannot"表达的是可能性条款。"shall"翻译为"应","should"翻译为"宜",两者不可以替换,在翻译时也不可替换为其他的表达。此外,情态动词的使用要和条款(表达)所属的类别严格对应,而标准化文件中的不同部分对不同类型的条款的使用也有限制。如在资料性附录和范围中不可以出现要求性条款,所以指示要求的"shall"和"shall not"也就不应该出现在资料性附录和范围中。除了情态动词之外,还有与情态动词相对应的等效表达,作为对情态动词的补充,具体的表述及其与情态动词的对应关系可见表1至表4(GB/T 1.2—2020:11–12)。

表1 要求

ISO/IEC标准化文件的助动词	国家标准化文件对应的能愿动词	ISO/IEC标准化文件在特殊情况下使用的等效表述	国家标准化文件在特殊情况下使用的等效表述
shall	应	is to is required to it is required that has to only … is permitted it is necessary	应该 只准许
shall not	不应	is not allowed [permitted] [acceptable] [permissible] is required to be not is required that … be not is not to be do not	不应该 不准许

表2 推荐

ISO/IEC标准化文件的助动词	国家标准化文件对应的能愿动词	ISO/IEC标准化文件在特殊情况下使用的等效表述	国家标准化文件在特殊情况下使用的等效表述
should	宜	it is recommended that ought to	推荐 建议
should not	不宜	it is not recommended that ought not to	不推荐 不建议

表3 允许

ISO/IEC标准化文件的助动词	国家标准化文件对应的能愿动词	ISO/IEC标准化文件在特殊情况下使用的等效表述	国家标准化文件在特殊情况下使用的等效表述
may	可	is permitted is allowed is permissible	可以 允许
may not	不必	it is not required that no…is required	可以不 无须

表4 能力和可能性

ISO/IEC标准化文件的助动词	国家标准化文件对应的能愿动词	ISO/IEC标准化文件在特殊情况下使用的等效表述	国家标准化文件在特殊情况下使用的等效表述
can	能 可能	be able to there is a possibility of it is possible to	能够 有可能
cannot	不能 不可能	be unable to there is no possibility of it is not possible to	不能够 没有可能

（二）普通名词专业化及特定名词的规定译法

（1）普通名词专业化

在翻译专业性较强的文本内容时，普通名词专业化是很常见的。表5列出了一些很常见的普通名词，但是当它们单独或与其他单词一起组成词组在齿轮类标准化文件中出现时，其对应的翻译通常不是我们日常熟悉的释义。如在日常生活中，"worm"最常用的词义为"蠕虫"，但在齿轮行业中，"worm"译为"蜗杆"，"worm gear"译为"蜗轮"，"gear pair"不是译为"齿轮对"，而是译为"齿轮副"，"worm pair"译为"蜗杆副"，"worm gear pair"译为"蜗轮副"；"wheel"最常用的释义为"车轮"，但在齿轮行业中，译为"大轮"，与"pinion""小轮"相对应；"stress"最常用的意思为"压力"，但在机械（齿轮）行业，"stress"通常译为"应力"，"contact stress"则译为"接触应力"；"clearance"和"backlash"在日常生活中常用的释义为"清除"和"反冲"，但出现在与齿轮相关的文本中时，两者分别指的是"齿顶隙"和"圆周侧隙"，有时候也简称为"顶隙"和"侧隙"，指的是两个不同位置处的间隙，在使用或表述时，切记不要混淆；"normal"在普通文本中通常译为"正常的"，但在齿轮类标准化文件中，大多译为"法向"，如"normal backlash"，译为"法向侧隙"；虽然"齿顶圆"和"齿根圆"分别为"tip circle"和"root circle"，但"tip relief"和"root relief"既不是翻译为"齿顶缓解"和"齿根缓解"，也不是译为"齿顶修形"和"齿根修形"，而是进一步演绎为"修缘"和"修根"；"crowning"在日常生活中多译为"加冕"，但在"profile crowning"中，译为"齿廓方向鼓形修形"；"translation"最基本的词义为"翻译、笔译"，但在特定语境下，有时需要译为"平移"，如"translation of a linear axis"译为"线性轴的平移"。

表5 普通名词专业化

单词	普通词义	专业词义
stress	压力	应力
allowable	允许的	许用（值）
translation	翻译	平移
blank	空白的	毛坯
normal	正常的	法向
clearance	清除	齿顶隙
backlash	反冲	圆周侧隙
solution	解决办法	溶液
manipulator	操纵器	机械臂
crowning	加冕	鼓形修形
tip circle	顶圆	齿顶圆
gear	装备	齿轮
worm	蠕虫	蜗杆
contact ratio	接触比	重合度
face width	面宽	齿宽
tooth depth	齿深	齿高
tip relief	顶部缓解	修缘
root relief	根部缓解	修根

（2）特定名词的规定译法

在标准化文件中，有一些特定的词或词组出现在特定的位置，其译法是固定的，不能换成其他表达。如在国标外文版的封面中，"××××－××－××（时间）发布""××××－××－××（时间）实施"和"×××（机构名）发布"分别译为"Issue date: ××××－××－××""Implementation date: ××××－××－××"和"Issued by（机构名）"，而不能随意选用其他词。目次中的"范围、术语、定义、符号、单位、缩略语"分别译为"scope, terms, definitions, symbols, units, abbreviated terms"。"规范性附录"和"资料性附录"应分别译为"Annex（normative）"和"Annex（informative）"，此处的"附录"不能译为"appendix"，也切不可将"normative"译为"规范的、标准的"或将"informative"译为"信息性的、知识性的"。"规范性引用文件"要译为"normative references"，这里的"文件"不能译为"documents"。在标准化文件中，"documents"具有特殊的含义，用来提及标准本身。根据 GB/T 1.2—2020，ISO/IEC 标准化文件在提及自身时，统一用"本文件"（this document）来进行表示（GB/T 1.2—2020：3）。在表达标准文件的文本层次时，中文标准中的"部分、章、条、段、列项、项"应分别译为"part, clause, subclause, paragraph, list, item"。在标准化文件中经常可以看到标准化文件的章标题或条标题只有一个单词"general"，该词在标准化文件中的译法也很有讲究，一般可译为"概述""通则"或"通用要求"。具体选哪一个要看下面段落的内容。如果所统领的段落全部是陈述性内容，不包含要求，则译为"概述"；如果段落内容既包含陈述性内容，也包含要求性条款，则译为"通则"；如果段落内容仅包含要求性条款，则译为"通用要求"。标准化文件正文中的示图下方在对符号或序号进行解释说明时，会用单词"key"来引领，这种情况下的"key"要按规定译为"标引序号说明："。与之类似，正文中公式下会用"where"来引出对公式中出现的符号的解释，此处的"where"统一译为"式中："，而不能译为"其中"或其他。

（三）术语的唯一性与词组的多样化译法

术语是在特定学科领域用来表示概念的称谓的集合。术语具有专业性、科学性、单义性、系统性和本地性。术语的确立要遵循唯一性原则。如果一个概念对应多个同义词，应当从中选取一个最恰当的作为首选术语。概念与术语要一一对应，即在某领域内构建的概念体系中，一个概念只由一个术语来表示（单名性），一个术语只表示一个概念（单义性）（白殿一等，2020：69）。

确立术语的最初目的是方便专业人员之间的交流、沟通和学习。但由于术语使用的广泛性、使用人员的复杂性和时空依附性，总体来看，术语是庞杂烦琐的，有时候甚至是艰涩而矛盾的。比如，在齿轮行业，同样一个概念，使用的人员可能来自高校、研究所或企业，因为背景的差异，不同的人对同一个概念的叫法可能会不同；而因为历史的演变，同一个概念的表述方式可能也会有差异，比如早些年代的专业书籍和当今时代的教科书对同一个概念的称谓也会有所区别。这是制定标准化文件的过程中在术语确立方面的一大难题。

如近期齿标委在主持修订 GB/T 10095.2[①] 的过程中，就计划对所采标的国际标准 ISO 1328—2: 2020（ISO 1328—2: 2020: 2）中的"master gear"一词重新确立称谓。"Master gear"用于齿轮综合测量。具体来说，为了检验一个产品齿轮（product gear）是否合格，通常需要使用一个加工精度较高的齿轮来与其进行对啮标定。"Master gear"最主要的目的是进行测量标定；其最主要的特征是精度比较高，虽然存在偏差，但其偏差可以忽略不计，在这种情况下常被看作是一个绝对精准的标准齿轮；在与产品齿轮进行啮合时，"master gear"大多时候充当的是主动齿轮（驱动齿轮），但也有少数时候充当被动齿轮（从动齿轮）。鉴于此，"master gear"在国内业界的叫法也非常多样，如主齿轮、母齿轮、基准齿轮、测量齿轮（GB/T 10095.2—2008: 2）、标准齿轮（测量标准齿轮）、标定齿轮、标准器、主测齿轮、双啮齿轮（双啮标准齿轮）、啮测齿轮、啮合齿轮、量仪齿轮等。这无疑为专业人员之间的交流和标准术语的确立带来了困难。此外，考虑到以上称谓大多是基于"master gear"某一方面的特性而确立，如"标准齿轮"仅考虑其精度，"测量齿轮"仅考虑其目的功用，"主齿轮"主要考虑"master gear"在与产品齿轮啮合时充当的角色，等等。虽然以上称谓的确定都具有一定的合理性，但也都有各自的局限，如"主齿轮"这一称谓很容易让人与"主动齿轮"混淆，而"master gear"又不总是充当主动齿轮。此外，由于"master gear"在齿轮类标准化文件和齿轮行业的其他应用场景中出现的频次较高，随着我国标准化文件外文版的推进，我们还要考虑中文术语在回译为英文时的便捷性。考虑到这一点，以上称谓如"标准齿轮"在回译为英文时，如果译者对专业知识和行业惯例的了解和熟悉程度不够，那么译者能将"标准齿轮"译为"master gear"的概率非常低，而一旦译为"standard gear"，又会与其他术语概念重叠混淆，这对整个行业的交流和发展将会产生十分不利的影响。鉴于此，齿标委秘书处与行业专家在标准讨论会上多次就"master gear"的译法进行了探讨。由于采取直译或意译的方法很难找到一个能全面顾及上述几个方面的适当的词，因此秘书处和专家经过讨论和投票后最终决定采取音译的方法，将"master gear"译为"码特齿轮"。码特齿轮被赋予了"master gear"的

---

① GB/T 10095.2 新版标准即将发布。

种种特性,在齿轮行业是一个新词,但相信在标准正式发布后,经过标准的宣贯和业内专业人员的普及,码特齿轮应该会在不久的将来成为业内专业人员耳熟能详的一个词。

(四)行业内约定俗成的译法

在齿轮类标准化文件中有很多长的词组或短语,其中英文表达在单词选用和字词排列次序方面很不对应,甚至可以说相差极大。但是因为这一组看似很不对应的中英文表述指示的概念相同,且在各自的语言体系中因为长期沿用而已经成为一种约定俗成的说法,因此在翻译时,要按照功能对等的原则,将这样的一对词组直接替换,直接沿用习惯的表达,不宜再造新的表述方式。如"cylindrical involute gears",比起按英文单词的顺序译为"圆柱渐开线齿轮",更多的是译为"渐开线圆柱齿轮"。类似地,"radial composite deviation, tooth-to-tooth"译为"一齿径向综合公差","profile form filter cutoff"译为"齿廓形状滤波器截止波长","pitch, transverse circular on measurement diameter"译为"测量圆上的端面齿距","working transverse pressure angle"译为"端面啮合角",等等。

表6 行业内约定俗成的译法

英文	中文
cylindrical involute gears	渐开线圆柱齿轮
root form diameter	齿根成形圆直径
root relief zone	修根区域
minimum length of tip relief	最小修缘长度
working transverse pressure angle	端面啮合角
single pitch deviation (individual)	任一单个齿距偏差
radial composite deviation, tooth-to-tooth	一齿径向综合公差
profile (helix) form filter cutoff	齿廓(螺旋线)形状滤波器截止波长
pitch, transverse circular on measurement diameter	测量圆上的端面齿距
cumulative pitch deviation (index deviation), individual	任一齿距累积偏差(任一分度偏差)
single flank composite tolerance (deviation), tooth-to-tooth	一齿切向综合公差(偏差)

（五）句子中会引起歧义的字词句的译法

ISO 14104：2017 讲的是齿轮磨削后表面回火的浸蚀检验，检验的过程中涉及使用不同的溶液以不同的方式（如浸泡、擦拭、喷涂等）对齿轮的表面进行浸蚀。在原文表 2 下方的注释 a "Uniform agitation of the parts while immersed in the respective baths and rinses is required to avoid a spotty etching condition as well as to accomplish complete neutralization"（ISO 14104：2017：5）中，"baths"和"rinses"这两个词的精准翻译就比较有难度。难点在于：第一，"bath"既有"泡澡"（对应语境为"清洗"）的意思，也有"浴盆"（对应语境为清洗用的"容器"）的意思；第二，如果"bath"取其"清洗"意，"rinse"也有"冲洗"的意思，而在大语境下，文中对容器、溶液和不同的清洗方式均有提及，那么这两个词究竟怎样翻译才更精准？最后通过对标准整体内容的研读和讨论，才确定将"bath"译为"浸泡"，将"rinse"译为"漂洗"，将该句译为"在浸泡和漂洗零件时，均应使齿面与溶液充分接触，以避免出现点状腐蚀，并实现完全中和"。由此可见，在翻译的过程中，有可能会遇到一些会产生歧义的字词，而遇到这样的问题，最终还是要回到原文去寻找答案。在翻译时，既要了解原文的整体内容，有时候也需要对文中的细节进行分析，这样才能使译文更加精准，表达更加易懂。

六、结语

标准化文件的制定与翻译密切相关，促使我国的标准化文件与国际接轨、靠拢是我国在"十四五"规划中的重大战略之一，结合当今跨学科发展的趋势和当前翻译研究界在应用翻译研究方面的匮乏，本文以齿轮类标准化文件的翻译为例，对齿轮类标准化文件翻译的特点和难点进行了剖析，希望未来有更多的翻译和研究人员能关注我国的标准化活动，参与标准化文件的翻译及其研究，为我国标准化事业的进一步发展添砖加瓦。

【参考文献】

[1] ISO 1328-2: 2020, *Cylindrical gears — ISO system of flank tolerance classification —*

Part 2: Definitions and allowable values of double flank radial composite deviations [S].

[2] ISO 14104: 2017, *Gears — Surface temper etch inspection after grinding, chemical method* [S].

[3] GB/T 1.1—2020, 标准化工作导则　第 1 部分：标准化文件的结构和起草规则 [S].

[4] GB/T 1.2—2020, 标准化工作导则　第 2 部分：以 ISO/IEC 标准化文件为基础的标准化文件起草规则 [S].

[5] GB/T 10095.2—2008, 圆柱齿轮　精度制　第 2 部分：径向综合偏差与径向跳动的定义和允许值 [S].

[6] 白殿一等，2020. 标准化文件的起草 [M]. 北京：中国标准出版社.

[7] 国标委联，2021. "十四五"推动高质量发展的国家标准体系建设规划 [Z]. 北京：国家标准化管理委员会秘书处.

[8] 刘智洋、高燕、邵姗姗，2017. 实施国家标准化战略　推动中国标准走出去 [J]. 中国标准化（6）：56–61.

Difficulties in the Translation of Gear Standardization Documents and Countermeasures

SAC/TC52 Zhengzhou Research Institute of Mechanical Engineering Co., Ltd.　GUO Qingqing

Jiangxi Normal University　Yibin University　YAN Bing

Abstract: Taking the translation of standardization documents as the research object, this research summarizes the formulation process, the group characteristics of translators, the general characteristics of the text and linguistic features, analyzes the translation difficulties and the countermeasures, and concludes that, while translating standardization documents, special attention should be paid to modal verbs, professional connotations of common words and phrases and the specified translations of certain words and phrases, the uniqueness of terms and diversified translations of phrases, the conventional translations in the industry and the translation of ambiguous words, phrases and clauses in sentences etc., in hope of providing some reference for future practice and research related to the translation of standardization documents.

Keywords: standardization document; translation; international discourse system; gears

中国高校校名中"科技"一词英译研究[①]

哈尔滨工业大学（威海） 李鹏宇[②] 孟宇[③]

【摘　要】2023年校名含"科技"一词的中国高校共计249所，约占中国高校总数的8%，但不同高校对"科技"的英译不尽相同，可总结为11种形式，另有36所高校未单独翻译校名中的"科技"。本文将此11种"科技"英译形式创新性地与教育部中国留学网提供的国外高校英文名称及其中文译名进行比对，并结合字典释义和国内高校"科技"一词的翻译情况，对362所国外高校中英校名进行分析后，认为"science and technology"是"科技"的最佳翻译，并提出关于高校校名中"科技"一词的翻译建议，助力中国高校校名英译符合国际习惯。

【关键词】中国高校；科技；校名英译

中国高校作为学术研究平台及文化交流载体，其国际影响力日益显著。鉴于高校校名英译在构建中国高校对外形象方面的重要影响，学界对此多予以关注，耿殿磊（2005）、余新兵（2007）、张顺生（2008）、王振国（2019）等人对高校校名英译均有论述。目前高校校名的英译研究主要由校名翻译结构和限定词汇表达两方面组成。校名翻译结构方面，于应机（2006）、侯志红（2010）、麦新转（2017）、唐仪和陈章（2023）等人多有研究，且已相对成熟；限定词汇表达方面可另分为办学规模类词汇（如"大学""学院"）和办学性质类词汇（如"师范""理工"）两部分研究，肖荷和谢红雨（2017）、陈苏玲和张顺生（2019）、付雨菱（2019）等

[①] 本文系2022哈尔滨工业大学项目"新兴交叉"融拓计划"面向国际传播能力建设的跨模态多语种语料平台研究与开发"、哈尔滨工业大学"通用英语D校本SPOC课程建设"（项目编号：2023KTZZ02）的阶段性研究成果。
[②] 李鹏宇（2002— ），本科在读。研究方向：公示语翻译、译名标准化等。邮箱：2197419794@qq.com。
[③] 孟宇（1979— ），博士。研究方向：外语教育政策与规划。邮箱：mengyuemma@126.com。

人均有论述。

虽然高校校名英译成果众多,但历来学者多关注校名翻译结构及办学规模类词汇,对限定词汇表达的细分含义关注较少。"大学""学院""师范"等词的英译选择已趋于固定,而"理工"常视作"理工类"思考,致使理工类下对"理工""科技""工业""工程"等词汇英译的详细研究较少,上述词汇英译方式即使参考国内外高校译法,也往往因例证数量偏少使得结论可信度偏低。房印杰(2012)曾创新性地构建语料库观察国内外"理工大学"英译方式,语料库的引入弥补了例证数量偏少的缺点,但又对学者利用计算机软件自行构建语料库的能力提出较高要求。为对此法加以改进,本文引入教育部留学服务中心提供的认证院校查询结果作为语料库进行研究,此方案相较自行构建语料库更加便捷,所得国外高校英文名及其中文译名权威性及准确性也相对较高。

本文研究对象为校名含"科技"一词的高校英文译名,通过对比国内外高校校名中"科技"一词的英译选择,得出符合国际习惯的"科技"英译建议。

一、中外高校校名中"科技"一词翻译选择

教育部《全国高等学校名单》(2023年6月19日发布)、《香港高等学校名单》(2021年9月17日更新)、《澳门高等学校名单》(2022年3月9日更新)及中国台湾地区教育主管部门《大专校院一览表》(2023年10月15日统计)显示,校名含"科技"一词的中国大陆高校共计194所,中国香港2所,中国澳门1所,中国台湾56所。其中,沈阳航空航天大学北方科技学院无可查官网,辽宁招生考试之窗显示,该校自2013年至今再未更新高考录取分数线,或已停止招生。山东杏林科技职业学院情况类似,山东省教育招生考试院查无该校2023年招生分数线。此外据陕西省教育厅相关通报,西安电子科技大学长安学院已于2018年停止办学。台湾中州科技大学官网显示该校已于2023年8月1日起停办。

去除上述4所停办高校后,校名含"科技"一词的中国大陆高校变更为191所,中国台湾高校变更为55所。全国校名含"科技"一词的高校共计249所。结合高校官网及其相关网站得知,不同高校对校名中"科技"一词的英译形式可总结为11种,详见表1。另有36所高校未对"科技"单独翻译,详见表2。各英译形式后高校依中文校名拼音升序排列。个别高校英文译名单词首字母大小写有误,本文均已更正。

表1 "科技"在中国高校校名中的11种英译形式

"科技"英译形式	使用此英译形式的高校中英文名称	对应高校（所）
science and technology	见附录1	122
technology		45
science & technology		30
polytechnic	北京电子科技职业学院 Beijing Polytechnic 杭州科技职业技术学院 Hangzhou Polytechnic 南京科技职业学院 Nanjing Polytechnic Institute 三明医学科技职业学院 Sanming Medical and Polytechnic Vocational College	4
technical	广东创新科技职业学院 Guangdong Innovative Technical College 广东茂名农林科技职业学院 Guangdong Maoming Agriculture & Forestry Technical College 内蒙古科技职业学院 Inner Mongolia Technical and Vocational College	3
technological	德州科技职业学院 Technological Vocational College of Dezhou 香港高等教育科技学院 Technological and Higher Education Institute of Hong Kong	2
sci-tech	长春科技学院 Changchun Sci-Tech University	1
S & T	黄河科技学院 Huanghe S & T University	1
science technology	北京科技经营管理学院 Beijing Science Technology and Management College	1
science	武汉工程科技学院 Wuhan University of Engineering Science	1
science and engineering	湖南科技学院 Hunan University of Science and Engineering	1

表2　未单独翻译校名中"科技"一词的36所中国高校及其中英文校名

高校中文校名	对应英文校名
成都农业科技职业学院	Chengdu Agricultural College
崇右影艺科技大学	Chungyu University of Film and Arts
大仁科技大学	Tajen University
德阳农业科技职业学院	Deyang Agricultural College
滇西科技师范学院	West Yunnan University
东南科技大学	Tungnan University
防灾科技学院	Institute of Disaster Prevention
辅英科技大学	Fooyin University
高苑科技大学	Kao Yuan University
杭州电子科技大学	Hangzhou Dianzi University
杭州电子科技大学信息工程学院	Hangzhou Dianzi University Information Engineering College
弘光科技大学	Hungkuang University
湖北生物科技职业学院	Hubei Vocational College of Bio-Technology
虎尾科技大学	Formosa University
环球科技大学	TransWorld University
江苏农牧科技职业学院	Jiangsu Agri-animal Husbandry Vocational College
江西生物科技职业学院	Jiangxi Biotech Vocational College
崑山科技大学	Kun Shan University
岭东科技大学	Ling Tung University
美和科技大学	Meiho University
侨光科技大学	Overseas Chinese University
青岛恒星科技学院	Hengxing University
青海农牧科技职业学院	Qinghai Agri-animal Husbandry Vocational College

（续表）

高校中文校名	对应英文校名
上海科技大学	ShanghaiTech University
圣约翰科技大学	St. John's University
树德科技大学	Shu-Te University
万能科技大学	Vanung University
吴凤科技大学	WuFeng University
西安电子科技大学	Xidian University
西安高新科技职业学院	Xi'an High-Tech University
西安科技大学高新学院	Xi'an Kedagaoxin University
西北农林科技大学	Northwest A&F University
醒吾科技大学	Hsing Wu University
远东科技大学	Far East University
浙江理工大学科技与艺术学院	Keyi College of Zhejiang Sci-Tech University
正修科技大学	Cheng Shiu University

表1显示，"science and technology"是"科技"最常使用的英译形式，使用此译法的高校约占校名含"科技"一词高校总数的49%，但仍有约51%的高校采用其余10种译法。将表1中11种译法分别输入教育部留学服务中心"认证院校查询"网页，发现国外高校校名中有30所包含"science and technology"、244所包含"technology"、34所含"polytechnic"、32所含"technical"、23所含"technological"、1所含"S & T"、189所含"science"。"science & technology""sci-tech""science technology"和"science and engineering"查无结果。

因该网页不区分输入内容与检索结果存在的字母大小写差异，故输入"S & T"后，网页检索出了新西兰Aspire2国际商务与技术学院（Aspire2 International Business & Technology）。观察发现，该校校名并不存在与"S & T"形式上相同的部分，因此暂无国外高校校名中包含"S & T"。由于不同译法间存在拼写重合情况，且可能以组合词或复数形式出现，在重新处理影响结果的因素后，校名含"technology"的国外高校为212所，含"science"的为34所。各译法在国外高校中文名中对应的不同翻译结果见表3。国外高校中英文名称见附录2。

179

表3 "science and technology" "technology" "polytechnic" "technical" "technological" "science" 在国外高校中文译名中对应的不同翻译

国外高校校名包含的词或词组	校名含该词或词组的高校数量	在中文校名中对应的翻译
science and technology	30所	"科技"26所、"科学与技术"3所、"理工"1所
technology	212所	"技术"97所、"理工"80所、"科技"20所、"工业"3所、"工艺"1所、"工（学）"1所、未译出6所、与其他词构成词组表意4所
polytechnic	34所	"理工"30所、"工（学）"3所、"技术"1所
technical	32所	"技术"27所、"理工"3所、"科技"1所、"工业"1所
technological	23所	"理工"14所、"技术"4所、"科技"4所、"工业"1所
science	34所	"科学"23所、"技术"3所、"医学"1所、未译出3所、与其他词构成词组表其他意4所

表2显示，52所国外高校校名中的"science and technology" "technology" "technical" "technological" 对应中文校名中的"科技"。利用表2数据可计算出上述4种英译形式译为"理工"时的使用率和关联度。某一译法的使用率和关联度越高，这一译法越适合作为"科技"英译选择。计算结果详见表4。计算公式为：

某一译法使用率＝该译法译为"科技"的次数／所有译法译为"科技"的次数

某一译法关联度＝该译法译为"科技"的次数／该译法对应所有中文翻译的数量总和

表4 "science and technology" "technology" "technical" "technological" 在国外高校中文名中译为"科技"时的使用率和关联度

词汇或词组	使用率	关联度
science and technology	0.51	0.87
technology	0.39	0.09
technical	0.02	0.03
technological	0.08	0.17

表 4 显示,"science and technology"的使用率及关联度相较于其余 3 种"科技"译法均为最高。"technology"虽有 0.39 的使用率,但与"科技"的关联度仅有 0.09。"technical"及"technological"的使用率及关联度均偏低。上述结果表明"science and technology"与"科技"含义关联程度高,这与国内高校常用此译法翻译校名中"科技"一词的现象一致。在国内其余 10 种"科技"译法中,"science & technology""sci-tech""science technology""S & T"均未在国外高校校名中发现;"polytechnic"和"science"虽然存在,但未在国外高校中文校名中译为"科技"。对于国内高校使用的 11 种"科技"英译形式,有必要对其含义及国外高校使用习惯进行分析。

二、"科技"一词不同英译形式分析

(一) science and technology、science & technology、science technology、science 和 technology

《牛津高阶英汉双解词典》(缩印本)分别对 science 和 technology 解释如下:

science	knowledge about the structure and behavior of the natural and physical world, based on facts that you can prove, for example by experiments 科学;自然科学
technology	scientific knowledge used in practical ways in industry, for example, in designing new machines 科技;工艺;工程技术;技术学;工艺学

"technology"是自然科学在特定领域的实际应用,即"科技",相较自然科学可译为"应用科学",其"工程技术"的含义与"理工"等同。据前文表 3 内容,"technology"在国外高校中文译名中译为"理工"的次数远多于"科技",国内也多以"technology"译"理工"。同时"technology"词条下亦有"science and technology 科学技术"的用例。因此,"science and technology"和"technology"均可译为"科学技术"或"科技",但"science and technology"更适合译为"科技","technology"则多用于"理工"。

"science & technology"与"science and technology"同义,使用"science & technology"增加了"科技"的翻译选择。以北京的 4 所"科技"高校为例:1988 年,北京科技大学(University of Science and Technology Beijing)更为现名;1992

年，北京电子科技学院（Beijing Electronic Science & Technology Institute）在北京电子专科学校的基础上成立；2003 年，北京科技职业学院（University for Science & Technology, Beijing）启用此名；2008 年，北京信息科技大学（Beijing Information Science & Technology University）正式挂牌。除最先使用"science and technology"的北京科技大学外，其余 3 所均使用"science & technology"翻译"科技"，以同北京科技大学英文名相区分。而这 3 所学校未使用"technology"，或因北京理工大学（Beijing Institute of Technology）于 1988 年更为现名时，已用"technology"表示"理工"。

"science technology" 仅见于北京科技经营管理学院（Beijing Science Technology and Management College），其英文名"Science Technology and Management"部分对应中文名应译为"Science and Technology and Management"或"Science, Technology and Management"，"science"和"technology"间需有连词或逗号相连表意。

当"science"单独使用时，倾向于以实验或推导得出的，"science"更适合译为"理科"或"理学"，《牛津高阶英汉双解词典》（缩印本）"science"词条下有用例"science students/teachers/courses 理科学生 / 教师 / 课程"，"science"也常用于高校理学院的翻译当中，如天津大学理学院（School of Science, Tianjin University）、甘肃农业大学理学院（Gansu Agricultural University College of Science）等，故不适用于翻译表意更为丰富的"科技"。

（二）Technical 和 Technological

《牛津高阶英汉双解词典》（缩印本）中对"technical"和"technological"的解释均有"技术的"含义，但前者相较后者多出"专门技术的；技巧的；技艺的"释义，英文解释为"connected with the skills needed for a particular job, sport, art, etc."。与附在"technology"下的"technological"的用例"technological advances 科技进步""technological change 科技革新"相比，"technical"强调在特定领域下掌握的技术能力及应用水平，"technological"强调科学技术层面带来的方法革新及发展状况。结合前文表 3 内容，在国外高校的中文译名中，"technical"多译为"技术"，"technological"多译为"理工"，都非"科技"的最佳翻译。

（三）Polytechnic

《牛津高阶英汉双解词典》（缩印本）解释"polytechnic"为"（in Britain in

the past) a college for higher education, especially in scientific and technical subjects. Most polytechnics are now called, and have the same status as, universities.（旧时英国的）理工学院（现已多改为大学）"。依表3显示，校名含"polytechnic"的34所国外高校中，30所的中文校名都将其译为"理工"，如美国的弗吉尼亚理工大学（Virginia Polytechnic Institute and State University）、加拿大的昆特兰理工大学（Kwantlen Polytechnic University）、阿富汗的喀布尔理工大学（Kabul Polytechnic University）等。我国的香港理工大学（The Hong Kong Polytechnic University）和澳门理工大学（Macao Polytechnic University）也均使用"polytechnic"译"理工"。从字典释义和国内外高校翻译情况来看，"polytechnic"都不适合翻译"科技"。

（四）Sci-Tech 和 S & T

《牛津英语词典》在线版将"sci-tech"解释为"Of or relating to science and technology as interrelated activities"，与"science and technology"同义。而用"S & T"表示"科技"，目前仅见于黄河科技学院（Huanghe S & T University）。相较于"sci-tech"，"S & T"只在结合中文校名时能准确表意。同时，上述两种缩写尚未在国外高校校名中发现，且缩写词组不宜出现在作为正式语体的高校校名中。

（五）Science and Engineering

《牛津高阶英汉双解词典》将"technology"解释为"scientific study and use of mechanical arts and applied sciences, eg engineering"。"engineering"是"technology"的表现形式之一，使用"science and technology"表达"科技"要比"science and engineering"的含义更广，"science and engineering"更适合译为"科学与工程"。

（六）略译校名中的"科技"一词

分析前文表2发现，249所"科技"高校中，去除湖北生物科技职业学院（Hubei Vocational College of Bio-Technology）、江西生物科技职业学院（Jiangxi Biotech Vocational College）、上海科技大学（Shanghai Tech University）、西安高新科技职业学院（Xi'an High-Tech University）、浙江理工大学科技与艺术学院（Keyi College of Zhejiang Sci-Tech University）5所将"科技"作为组合词的一部分译出的高校，有31所未单独翻译校名中"科技"一词。

随着我国高校办学规模不断扩大，办学层次日趋多元，中文校名也在随之变化，如"东北重工机械学院"更名为"燕山大学"。中文校名作为高校形象标识之一不会轻易改变，变更时也多改称"学院"为"大学"，如"信阳师范学院"改称"信阳师范大学"，"嘉兴学院"改称"嘉兴大学"等。在中文校名短时间难以改变的情况下，借助英文校名能更快"达成"扩大办学规模的目标，如滇西科技师范学院（West Yunnan University）、青岛恒星科技学院（Hengxing University）等。而这种不对等翻译，却容易造成对办学规模理解上的偏差，同时降低学校校名辨识度，反而不利于高校对外形象建设。值得注意的是，中国台湾私立高校多未对校名中"科技"一词进行翻译，如大仁科技大学（Tajen University）、美和科技大学（Meiho University）等，或因中国台湾拥有55所"科技"高校，约逾中国台湾高校总数三分之一，不译"科技"反而在一定程度上提升了学校辨识度。

当校名中包含其他表示办学特色的词汇时，忽略"科技"的翻译更易突出学校主要办学特色及办学情况，如成都农业科技职业学院（Chengdu Agricultural College）、防灾科技学院（Institute of Disaster Prevention）、西北农林科技大学（Northwest A&F University）等。同时，采用汉语拼音构成英文名也可提高学校辨识度，西安电子科技大学（Xidian University）将其知名简称"西电"作为英文名主体，与北京航空航天大学（Beihang University）校名英译方式有异曲同工之妙。西安科技大学高新学院（Xi'an Kedagaoxin University）将"科大高新"拼音融入英文校名，同西安科技大学（Xi'an University of Science and Technology）英文名相比差异明显，更容易区分彼此，避免将前者看作是后者下属的二级学院。上述英文校名虽未单独翻译"科技"，却未造成明显的表意歧义，可视为合理的略译。

同一地区"科技"大学出于竞争目的也会选择不同英文校名。云林科技大学（Yunlin University of Science & Technology）和虎尾科技大学（Formosa University）均建于中国台湾云林县，前者建校时间晚于后者，但早于后者在1997年改称此名。后者原名"云林工业专科学校"，随办学层次及规模扩大更名为"虎尾技术学院"，至2004年改称现名。作为云林县下辖的虎尾镇，知名度相较"云林"更低，从"云林"变为"虎尾"，中文名称来看似乎自"降"水平。或因此缘故，该校采用"Formosa University"作为英文名。《柯林斯英语词典》在线版将"Formosa"解释为"the former name of Taiwan"。"Formosa"具有殖民色彩，且"Formosa University"无法回译为"虎尾科技大学"，不如云林科技大学的英文名一目了然。

三、中国高校校名中"科技"一词英译建议

我国校名含"科技"一词的高校数量众多，因缺乏统一命名规范，学校多自行选择"科技"翻译形式，或借鉴国外高校校名译法。同时，同一地区常设有多所办学规模相近、办学层次相当、办学学科重合、办学性质相似的高校，当有高校率先将"science and technology"用于校名时，后来者为避免使用重复翻译造成认知混淆，只能另寻他法，采用含义相近的"technology"或形式不同含义相同的"science & technology"。

对于早已用"technology""science & technology"等其他"科技"翻译校名的高校可不做更改，但对于即将成立、合并或并入以及因办学规模扩大而欲更名的高校，应优先使用"science and technology"，在被其他高校先行使用的前提下，再考虑使用"science & technology"。"technology""polytechnic"和"technological"常用于翻译"理工"；"technical"常用来翻译"技术"；"science technology""science""technology"和"science and engineering"均未对应国外高校中文校名中"科技"一词；"sci-tech"和"S & T"作为缩写形式不适合置入高校校名当中。综上，"science and technology"是"科技"的最佳翻译。

此外，如略译"科技"后不影响对英文校名的理解，有助于突出学校办学特色，或因使用学校知名中文简称的拼音作为校名主题而不单译"科技"，则可选择不译。

四、结语

依照《全国高等学校名单》，2019年至2023年，仅中国内地校名含"科技"一词的普通高等学校就从177所增至194所。面对数量众多的"科技"高校，在英文名中使用准确得当的"科技"翻译，有助于我国高校对外形象建构，提升不同学校间的辨别度，更好地服务于高校国际化发展趋势。

【参考文献】

[1] 澳门高等学校名单［EB/OL］．中华人民共和国教育部．检索日期：2023年12月20日．网址：http://www.moe.gov.cn/jyb_xxgk/s5743/s5744/A20/202203/t20220310_606145.html.

[2] 本校概况［EB/OL］．云林科技大学．检索日期：2024年1月21日．网址：https://www.yuntech.edu.tw/index.php/2019-04-02-07-04-39/1/2019-04-02-07-23-55.

[3] 陈苏玲、张顺生，2019．高校校名中"师范"一词的英译与思考［J］．上海理工大学学报（社会科学版），41（01）：30–35.

[4] 大专校院一览表［DB/OL］．检索日期：2023年12月20日．网址：https://udb.moe.edu.tw/ulist/search.

[5] 房印杰，2012．"理工大学"英译的语料库调查［J］．北京邮电大学学报（社会科学版），14（02）：117–121.

[6] 付雨菱，2019．中国高校校名英译——以"理工"与"师范"院校为例［J］．中国科技术语，21（06）：42–46.

[7] 耿殿磊，2005．中国大学校名英译研究［J］．术语标准化与信息技术，（04）：15–20.

[8] 侯志红，2010．山西省高校校名英文翻译实证研究［J］．长治学院学报，27（03）：54–57.

[9] 霍恩比，2019．牛津高阶英汉双解词典（缩印本）［M］．第九版．北京：商务印书馆．

[10] 霍恩比，1994．牛津高阶英汉双解词典［M］．第四版．香港：牛津大学出版社．

[11] 教育部关于同意嘉兴学院更名为嘉兴大学的函［EB/OL］．检索日期：2024年1月21日．网址：http://www.moe.gov.cn/srcsite/A03/s181/202312/t20231214_1094623.html.

[12] 教育部关于同意信阳师范学院更名为信阳师范大学的函［EB/OL］．中华人民共和国教育部．检索日期：2024年1月21日．网址：http://www.moe.gov.cn/srcsite/A03/s181/202306/t20230616_1064614.html.

[13] 历史回顾［EB/OL］．北京电子科技学院．检索日期：2024年1月20日．网址：https://www.besti.edu.cn/201/64.html.

[14] 历史沿革［EB/OL］．北京理工大学．检索日期：2024年1月20日．网址：https://www.bit.edu.cn/gbxxgk/lsyg_sjb/index.htm.

[15] 历史沿革［EB/OL］．北京信息科技大学．检索日期：2024年1月20日．网址：https://www.bistu.edu.cn/xxgk/lsyg/.

[16] 辽宁招生考试之窗［DB/OL］．检索日期：2023年12月22日．网址：https://www.lnzsks.com/listinfo/NewsList_1104_1.html.

[17] 麦新转，2017．大学校名英译探微［J］．贺州学院学报，33（02）：48–52.

[18] 全国高等学校名单查询［DB/OL］．检索日期：2023年12月20日．网址：https://hudong.moe.gov.cn/qggxmd/#.

[19] 山东省教育招生考试院 [DB/OL]．检索日期：2023 年 12 月 22 日．网址：https://www.sdzk.cn/Default.aspx.

[20] 陕西省教育厅关于民办高校．独立学院 2018 年度检查结果的通报 [EB/OL]．陕西省教育厅．检索日期：2023 年 12 月 22 日．网址：http://jyt.shaanxi.gov.cn/news/jiaoyutingwenjian/201905/08/15562.html.

[21] 唐仪、陈章，2023．大学校名的英语命名与翻译问题及其理论依据 [J]．外国语（上海外国语大学学报），46（06）：120–128.

[22] 王振国，2019．内地公办本科院校校名英译情况研究 [J]．湖北第二师范学院学报，36（05）：104–108.

[23] 香港高等学校名单 [EB/OL]．中华人民共和国教育部．检索日期：2023 年 12 月 20 日．网址：http://www.moe.gov.cn/jyb_xxgk/s5743/s5744/A20/202109/t20210923_566126.html.

[24] 肖荷、谢红雨．从社会语言学角度看高校校名英译情况 [J]．海外英语，2017（01）：140+146.

[25] 校史沿革 [EB/OL]．虎尾科技大学．检索日期：2024 年 1 月 21 日．网址：https://www.nfu.edu.tw/zh/aboutnfu/history.

[26] 学校简介 [EB/OL]．北京科技大学．检索日期：2024 年 1 月 20 日．网址：https://www.ustb.edu.cn/xxgk/xxjj/index.htm.

[27] 学校简介 [EB/OL]．燕山大学．检索日期：2024 年 1 月 21 日．网址：http://www.ysu.edu.cn/xxgk/xxjj.htm.

[28] 学校沿革 [EB/OL]．北京科技职业学院．检索日期：2024 年 1 月 20 日．网址：https://www.5aaa.com/history/.

[29] 于应机，2006．兼谈理工类大学的校名英译问题 [J]．宁波工程学院学报，(01)：59–62.

[30] 余新兵，2007．中国大学校名英译的现状及其分析 [J]．河北理工大学学报（社会科学版），(04)：172–175.

[31] 张顺生，2008．"理工学院"和"工学院"的英译与思考 [J]．中国科技翻译（04）：33–36.

[32] 中国留学网认证院校查询 [DB/OL]．检索日期：2023 年 12 月 22 日．网址：https://yxcx.cscse.edu.cn/rzyxmd.

[33] 中州科技大学 [EB/OL]．检索日期：2023 年 12 月 22 日．网址：https://www.ccut.edu.tw/.

[34] HarperCollins Publishers. *Collins English Dictionary* [M/OL]. Retrieved from https://www.collinsdictionary.com/dictionary/english/formosa. Accessed January, 2024.

[35] Oxford University Press. *Oxford English Dictionary* [M/OL]. Retrieved from https://www.oed.com/search/dictionary/?scope=Entries&q=sci-tech. Accessed January, 2024.

A Study on English Translation of "*Ke Ji*" in Names of Chinese Colleges and Universities

Harbin Institute of Technology, Weihai　　LI Pengyu, MENG Yu

Abstract: In 2023, there are 249 Chinese colleges and universities with the word "*Ke Ji*" in their names, accounting for about 8% of Chinese colleges and universities in total, but there are 11 different English translations for "*Ke Ji*", and 36 colleges and universities have not translated "*Ke Ji*" in their names at all. This paper compares 11 English translations of "*Ke Ji*" with the English names and Chinese translations of 362 foreign colleges and universities provided by the Chinese Service Center for Scholarly Exchange of the Ministry of Education, analyzing the translations for "*Ke Ji*" used in domestic colleges and universities with the interpretations from dictionaries. It concludes that "science and technology" is the most appropriate translation for "*Ke Ji*", which may help the English names of Chinese colleges and universities conform to international translation conventions.

Keywords: Chinese colleges and universities; *Ke Ji*; English translations of names of Chinese colleges and universities

附录 1

	使用此翻译的高校（附英文名）
science and technology	1. 北京科技大学 University of Science and Technology Beijing 2. 北京科技大学天津学院 Tianjin College, University of Science and Technology Beijing 3. 河北科技大学 Hebei University of Science and Technology 4. 河北科技学院 Hebei College of Science and Technology 5. 河北农业大学现代科技学院 College of Modern Science and Technology Hebei Agricultural University 6. 唐山科技职业技术学院 Tangshan Vocational College of Science and Technology 7. 石家庄科技职业学院 Shijiazhuang Science and Technology Career Academy 8. 邯郸科技职业学院 Handan Vocational College of Science and Technology 9. 太原科技大学 Taiyuan University of Science and Technology 10. 山西应用科技学院 Shanxi College of Applied Science and Technology 11. 山西工程科技职业大学 Shanxi Vocational University of Engineering Science and Technology 12. 山西科技学院 Shanxi Institute of Science and Technology 13. 辽宁科技大学 University of Science and Technology Liaoning 14. 辽宁科技学院 Liaoning Institute of Science and Technology 15. 大连科技学院 Dalian University of Science and Technology 16. 沈阳科技学院 Shenyang Institute of Science and Technology 17. 吉林农业科技学院 Jilin Agricultural Science and Technology University 18. 吉林科技职业技术学院 Jilin Science and Technology Vocational College 19. 黑龙江科技大学 Heilongjiang University of Science and Technology 20. 江苏科技大学 Jiangsu University of Science and Technology 21. 苏州科技大学 Suzhou University of Science and Technology 22. 苏州科技大学天平学院 Tianping College of Suzhou University of Science and Technology 23. 江苏科技大学苏州理工学院 Suzhou Institute of Technology, Jiangsu University of Science and Technology 24. 无锡科技职业学院 Wuxi Vocational College of Science and Technology 25. 南通科技职业学院 Nantong College of Science and Technology 26. 昆山登云科技职业学院 Kunshan Dengyun College of Science and Technology 27. 中国计量大学现代科技学院 China Jiliang University College of Modern Science and Technology 28. 浙江同济科技职业学院 Zhejiang Tongji Vocational College of Science and Technology 29. 安徽科技学院 Anhui Science and Technology University 30. 阜阳科技职业学院 Fu Yang Vocational College of Science and Technology

(续表)

	使用此翻译的高校（附英文名）
science and technology	31. 合肥科技职业学院 Hefei Science and Technology College 32. 闽南科技学院 Minnan Science and Technology College 33. 福州科技职业技术学院 Fuzhou Science and Technology College 34. 厦门安防科技职业学院 Xiamen Security Science and Technology College 35. 江西应用科技学院 Jiangxi Institute of Applied Science and Technology 36. 南昌航空大学科技学院 Science and Technology College of NCHU 37. 赣南科技学院 Gannan University of Science and Technology 38. 赣南师范大学科技学院 Science and Technology College Gannan Normal University 39. 江西科技职业学院 Jiangxi Vocational College of Science and Technology 40. 赣西科技职业学院 Ganxi Vocational College of Science and Technology 41. 共青科技职业学院 Gongqing Institute of Science and Technology 42. 山东科技大学 Shandong University of Science and Technology 43. 潍坊科技学院 Weifang University of Science and Technology 44. 泰山科技学院 Taishan College of Science and Technology 45. 烟台科技学院 Yantai Institute of Science and Technology 46. 山东科技职业学院 Shandong Vocational College of Science and Technology 47. 山东力明科技职业学院 Shandong Liming Science and Technology Vocational College 48. 东营科技职业学院 Dongying Vocational College of Science and Technology 49. 临沂科技职业学院 Linyi Vocational University of Science and Technology 50. 青岛航空科技职业学院 Qingdao Vocational College of Aeronautical Science and Technology 51. 滨州科技职业学院 Binzhou College of Science and Technology 52. 潍坊食品科技职业学院 Weifang Vocational College of Food Science and Technology 53. 烟台城市科技职业学院 Yantai City College of Science and Technology 54. 河南科技大学 Henan University of Science and Technology 55. 河南科技学院 Henan Institute of Science and Technology 56. 郑州科技学院 Zhengzhou University of Science and Technology 57. 中原科技学院 Zhongyuan Institute of Science and Technology 58. 河南科技职业大学 Henan Vocational University of Science and Technology 59. 洛阳科技职业学院 Luoyang Vocational College of Science and Technology 60. 南阳科技职业学院 Nanyang Vocational College of Science and Technology 61. 华中科技大学 Huazhong University of Science and Technology 62. 武汉科技大学 Wuhan University of Science and Technology 63. 湖北科技学院 Hubei University of Science and Technology 64. 三峡大学科技学院 College of Science and Technology of China Three Gorges University

（续表）

	使用此翻译的高校（附英文名）
science and technology	66. 武汉科技职业学院 Wuhan Vocational College of Science and Technology 67. 黄冈科技职业学院 Huanggang College of Science and Technology 68. 湖北科技职业学院 Hubei Science and Technology College 69. 宜昌科技职业学院 Yichang Vocational College of Science and Technology 70. 湖南科技大学 Hunan University of Science and Technology 71. 湖南人文科技学院 Hunan University of Humanities, Science and Technology 72. 湖南工业大学科技学院 College of Science and Technology HNUT 73. 湖南科技大学潇湘学院 Xiaoxiang College, Hunan University of Science and Technology 74. 湖南科技职业学院 Hunan Vocational College of Science and Technology 75. 常德科技职业技术学院 Changde College of Science and Technology 76. 衡阳科技职业学院 Hengyang Vocational College of Science and Technology 77. 电子科技大学中山学院 University of Electronic Science and Technology of China, Zhongshan Institute 78. 湛江科技学院 Zhanjiang University of Science and Technology 79. 广州应用科技学院 Guangzhou College of Applied Science and Technology 80. 珠海科技学院 Zhuhai College of Science and Technology 81. 广州科技职业技术大学 Guangzhou Vocational University of Science and Technology 82. 南方科技大学 Southern University of Science and Technology 83. 香港科技大学（广州） The Hong Kong University of Science and Technology (Guangzhou) 84. 广州华立科技职业学院 Guangzhou Huali Science and Technology Vocational College 85. 广西科技大学 Guangxi University of Science and Technology 86. 海南科技职业大学 Hainan Vocational University of Science and Technology 87. 重庆城市科技学院 Chongqing Metropolitan College of Science and Technology 88. 重庆科技职业学院 Chongqing Vocational College of Science and Technology 89. 电子科技大学 University of Electronic Science and Technology of China 90. 西南科技大学 Southwest University of Science and Technology 91. 电子科技大学成都学院 Chengdu College of University of Electronic Science and Technology of China 92. 南充科技职业学院 Nanchong Vocational College of Science and Technology 93. 资阳环境科技职业学院 Ziyang College of Environmental Science and Technology 94. 贵州黔南科技学院 Guizhou Qiannan College of Science and Technology 95. 贵阳信息科技学院 Guiyang Institute of Information Science and Technology 96. 贵州电子科技职业学院 Guizhou College of Electronic Science and Technology 97. 西安科技大学 Xi'an University of Science and Technology 98. 兰州博文科技学院 Lanzhou Bowen College of Science and Technology

(续表)

	使用此翻译的高校（附英文名）
science and technology	99. 兰州信息科技学院 Lanzhou University of Information Science and Technology 100. 银川科技学院 Yinchuan University of Science and Technology 101. 新疆科技职业技术学院 XinJiang Science and Technology Career Technical College 102. 香港科技大学 The Hong Kong University of Science and Technology 103. 澳门科技大学 Macau University of Science and Technology 104. 台湾科技大学 Taiwan University of Science and Technology 105. 屏东科技大学 Pingdong University of Science and Technology 106. 澎湖科技大学 Penghu University of Science and Technology 107. 台中科技大学 Taichung University of Science and Technology 108. 高雄科技大学 Kaohsiung University of Science and Technology 109. 南台科技大学 Southern Taiwan University of Science and Technology 110. 龙华科技大学 Lunghwa University of Science and Technology 111. 明新科技大学 Minghsin University of Science and Technology 112. 健行科技大学 Chien Hsin University of Science and Technology 113. 中台科技大学 Central Taiwan University of Science and Technology 114. 德明财经科技大学 Takming University of Science and Technology 115. 中华科技大学 China University of Science and Technology 116. 育达科技大学 Yu Da University of Science and Technology 117. 修平科技大学 Hsiuping University of Science and Technology 118. 长庚科技大学 Chang Gung University of Science and Technology 119. 台北城市科技大学 Taipei City University of Science and Technology 120. 敏实科技大学 Minth University of Science and Technology 121. 慈济科技大学 Tzu Chi University of Science and Technology 122. 亚东科技大学 Asia Eastern University of Science and Technology
technology	1. 河北科技工程职业技术大学 Hebei Vocational University of Technology and Engineering 2. 石家庄科技信息职业学院 Shijiazhuang Vocational College of Technology & Information 3. 衡水健康科技职业学院 Hengshui Health Technology 4. 长春电子科技学院 Changchun College of Electronic Technology 5. 吉林建筑科技学院 Jilin University of Architecture and Technology 6. 金陵科技学院 Jinling Institute of Technology 7. 安徽冶金科技职业学院 Anhui Vocational College of Metallurgy and Technology 8. 安徽中澳科技职业学院 Anhui Zhongao Institute of Technology 9. 安徽国防科技职业学院 Anhui Vocational College of Defense Technology 10. 江西科技学院 Jiangxi University of Technology 11. 江西新能源科技职业学院 Jiangxi New Energy Technology Institute

(续表)

	使用此翻译的高校（附英文名）
technology	12. 河南开封科技传媒学院 Technology & Media University of Henan Kaifeng 13. 郑州信息科技职业学院 Zhengzhou Vocational College of Information Technology 14. 郑州智能科技职业学院 Zhengzhou Vocational College of Intelligent Technology 15. 襄阳科技职业学院 Xiangyang Vocational College of Technology 16. 中南林业科技大学 Central South University of Forestry & Technology 17. 中南林业科技大学涉外学院 Swan College, Central South University of Forestry and Technology 18. 湖南铁路科技职业技术学院 Hunan Vocational College of Railway Technology 19. 湖南电子科技职业学院 Hunan Vocational College of Electronic and Technology 20. 广州科技贸易职业学院 Guangzhou Vocational College of Technology & Business 21. 桂林电子科技大学 Guilin University of Electronic Technology 22. 桂林信息科技学院 Guilin Institute of Information Technology 23. 重庆建筑科技职业学院 Chongqing College of Architecture and Technology 24. 四川工业科技学院 Sichuan Institute of Industrial Technology 25. 贵阳人文科技学院 Guiyang Institute of Humanities and Technology 26. 遵义医科大学医学与科技学院 Medicine & Technology College of Zunyi Medical University 27. 云南科技信息职业学院 Yunnan Institute of Technology and Information 28. 西安建筑科技大学 Xi'an University of Architecture and Technology 29. 西安建筑科技大学华清学院 Xi'an University of Architecture and Technology Huaqing College 30. 榆林能源科技职业学院 Yulin Energy Technology Vocational College 31. 台北科技大学 Taipei University of Technology 32. 勤益科技大学 Chin-Yi University of Technology 33. 朝阳科技大学 Chaoyang University of Technology 34. 建国科技大学 Chienkuo Technology University 35. 明志科技大学 MIng Chi University of Technology 36. 中国科技大学 China University of Technology 37. 台南应用科技大学 Tainan University of Technology 38. 元培医事科技大学 Yuanpei University of Medical Technology 39. 中华医事科技大学 Chung Hwa University of Medical Technology 40. 南开科技大学 Nan Kai University of Technology 41. 华夏科技大学 Hwa Hsia University of Technology 42. 致理科技大学 Chihlee University of Technology 43. 宏国德霖科技大学 Hungkuo Delin University of Technology 44. 南亚技术学院 Nanya Institute of Technology 45. 台北海洋科技大学 Taipei University of Marine University

（续表）

	使用此翻译的高校（附英文名）
Science & Technology	1. 北京电子科技学院 Beijing Electronic Science & Technology Institute 2. 北京信息科技大学 Beijing Information Science & Technology University 3. 北京科技职业学院 University for Science & Technology, Beijing 4. 天津科技大学 Tianjin University of Science & Technology 5. 河北科技师范学院 Hebei Normal University of Science & Technology 6. 华北科技学院 North China Institute of Science & Technology 7. 青岛科技大学 Qingdao University of Science & Technology 8. 宣化科技职业学院 Xuanhua Vocational College of Science & Technology 9. 内蒙古科技大学 Inner Mongolia University of Science & Technology 10. 浙江科技学院 Zhejiang University of Science & Technology 11. 台州科技职业学院 Taizhou Vocational College of Science & Technology 12. 温州科技职业学院 Wenzhou Vocational College of Science & Technology 13. 万博科技职业学院 Wanbo Institute of Science & Technology 14. 漳州科技学院 Zhangzhou College of Science & Technology 15. 江西科技师范大学 Jiangxi Science & Technology Normal University 16. 枣庄科技职业学院 ZaoZhuang Vocational College of Science & Technology 17. 濮阳科技职业学院 Puyang Vocational College of Science & Technology 18. 湖南农业大学东方科技学院 Orient Science & Technology College of Hunan Agricultural University 19. 广东科技学院 Guangdong University of Science & Technology 20. 广西科技师范学院 Guangxi Science & Technology Normal University 21. 广西科技职业学院 Guangxi Vocational University of Science & Technology 22. 重庆科技学院 Chongqing University of Science & Technology 23. 重庆人文科技学院 Chongqing College of Humanities, Science & Technology 24. 四川科技职业学院 University for Science & Technology Sichuan 25. 陕西科技大学 Shaanxi University of Science & Technology 26. 陕西科技大学镐京学院 Hao Jing College of Shaanxi University of Science & Technology 27. 兰州科技职业学院 Lanzhou Vocational College of Science & Technology 28. 新疆科技学院 Xinjiang University of Science & Technology 29. 云林科技大学 Yunlin University of Science & Technology 30. 景文科技大学 Jinwen University of Science & Technology

注：个别高校英文译名中单词字母大小写有误，此表均已更正。

附录 2

国外高校英文校名包含的词或词组	校名含该词或词组的国外高校 （按照学校所属国家及中文译名拼音首字母升序排列）
science and technology	**英文校名中"science and technology"译为"科技"的国外高校：26 所** 1. 埃　　及　埃及日本科技大学 (Egypt-Japan University of Science and Technology) 2. 巴基斯坦　本努科技大学 (University of Science and Technology, Bannu) 3. 巴基斯坦　科哈特科技大学 (Kohat University of Science and Technology) 4. 巴基斯坦　沙希德佐勒菲卡尔·阿里·布托科技学院 (Shaheed Zulfikar Ali Bhutto Institute of Science and Technology) 5. 巴基斯坦　首都科技大学 (Capital University of Science and Technology) 6. 菲 律 宾　雷省国立科技大学 (Nueva Ecija University of Science and Technology) 7. 菲 律 宾　伊洛伊洛科技大学 (Iloilo Science and Technology University) 8. 加　　纳　恩克鲁玛科技大学 (Kwame Nkrumah University of Science and Technology) 9. 黎 巴 嫩　美国科技大学 (American University of Science and Technology) 10. 马来西亚　马来西亚科技大学 (Malaysia University of Science and Technology) 11. 美　　国　哈里斯堡科技大学 (The Harrisburg University of Science and Technology) 12. 美　　国　密苏里科技大学 (Missouri University of Science and Technology) 13. 蒙　　古　蒙古科技大学 (Mongolian University of Science and Technology) 14. 孟加拉国　阿萨努拉科技大学 (Ahsanullah University of Science and Technology) 15. 纳米比亚　纳米比亚科技大学 (Namibia University of Science and Technology) 16. 尼日利亚　武迪尔卡诺科技大学 (Kano University of Science and Technology, Wudil) 17. 挪　　威　挪威科技大学 (Norwegian University of Science and Technology) 18. 沙特阿拉伯　阿卜杜拉国王科技大学 (King Abdullah University of Science and Technology) 19. 苏　　丹　苏丹科技大学 (Sudan University of Science and Technology) 20. 乌干达姆　巴拉拉科技大学 (Mbarara University of Science and Technology) 21. 也　　门　科技大学 (University of Science and Technology) 22. 伊　　朗　伊朗科技大学 (Iran University of Science and Technology) 23. 印　　度　古鲁杰默贝什沃尔科技大学 (Guru Jambeshwar University of Science and Technology) 24. 印　　度　科钦科技大学 (Cochin University of Science and Technology)

（续表）

science and technology	25. 印　　度　彭奈亚拉马佳亚科技学院 (Ponnaiyah Ramajayam Institute of Science and Technology) 26. 约　　旦　约旦科技大学 (Jordan University of Science and Technology) 英文校名中"science and technology"译为"科学与技术"的国外高校：**3** 所 1. 奥地利　奥地利科学与技术学院 (Institute of Science and Technology Austria) 2. 菲律宾　罗德里格斯科学与技术学院 (Eulogio "Amang" Rodriguez Institute of Science and Technology) 3. 印　　度　希普尔印度工程科学与技术学院 (Indian Institute of Engineering Science and Technology, Shibpur) 英文校名中"science and technology"译为"理工"的国外高校：**1** 所 1. 阿联酋　马斯达尔理工学院 (Masdar Institute of Science and Technology)
technology	英文校名中"technology"译为"技术"的国外高校：**97** 所 1. 埃　　及　坦塔高等工程技术学院 (Tanta Higher Institute of Engineering and Technology) 2. 澳大利亚　埃斯伯利商业技术学院 (Eynesbury Institute of Business and Technology) 3. 澳大利亚　国际商业与技术学院 (International Institute of Business and Technology) 4. 澳大利亚　堪培拉技术学院 (Canberra Institute of Technology) 5. 澳大利亚　昆士兰商业技术学院 (Queensland Institute of Business and Technology) 6. 澳大利亚　墨尔本技术学院 (Melbourne Institute of Technology) 7. 澳大利亚　墨尔本商业技术学院 (Melbourne Institute of Business and Technology) 8. 澳大利亚　南澳大利亚商业技术学院 (South Australian Institute of Business and Technology) 9. 澳大利亚　悉尼商业技术学院 (Sydney Institute of Business and Technology) 10. 澳大利亚　信息技术学院 (Academy of Information Technology) 11. 澳大利亚　中央技术学院 (Central Institute of Technology) 12. 巴基斯坦　COMSATS 信息技术学院 (COMSATS Institute of Information Technology) 13. 巴基斯坦　白沙瓦工程技术大学 (University of Engineering and Technology, Peshawar) 14. 巴基斯坦　白沙瓦萨哈德科学与信息技术大学 (Sarhad University of Science & Information Technology, Peshawar) 15. 巴基斯坦　古兰伊沙克汗工程科学技术研究所 (Ghulam Ishaq Khan Institute of Engineering Sciences and Technology)

(续表)

technology	16. 巴基斯坦	国立科学与技术大学 (National University of Sciences and Technology)
	17. 巴基斯坦	空间技术学院 (Institute of Space Technology)
	18. 巴基斯坦	拉合尔工程与技术大学 (University of Engineering and Technology, Lahore)
	19. 巴基斯坦	拉希姆亚尔汗哈瓦德法雷德工程与信息技术大学 (Khwaja Fareed University of Engineering & Information Technology, Rahim Yar Khan)
	20. 巴基斯坦	内德工程技术大学 (NED University of Engineering and Technology)
	21. 巴基斯坦	塔西拉工程技术大学 (University of Engineering and Technology, Taxila)
	22. 波　　兰	热舒夫信息技术与管理大学 (University of Information Technology and Management in Rzeszow)
	23. 波　　兰	西波美拉尼亚技术大学 (West Pomeranian University of Technology in Szczecin)
	24. 丹　　麦	哥本哈根设计与技术学院 (The Copenhagen School of Design and Technology)
	25. 丹　　麦	西兰商务与技术学院 (Zealand Institute of Business and Technology)
	26. 德　　国	柏林欧洲管理与技术学院 (ESMT European School of Management and Technology)
	27. 法　　国	艾万西提技术、商业与社会学院 (Aivancity School for Technology, Business & Society)
	28. 法　　国	信息技术学院 (SUPINFO Institute of Information Technology)
	29. 菲 律 宾	菲律宾南部农商与海洋水产技术学院 (Southern Philippines Agri-Business and Marine and Aquatic School of Technology)
	30. 加 拿 大	百年理工应用艺术与技术学院 (Centennial College of Applied Arts and Technology)
	31. 加 拿 大	北方应用艺术与技术学院 (Northern College of Applied Arts and Technology)
	32. 加 拿 大	德汉姆应用艺术与技术学院 (Durham College of Applied Arts and Technology)
	33. 加 拿 大	范莎应用艺术与技术学院 (Fanshawe College of Applied Arts and Technology)
	34. 加 拿 大	弗莱明应用艺术与技术学院 (Sir Sandford Fleming College of Applied Arts and Technology)
	35. 加 拿 大	卡纳多应用艺术与技术学院 (Canadore College of Applied Arts and Technology)

(续表)

technology	36. 加拿大	坎伯伦应用艺术与技术学院 (Cambrian College of Applied Arts and Technology)
	37. 加拿大	莱姆顿应用艺术与技术学院 (Lambton College of Applied Arts and Technology)
	38. 加拿大	联邦应用艺术与技术学院 (Confederation College of Applied Arts and Technology)
	39. 加拿大	曼尼托巴贸易与技术学院 (Manitoba Institute of Trades and Technology)
	40. 加拿大	莫霍克应用艺术与技术学院 (Mohawk College of Applied Arts and Technology)
	41. 加拿大	尼亚加拉应用艺术与技术学院 (Niagara College of Applied Arts and Technology)
	42. 加拿大	乔治布朗应用艺术与技术学院 (George Brown College of Applied Arts and Technology)
	43. 加拿大	乔治亚应用艺术与技术学院 (Georgian College of Applied Arts and Technology)
	44. 加拿大	圣克莱尔应用艺术与技术学院 (St. Clair College of Applied Arts and Technology)
	45. 加拿大	圣劳伦斯应用艺术与技术学院 (St. Lawrence College of Applied Arts and Technology)
	46. 加拿大	圣力嘉应用艺术与技术学院 (Seneca College of Applied Arts and Technology)
	47. 加拿大	索尔特应用艺术与技术学院 (Sault College of Applied Arts and Technology)
	48. 加拿大	亚岗昆应用艺术与技术学院 (Algonquin College of Applied Arts and Technology)
	49. 肯尼亚	乔莫肯雅塔农业与技术大学 (Jomo Kenyatta University of Agriculture and Technology)
	50. 马来西亚	亚太技术与创新大学 (Asia Pacific University of Technology and Innovation)
	51. 马来西亚	亚太信息技术学院 (Asia Pacific Institute of Information Technology)
	52. 美国	俄克拉荷马州立大学技术学院 (Oklahoma State University Institute of Technology)
	53. 美国	南达科他矿业与技术学院 (South Dakota School of Mines and Technology)
	54. 美国	纽约市立大学纽约市立技术学院 (The City University of New York, New York City College of Technology)

(续表)

technology	55. 美　　国	纽约州立大学科贝尔斯基农业技术学院 (State University of New York College of Agriculture and Technology at Cobleskill)	
	56. 美　　国	纽约州立大学莫里斯维尔农业技术学院 (State University of New York College of Agriculture & Technology at Morrisville)	
	57. 美　　国	纽约州立大学时装技术学院 (State University of New York, Fashion Institute of Technology)	
	58. 美　　国	斯巴达航空技术学院 (Spartan College of Aeronautics and Technology)	
	59. 美　　国	先进技术大学 (University of Advancing Technology)	
	60. 美　　国	新墨西哥矿业技术学院 (New Mexico Institute of Mining and Technology)	
	61. 蒙　　古	蒙古工程技术学院 (Mongolia Institute of Engineering and Technology)	
	62. 斯洛伐克	斯洛伐克技术大学 (Slovak University of Technology in Bratislava)	
	63. 泰　　国	北曼谷先皇技术学院 (King Mongkut's University of Technology North Bangkok)	
	64. 泰　　国	拉卡邦先皇技术学院 (King Mongkut's Institute of Technology Ladkrabang)	
	65. 特立尼达和多巴哥	特立尼达和多巴哥科学、技术与应用艺术学院 (College of Science, Technology and Applied Arts of Trinidad and Tobago)	
	66. 乌 克 兰	国家科学中心"哈尔科夫物理与技术研究所" (National Science Center "Kharkov Institute of Physics and Technology")	
	67. 乌 克 兰	乌克兰国立化学技术大学 (Ukrainian State University of Chemical Technology)	
	68. 乌兹别克斯坦	纳曼干工程技术学院 (Namangan Institute of Engineering and Technology)	
	69. 新 西 兰	Aspire 2 国际商务与技术学院 (Aspire 2 International Business & Technology)	
	70. 匈 牙 利	布达佩斯技术与经济大学 (Budapest University of Technology and Economics)	
	71. 牙 买 加	牙买加技术大学 (University of Technology, Jamaica)	
	72. 印　　度	阿拉哈巴德莫蒂尔·尼赫鲁国家技术学院 (Motilal Nehru National Institute of Technology Allahabad)	
	73. 印　　度	蒂鲁吉拉伯利国家技术学院 (National Institute of Technology Tiruchirapalli)	
	74. 印　　度	杜尔加布尔国家技术学院 (National Institute of Technology, Durgapur)	

（续表）

technology	75.	印　度	甘地技术管理大学 (Gandhi Institute of Technology and Management University)
	76.	印　度	戈芬德巴拉布彭特农业技术大学 (G.B. Pant University of Agriculture & Technology)
	77.	印　度	哈米尔普尔国家技术学院 (National Institute of Technology, Hamirpur)
	78.	印　度	化学技术学院 (Institute of Chemical Technology)
	79.	印　度	加济阿巴德管理技术学院 (Institute of Management Technology, Ghaziabad)
	80.	印　度	贾姆谢德布尔国家技术学院 (National Institute of Technology Jamshedpur)
	81.	印　度	贾伊比信息技术大学 (Jaypee University of Information Technology)
	82.	印　度	贾伊比信息技术学院 (Jaypee Institute of Information Technology)
	83.	印　度	羯陵伽工业技术学院 (Kalinga Institute of Industrial Technology)
	84.	印　度	卡利卡特国家技术学院 (National Institute of Technology Calicut)
	85.	印　度	卡伦扬技术与科学学院 (Karunya Institute of Technology and Sciences)
	86.	印　度	卡纳塔克邦塞阿斯卡尔国家技术学院 (National Institute of Technology Karnataka, Surathkal)
	87.	印　度	鲁尔克拉国家技术学院 (National Institute of Technology Rourkela)
	88.	印　度	那加兰国家技术学院 (National Institute of Technology Nagaland)
	89.	印　度	普纳高级技术国防学院 (Defence Institute of Advanced Technology, Pune)
	90.	印　度	萨帕工程与技术学院 (Thapar Institute of Engineering & Technology)
	91.	印　度	山姆希金波顿农业、技术与科学研究所 (Sam Higginbottom Institute of Agriculture, Technology & Sciences)
	92.	印　度	圣隆格奥瓦尔工程技术学院 (Sant Longowal Institute of Engineering and Technology)
	93.	印　度	瓦兰加尔国家技术学院 (National Institute of Technology Warangal)
	94.	印　度	西孟加拉邦毛拉·阿布·卡拉姆·阿扎德技术大学 (Maulana Abul Kalam Azad University of Technology, West Bengal)
	95.	越　南	LADEC 工程技术职业学院 (LaDec Vocational College of Engineering and Technology)
	96.	越　南	胡志明市技术大学 (Ho Chi Minh City University of Technology)
	97.	越　南	越南胡志明市国家大学附属技术大学 (Vietnam National University Ho Chi Minh City-University of Technology)
	英文校名中"technology"译为"理工"的国外高校：80 所		
	1.	爱尔兰	邓多克理工学院 (Dundalk Institute of Technology)

(续表)

technology	2.	爱 尔 兰	邓莱里文艺理工学院 (Dun Laoghaire Institute of Art, Design and Technology)
	3.	爱沙尼亚	塔林理工大学 (Tallinn University of Technology)
	4.	澳大利亚	皇家墨尔本理工大学 (Royal Melbourne Institute of Technology)
	5.	澳大利亚	维多利亚理工学院 (Victorian Institute of Technology)
	6.	菲 律 宾	棉兰老州立大学伊利甘理工学院 (Mindanao State University - Iligan Institute of Technology)
	7.	菲 律 宾	西部理工学院 (Western Institute of Technology)
	8.	加 拿 大	安省理工大学 (University of Ontario Institute of Technology)
	9.	加 拿 大	北阿尔伯塔理工学院 (Northern Alberta Institute of Technology)
	10.	加 拿 大	不列颠哥伦比亚理工学院 (British Columbia Institute of Technology)
	11.	加 拿 大	南阿尔伯塔理工学院 (Southern Alberta Institute of Technology)
	12.	加 拿 大	纽约理工学院温哥华分校 (New York Institute of Technology, Vancouver Campus)
	13.	加 纳	阿克拉理工学院 (Accra Institute of Technology)
	14.	柬 埔 寨	IIC 理工大学 (IIC University of Technology)
	15.	捷 克	布尔诺理工大学 (Brno University of Technology)
	16.	津巴布韦	奇伊诺理工大学 (Chinhoyi Universtiy of Technology)
	17.	美 国	迪吉彭理工学院 (DigiPen Institute of Technology)
	18.	美 国	佛罗里达理工学院 (Florida Institute of Technology)
	19.	美 国	华盛顿湖理工学院 (Lake Washington Institute of Technology)
	20.	美 国	加利福尼亚理工学院 (California Institute of Technology)
	21.	美 国	拉马尔理工学院 (Lamar Institute of Technology)
	22.	美 国	罗切斯特理工学院 (Rochester Institute of Technology)
	23.	美 国	罗斯霍曼理工学院 (Rose-Hulman Institute of Technology)
	24.	美 国	麻省理工学院 (Massachusetts Institute of Technology)
	25.	美 国	纽约理工学院 (New York Institute of Technology)
	26.	美 国	史蒂文斯理工学院 (Stevens Institute of Technology)
	27.	美 国	温特沃斯理工学院 (Wentworth Institute of Technology)
	28.	美 国	新英格兰理工学院 (New England Institute of Technology)
	29.	美 国	新泽西理工学院 (New Jersey Institute of Technology)
	30.	美 国	伊利诺伊理工学院 (Illinois Institute of Technology)
	31.	美 国	佐治亚理工学院 (The Georgia Institute of Technology)
	32.	南 非	德班理工大学 (Durban University of Technology)
	33.	南 非	里奇菲尔德理工学院 (Richfield Graduate Institute of Technology)
	34.	南 非	自由州中央理工大学 (Central University of Technology, Free State)

（续表）

technology	35. 尼日利亚	阿库雷联邦理工大学 (The Federal University of Technology, Akure)
	36. 瑞　　典	布莱京理工学院 (Blekinge Institute of Technology)
	37. 瑞　　典	查尔姆斯理工大学 (Chalmers University of Technology)
	38. 塞浦路斯	弗雷德里克理工学院 (Frederick Institute of Technology)
	39. 泰　　国	东方皇家理工大学 (Rajamangala University of Technology Tawan-ok)
	40. 泰　　国	兰那皇家理工大学 (Rajamangala University of Technology Lanna)
	41. 泰　　国	兰塔纳功欣皇家理工大学 (Rajamangala University of Technology Rattanakosin)
	42. 泰　　国	马汉科理工大学 (Mahanakorn University of Technology)
	43. 泰　　国	曼谷皇家理工大学 (Rajamangala University of Technology Krungthep)
	44. 泰　　国	帕纳空皇家理工大学 (Rajamangala University of Technology Phra Nakhon)
	45. 泰　　国	苏兰拉里理工大学 (Suranaree University of Technology)
	46. 泰　　国	素万那普理工学院 (Suvarnabhumi Institute of Technology)
	47. 泰　　国	塔亚武里皇家理工大学 (Rajamangala University of Technology Thanyaburi)
	48. 泰　　国	亚洲理工学院 (Asian Institute of Technology)
	49. 新 加 坡	新加坡理工大学 (Singapore Institute of Technology)
	50. 新 西 兰	奥克兰理工大学 (Auckland University of Technology)
	51. 新 西 兰	怀卡托理工学院 (Waikato Institute of Technology)
	52. 新 西 兰	惠灵顿理工学院 (Wellington Institute of Technology)
	53. 新 西 兰	联合理工学院 (Unitec Institute of Technology)
	54. 新 西 兰	曼努考理工学院 (Manukau Institute of Technology)
	55. 新 西 兰	南方理工学院 (Southern Institute of Technology)
	56. 新 西 兰	尼尔森马尔伯勒理工学院 (Nelson Marlborough Institute of Technology)
	57. 新 西 兰	西方理工学院 (Western Institute of Technology at Taranaki)
	58. 新 西 兰	新西兰国立中部理工学院 (Toi Ohomai Institute of Technology)
	59. 伊　　朗	阿米尔卡理工大学 (Amirkabir University of Technology)
	60. 伊　　朗	萨贾德理工大学 (Sadjad University of Technology)
	61. 伊　　朗	沙赫鲁德理工大学 (Shahrood University of Technology)
	62. 伊　　朗	沙里夫理工大学 (Sharif University of Technology)
	63. 伊　　朗	设拉子理工大学 (Shiraz University Of Technology)
	64. 伊　　朗	伊斯法罕理工大学 (Isfahan University of Technology)
	65. 以 色 列	以色列理工学院 (Technion — Israel Institute of Technology)
	66. 印　　度	巴拉理工学院 (Birla Institute of Technology)

(续表)

technology	67.	印　度	印度理工学院丹巴德分校（印度矿业学院）(Indian Institute of Technology (Indian School of Mines), Dhanbad)
	68.	印　度	印度理工学院德里分校 (Indian Institute of Technology Delhi)
	69.	印　度	印度理工学院甘地讷格尔分校 (Indian Institute of Technology Gandhinagar)
	70.	印　度	印度理工学院古瓦哈提分校 (Indian Institute of Technology Guwahati)
	71.	印　度	印度理工学院海德巴拉分校 (Indian Institute of Technology Hyderabad)
	72.	印　度	印度理工学院焦特布尔分校 (Indian Institute of Technology Jodhpur)
	73.	印　度	印度理工学院卡拉格普尔分校 (Indian Institute of Technology Kharagpur)
	74.	印　度	印度理工学院坎普尔分校 (Indian Institute of Technology Kanpur)
	75.	印　度	印度理工学院鲁基分校 (Indian Institute of Technology Roorkee)
	76.	印　度	印度理工学院马德拉斯分校 (Indian Institute of Technology Madras)
	77.	印　度	印度理工学院曼迪分校 (Indian Institute of Technology Mandi)
	78.	印　度	印度理工学院孟买分校 (Indian Institute of Technology Bombay)
	79.	印　度	印度理工学院瓦拉纳西分校（巴纳拉斯印度大学）(Indian Institute of Technology (Banaras Hindu University), Varanasi)
	80.	印　度	印度理工学院印多尔分校 (Indian Institute of Technology Indore)

英文校名中"technology"译为"科技"的国外高校：20 所

1. 阿尔及利亚　胡阿里布迈丁科技大学 (University of Sciences and Technology Houari Boumediene)
2. 澳大利亚　昆士兰科技大学 (Queensland University of Technology)
3. 澳大利亚　斯文本科技大学 (Swinburne University of Technology)
4. 澳大利亚　悉尼科技大学 (University of Technology Sydney)
5. 澳大利亚　悉尼科技大学 Insearch 学院 (University of Technology Sydney Insearch)
6. 巴基斯坦　联邦乌尔都文学与科技大学 (Federal Urdu University of Arts, Sciences and Technology)
7. 菲律宾　马普尔科技学院 (Mapua Institute of Technology)
8. 马来西亚　林国荣创意科技大学 (Limkokwing University of Creative Technology)
9. 马来西亚　马来西亚双德科技大学 (Twintech International University College of Technology)
10. 马来西亚　沙捞越科技大学 (University of Technology Sarawak)

(续表)

technology	11. 马来西亚　双德国际科技大学学院 (International University College of Technology Twintech) 12. 美　　　国　沃恩航空科技学院 (Vaughn College of Aeronautics and Technology) 13. 南　　　非　茨瓦尼科技大学 (Tshwane University of Technology) 14. 南　　　非　开普半岛科技大学 (Cape Peninsula University of Technology) 15. 泰　　　国　泰国国王科技大学 (King Mongkut's University of Technology Thonburi) 16. 新 加 坡　新加坡科技与设计大学 (Singapore University of Technology and Design) 17. 新 西 兰　东部科技理工学院 (Eastern Institute of Technology) 18. 伊　　　朗　萨汉德科技大学 (Sahand University of Technology) 19. 意 大 利　万神殿设计与科技学院 (Istituto Pantheon Design & Technology) 20. 印　　　度　比久伯德纳耶格科技大学 (Biju Patnaik University of Technology) **英文校名中"technology"译为"工业"的国外高校：3 所** 1. 芬　　　兰　拉彭兰塔－拉赫蒂工业大学 (Lappeenranta-Lahti University of Technology LUT) 2. 立 陶 宛　考纳斯工业大学 (Kaunas University of Technology) 3. 瑞　　　典　吕勒奥工业大学 (Luleå University of Technology) **英文校名中"technology"译为"工艺"的国外高校：1 所** 1. 马来西亚　第一工艺学院 (Pertama Institute of Technology) **英文校名中"technology"译为"工（学）"的国外高校：1 所** 1. 瑞　　　典　皇家工学院 (Royal Institute of Technology) **未译出"technology"的国外高校：6 所** 1. 加 拿 大　汉伯学院 (Humber College Institute of Technology and Advanced Learning) 2. 加 拿 大　康奈斯托加学院 (Conestoga College Institute of Technology and Advanced Learning) 3. 加 拿 大　谢尔丹学院 (Sheridan College Institute of Technology and Advanced Learning) 4. 美　　　国　纽约州立大学阿尔弗雷德分校 (State University of New York, College of Technology at Alfred) 5. 美　　　国　纽约州立大学德里分校 (State University of New York, College of Technology at Delhi) 6. 美　　　国　纽约州立大学坎顿分校 (State University of New York College of Technology at Canton)

（续表）

technology	**"technology"与其他词构成词组表意：4 所** 1. 印度　SRM 科技学院 (SRM Institute of Sciences and Technology) 2. 印度　巴拉科技学院 (The Birla Institute of Technology and Science) 3. 印度　艺术科技研究学院（萨斯特拉）(Shanmugha Arts, Science, Technology & Research Academy (SASTRA)) 4. 印度　印度斯坦科技学院 (Hindustan Institute of Technology and Science)
polytechnic	**英文校名中"polytechnic"译为"理工"的国外高校：30 所** 1. 阿富汗　喀布尔理工大学 (Kabul Polytechnic University) 2. 澳大利亚　澳大拉西亚理工学院 (Academies Australasia Polytechnic) 3. 澳大利亚　澳大利亚理工学院 (Polytechnic Institute Australia) 4. 澳大利亚　墨尔本理工学院 (Melbourne Polytechnic) 5. 菲律宾　菲律宾理工大学 (Polytechnic University of the Philippines) 6. 菲律宾　拉古纳国立理工大学 (Laguna State Polytechnic University) 7. 加拿大　昆特兰理工大学 (Kwantlen Polytechnic University) 8. 加拿大　萨斯卡彻温理工学院 (Saskatchewan Polytechnic) 9. 罗马尼亚　布加勒斯特理工大学 (Polytechnic University of Bucharest) 10. 美国　弗吉尼亚理工大学 (Virginia Polytechnic Institute and State University) 11. 美国　加利福尼亚州立理工大学波莫纳分校 (California State Polytechnic University, Pomona) 12. 美国　加利福尼亚州立理工大学圣路易斯奥比斯波分校 (California Polytechnic State University, San Luis Obispo) 13. 美国　纽约州立大学理工学院 (State University of New York Polytechnic Institute) 14. 美国　仁斯利尔理工学院 (Rensselaer Polytechnic Institute) 15. 美国　伍斯特理工学院 (Worcester Polytechnic Institute) 16. 乌克兰　敖德萨国立理工大学 (Odessa Polytechnic National University) 17. 乌克兰　国际技术大学"尼古拉耶夫理工学院" (International Technological University "Mykolayiv Polytechnics") 18. 乌克兰　切尔尼戈夫国立理工大学 (Chernihiv Polytechnic National University) 19. 乌兹别克斯坦　塔什干都灵理工大学 (Turin Polytechnic University in Tashkent) 20. 新加坡　淡马锡理工学院 (Temasek Polytechnic) 21. 新加坡　共和理工学院 (Republic Polytechnic) 22. 新加坡　南洋理工学院 (Nanyang Polytechnic) 23. 新加坡　新加坡理工学院 (Singapore Polytechnic) 24. 新加坡　义安理工学院 (Ngee Ann Polytechnic)

（续表）

polytechnic	25. 新　西　兰　奥塔戈理工学院 (Otago Polytechnic) 26. 新　西　兰　北地理工学院 (Northland Polytechnic) 27. 新　西　兰　泰普迪尼理工学院 (Tai Poutini Polytechnic) 28. 新　西　兰　维特利亚理工学院 (Whitireia Community Polytechnic) 29. 新　西　兰　新西兰开放理工学院 (Open Polytechnic of New Zealand) 30. 亚美尼亚　亚美尼亚国立理工大学 (National Polytechnic University of Armenia) **英文校名中"polytechnic"译为"工（学）"的国外高校：3 所** 1. 乌　克　兰　国立大学扎波罗热工学院 ("Zaporizhzhia Polytechnic" National University) 2. 乌　克　兰　国立技术大学哈尔科夫工学院 (National Technical University "Kharkiv Polytechnic Institute") 3. 乌　克　兰　乌克兰国立技术大学基辅工学院 (National Technical University of Ukraine "Igor Sikorsky Kyiv Polytechnic Institute") **英文校名中"polytechnic"译为"技术"的国外高校：1 所** 1. 乌　克　兰　利沃夫国立技术大学 (Lviv Polytechnic National University)
technical	**英文校名中"technical"译为"技术"的国外高校：27 所** 1. 土　耳　其　埃斯基谢尔技术大学 (Eskisehir Technical University) 2. 捷　　　克　奥斯特拉发技术大学 (VSB-Technical University of Ostrava) 3. 捷　　　克　布拉格捷克技术大学 (Czech Technical University in Prague) 4. 乌　克　兰　顿涅茨克国立技术大学 (Donetsk National Technical University) 5. 丹　　　麦　丹麦技术大学 (Technical University of Denmark) 6. 美　　　国　福赛斯技术社区学院 (Forsyth Technical Community College) 7. 乌　克　兰　国立技术大学哈尔科夫工学院 (National Technical University "Kharkiv Polytechnic Institute") 8. 乌　克　兰　赫尔松国立技术大学 (Kherson National Technical University) 9. 土　耳　其　吉布斯技术大学 (Gebze Technical University) 10. 美　　　国　克洛弗帕克技术学院 (Clover Park Technical College) 11. 捷　　　克　利贝雷茨技术大学 (Technical University of Liberec) 12. 美　　　国　麦迪逊区技术学院 (Madison Area Technical College) 13. 摩尔多瓦　摩尔多瓦技术大学 (Technical University of Moldova) 14. 印　　　度　旁遮普技术大学 (Punjab Technical University) 15. 保加利亚　索非亚技术大学 (Technical University of Sofia) 16. 美　　　国　特拉华社区技术学院 (Delaware Technical Community College) 17. 乌兹别克斯坦　塔什干国立技术大学 (Tashkent State Technical University named after Islam Karimov)

(续表)

technicaltechnical	18. 乌克兰　乌克兰国立技术大学基辅工学院 (National Technical University of Ukraine "Igor Sikorsky Kyiv Polytechnic Institute") 19. 立陶宛　维尔纽斯格迪米纳斯技术大学 (Vilnius Gediminas Technical University) 20. 美　国　维克技术社区学院 (Wake Technical Community College) 21. 乌克兰　文尼察国立技术大学 (Vinnytsia National Technical University) 22. 土耳其　伊斯坦布尔技术大学 (Istanbul Technical University) 23. 乌克兰　亚速滨海国立技术大学 (Pryazovskyi State Technical University) 24. 土耳其　伊尔迪兹技术大学 (Yildiz Technical University) 25. 乌克兰　伊万诺-弗兰科夫斯克国立石油天然气技术大学 (Ivano-Frankivsk National Technical University of Oil and Gas) 26. 希　腊　雅典国立技术大学 (National Technical University of Athens) 27. 乌克兰　中乌克兰国立技术大学 (Central Ukrainian National Technical University) **英文校名中"technical"译为"理工"的国外高校：3 所** 1.　阿塞拜疆　阿塞拜疆理工大学 (Azerbaijan Technical University) 2.　美　　国　科罗拉多理工大学 (Colorado Technical University) 3.　拉脱维亚　里加理工大学 (Riga Technical University) **英文校名中"technical"译为"科技"的国外高校：1 所** 1.　土　耳　其　中东科技大学 (Middle East Technical University) **英文校名中"technical"译为"工业"的国外高校：1 所** 1.　格鲁吉亚　格鲁吉亚工业大学 (Georgian Technical University)
technological	**英文校名中"technological"译为"理工"的国外高校：14 所** 1.　印　　度　德里技术大学 (Delhi Technological University) 2.　爱尔兰　都柏林理工大学 (Technological University Dublin) 3.　爱尔兰　东南理工大学 (South East Technological University) 4.　爱尔兰　大西洋理工大学 (Atlantic Technological University) 5.　美　国　劳伦斯理工大学 (Lawrence Technological University) 6.　加拿大　劳伦斯理工大学多伦多分校 (Lawrence Technological University (Ontario), Toronto Campus) 7.　加拿大　劳伦斯理工大学温哥华分校 (Lawrence Technological University, Vancouver) 8.　爱尔兰　芒斯特省理工大学 (Munster Technological University) 9.　缅　甸　曼德勒理工大学 (Technological University (Mandalay)) 10.　美　国　密歇根理工大学 (Michigan Technological University) 11.　新加坡　南洋理工大学 (Nanyang Technological University)

(续表)

technological	12. 乌 克 兰　切尔卡瑟国立理工大学 (Cherkasy State Technological University) 13. 美　　国　田纳西理工大学 (Tennessee Technological University) 14. 爱 尔 兰　香农理工大学 – 中部中西部 (Technological University of the Shannon: Midlands Midwest) **英文校名中"technological"译为"技术"的国外高校：4 所** 1. 菲 律 宾　菲律宾技术学院 (Technological Institute of the Philippines) 2. 美　　国　国际技术大学 (International Technological University) 3. 乌 克 兰　国际技术大学"尼古拉耶夫理工学院"(International Technological University "Mykolayiv Polytechnics") 4. 印　　度　古吉拉特技术大学 (Gujarat Technological University) **英文校名中"technological"译为"科技"的国外高校：4 所** 1. 菲 律 宾　菲律宾科技大学 (Technological University of the Philippines) 2. 印　　度　尼赫鲁科技大学 (Jawaharlal Nehru Technological University) 3. 印　　度　尼赫鲁科技大学阿嫩达布尔 (Jawaharlal Nehru Technological University Anantapur) 4. 印　　度　韦斯科技大学 (Visvesvaraya Technological University) **英文校名中"technological"译为"工业"的国外高校：1 所** 1. 美　　国　丰田工业大学芝加哥分校 (The Toyota Technological Institute at Chicago)
science	**英文校名中"science"译为"科学"的国外高校：23 所** 1. 美　　国　北德克萨斯大学沃思堡健康科学中心 (University of North Texas Health Science Center at Fort Worth) 2. 津巴布韦　宾杜拉教育科学大学 (Bindura University of Science Education) 3. 美　　国　德克萨斯大学圣安东尼奥健康科学中心 (The University of Texas Health Science Center at San Antonio) 4. 印　　度　达亚南达萨格尔艺术、科学与商业学院 (Dayananda Sagar College of Arts, Science and Commerce) 5. 美　　国　德克萨斯大学休斯顿健康科学中心 (The University of Texas Health Science Center at Houston) 6. 美　　国　俄勒冈健康与科学大学 (Oregon Health and Science University) 7. 意 大 利　格兰萨索科学研究院 (Gran Sasso Science Institute - Scuola di Dottorato Internazionale) 8. 马来西亚　管理与科学大学 (Management and Science University) 9. 美　　国　库伯高级科学艺术联合学院 (Cooper Union for the Advancement of Science and Art) 10. 印　　度　孟加拉邦工程与科学大学 (Bengal Engineering and Science University, Shibpur)

(续表)

science	11. 美　　国　纽约州立大学环境科学与林业学院 (State University of New York College of Environmental Science and Forestry) 12. 牙买加　农业、科学与教育学院 (College of Agriculture, Science and Education) 13. 美　　国　纽约州立大学布鲁克林医学科学中心 (State University of New York, Health Science Center at Brooklyn) 14. 印　　度　苏卢尔拉斯纳韦苏布拉马尼亚姆艺术科学学院 (Rathnavel Subramaniam College of Arts & Science, Sulur) 15. 印　　度　特里凡得琅印度科学教育与研究学院 (Indian Institute of Science Education and Research, Thiruvananthapuram) 16. 美　　国　太平洋健康与科学学院 (Pacific College of Health and Science) 17. 乌克兰　乌克兰国家农业科学院动物育种与遗传学研究所 (Institute of Animal Breeding and Genetics of National Academy of Agrarian Science of Ukraine) 18. 以色列　魏茨曼科学研究所 (Weizmann Institute of Science) 19. 乌克兰　乌克兰国家科学院核研究所 (Institute for Nuclear Research of National Academy of Science of Ukraine) 20. 印　　度　谢思 R. A. 学学院 (Sheth R.A. College of Science) 21. 越　　南　越南胡志明市国家大学附属科学大学 (Vietnam National University Ho Chi Minh City-University of Science) 22. 印　　度　印度科学学院 (Indian Institute of Science) 23. 印　　度　印度教育与研究科学学院莫哈利分校 (Indian Institute of Science Education and Research Mohali) **英文校名中"science"译为"技术"的国外高校：3 所** 1. 巴基斯坦　白沙瓦萨哈德科学与信息技术大学 (Sarhad University of Science & Information Technology, Peshawar) 2. 乌　克　兰　国家科学中心"哈尔科夫物理与技术研究所" (National Science Center «Kharkov Institute of Physics and Technology») 3. 特立尼达和多巴哥　特立尼达和多巴哥科学、技术与应用艺术学院 (College of Science, Technology and Applied Arts of Trinidad and Tobago) **英文校名中"science"译为"医学"的国外高校：1 所** 1. 美　　国　田纳西大学健康医学中心 (The University of Tennessee Health Science Center) **未译出"science"的国外高校：3 所** 1. 英　　国　伦敦政治经济学院 (The London School of Economics and Political Science)

(续表)

science	2. 美　国　罗莎琳德富兰克林医科大学 (Rosalind Franklin University of Medicine and Science) 3. 美　国　梅奥临床医学院 (Mayo Clinic College of Medicine and Science) **"science"** 与其他词构成词组表意：4 所 1. 印　度　巴拉科技学院 (The Birla Institute of Technology and Science) 2. 波　兰　克拉科夫 AGH 科技大学 (AGH University of Science and Techonolgy) 3. 印　度　艺术科技研究学院（萨斯特拉）(Shanmugha Arts, Science, Technology & Research Academy (SASTRA)) 4. 印　度　印度斯坦科技学院 (Hindustan Institute of Technology and Science)

会议与述评

MEETING AND REVIEW

《字幕翻译：概念与实践》述评[①]

广东外语外贸大学　王芷珊[②]　苏雯超[③]

【摘　要】 随着大量本土视听产品走出去、一批海外视听产品引进来，字幕翻译成为破除语言障碍、促进视听产品跨越国界传播、推动各国文化交流的重要环节。何塞·迪亚兹–辛塔斯（Jorge Díaz-Cintas）与艾琳·雷梅尔（Aline Remael）继《视听翻译：字幕翻译（*Audiovisual Translation: Subtitling*）》（2014）后再度合作，合力撰写《字幕翻译：概念与实践（*Subtitling: Concepts and Practices*）》（2021）。作为教材，该书结合当下翻译技术发展，深度展现字幕翻译的学术与行业发展动态，为字幕翻译学习者、研究人员与字幕译员展现了字幕翻译研究的基本框架与字幕翻译行业规范。

【关键词】 字幕翻译；文化传播；视听翻译

一、引言

如今，视听产品跨国传播迅速。一方面，海外电影、电视剧纷纷引进国内；另一方面，一批高质量电影、电视剧、纪录片等视听产品走出国门，展现出爱好和平、文化底蕴丰富的中国形象。在这一过程中，字幕翻译作为视听翻译中的一种形式，

[①] 基金项目：本文为广东省本科高校教学质量与教学改革工程建设项目"面向新文科的计算机辅助翻译课程教学改革与实践"（粤教高函〔2024〕9号）的阶段性成果。
[②] 王芷珊，广东外语外贸大学高级翻译学院硕士研究生，研究方向为视听翻译、多模态翻译、认知翻译学。邮箱：franceswong2022@163.com。
[③] 苏雯超，广东外语外贸大学高级翻译学院教授，研究方向为认知翻译学、翻译技术、翻译教学。邮箱：suwenchao0617@126.com。

成为破除语言与文化障碍的重要环节。熟悉字幕翻译的基本概念、实践流程、学术发展以及行业进步有助于字幕翻译的研究与实践发展，推动视听产品走向海外，助力文化对外传播。在这一背景下，视听翻译研究著名学者何塞·迪亚兹–辛塔斯（Jorge Díaz-Cintas）与艾琳·雷梅尔（Aline Remael）的力作《字幕翻译：概念与实践（Subtitling: Concepts and Practices）》（2021）成为指导字幕翻译研究与实践入门的重要教材。

《字幕翻译：概念与实践》于 2021 年由劳特利奇出版社出版，全书共由九章组成。该书聚焦字幕翻译的研究与实践，凝结字幕翻译的学术发展与行业进步，结合时下翻译相关技术如计算机辅助翻译、语音识别等为字幕翻译研究与实践带来的机遇与挑战，为读者带来了富有时代性、内容全面的字幕翻译介绍。

二、主要内容

该书第一章回顾了视听翻译在翻译研究中的地位演变与发展，介绍了"视听翻译"这一术语的命名演变与视听翻译常见的翻译形式。随后，作者聚焦字幕的制作与翻译，对字幕进行分类，并在章末简单介绍了插卡字幕。

第二章从字幕的制作与翻译出发，详细介绍字幕翻译的制作过程、参与主体、资源配置以及字幕译员的必备素养、培训活动。作者在章末指出，字幕翻译理应实现"产学研融合"，凝聚行业、高校与学界的发展成果，提升字幕翻译的质量。

第三章从符号学视角出发探讨字幕翻译。章节开篇点明视听产品具有多模态性质，凝结了文字符号、图像符号与声音符号，各类符号相互互动、建构意义、传达信息。作者指出视听产品的多模态性质是译员在翻译视听产品过程中遇到的重要难点，强调译员在字幕翻译过程中必须注重符号资源之间的互动以及视听文本整体的连贯性，单纯考虑语言层面的翻译难以保证字幕翻译的质量。

第四章的主题是字幕翻译的时空限制。本章指出当代字幕译员集翻译素养与字幕制作技能于一体的重要性，介绍了字幕翻译与制作过程中字幕的行数限制、位置、字体设置以及每行字幕的字数限制与字幕分行。

第五章主要介绍字幕翻译的形式与文本特点，重点探讨字幕翻译的可读性与易读性、字幕文本的呈现特点与字幕翻译的质量评估。在这一章节中，作者附上大量实例，详细介绍了标点符号、字体样式、字体颜色等在字幕中的运用，为字幕译员进行实操提供全面的指导。同时，作者详述了字幕翻译质量衡量标准，介绍了实时语内字幕质量评估 NER 模型（Romero-Fresco & Martínez, 2015）与语际字幕翻译质量评估 FAR 模型（Pedersen, 2017）等字幕翻译质量评估模型。

第六章围绕字幕翻译的多模态性质以及字幕的时空限制因素，详细介绍字幕翻译的语言特点。本章强调，字幕翻译有别于以往的文本翻译活动，字幕翻译跨越不同模态，存在时空限制。与影片的原声原文本相比，字幕翻译的语言文本具有简化趋势，更注重衔接性与连贯性，字幕分行遵循语义独立与完整。

第七章的标题是"字幕翻译中的语言变异与歌曲"。本章介绍了字幕翻译文本中语言变异的使用及其对字幕翻译的挑战。在探讨歌曲翻译时，作者指出，歌曲种类繁多，歌曲包含多样的语言变异，在字幕翻译的时空限制下，观众在听音乐的同时还需阅读歌词字幕，因此歌曲的字幕翻译具有一定难度。作者引用实例，围绕"翻译什么""怎么翻译"讲述如何对视听作品中的歌曲进行字幕翻译。

第八章以字幕翻译中的文化指涉、幽默元素以及意识形态为主题，探讨了字幕翻译中译员常见的翻译难题。本章首先聚焦文化指涉的翻译，探讨了文化指涉的内涵定义、分类与翻译难点，如兰扎托（Ranzato, 2016）提出的"现实世界指涉"和"互文指涉"以及彼得森（Pedersen, 2011）提出的"语言外文化指涉"及其翻译策略。在探讨字幕翻译中的幽默元素时，作者介绍字幕翻译研究常用的幽默相关理论，并以大量字幕翻译实例讲述如何传递幽默元素。在介绍字幕翻译的意识形态因素时，作者主要强调历史、文化、社会、政治、译者隐身、字幕翻译规则、视听产品发行规则等因素对字幕翻译的影响。

第九章以技术发展为主题，探讨了字幕翻译过程中的各项技术工具。本章回顾了字幕翻译实践历史中所用的技术，如计算机辅助翻译、字幕制作软件、通用模板等，探讨机器翻译、语音识别技术如何赋能字幕翻译，最后聚焦于云端技术，简单介绍了基于云端的字幕翻译平台工作界面与流程，展望未来技术与字幕翻译的共同发展。

三、简评

面对中国文化"走出去"的战略需要，视听产品成为对外讲好中国故事的重要媒介，以字幕翻译为首的视听翻译成为传播中国声音必不可少的环节，培养素质高、能力强的字幕译员具有重要现实意义，而人才培养离不开学术研究的进步与教材的发展。在现阶段，国内翻译学界对视听翻译的整体关注度不高（闫晓珊、蓝红军，2021），以视听翻译为主题的教材只占微小比重（肖维青、杜磊，2020）。

《字幕翻译：概念与实践》关注字幕翻译的理论基础与专业实践，能为专注于字幕翻译的学者和译员提供全面的指导，促进字幕翻译研究发展，优化字幕翻译实践质量，具有重要的述评意义。

从字幕翻译的学术研究看，该书概述了字幕翻译的重要理论，为学者提供了基本的研究视角与大量研究话题，有利于夯实字幕翻译研究基础。具体来说，该书呈现了字幕翻译的历史发展与行业进步，有利于学者了解字幕翻译兴起的社会历史文化因素，洞悉字幕翻译行业的发展动态，推动以考察字幕翻译历史、影视翻译历史为主题的研究，丰富字幕翻译研究土壤；该书介绍了字幕翻译的时空限制与相关主题研究，有利于调动字幕翻译学者思考基于本国语言的字幕翻译时空限制，探讨字幕翻译在技术层面的挑战；该书强调了视听文本的多模态性质，概述了多模态理论、符号学理论的核心观点，阐明了各类符号资源互动协作、传递文本信息的重要作用，有利于促进学者开展以多模态理论为框架的字幕翻译研究；同时，该书引入电影学、语言学等其他学科的理论发展与研究成果，展现了字幕翻译跨学科、多学科交叉融合的特点，有利于培养学者的跨学科、多学科融合意识，为字幕翻译研究提供新活力；该书还介绍关于语言变异的字幕翻译研究，为学者提供崭新的研究话题，有利于推动学者思考视听产品的方言字幕翻译问题，保留视听产品中的语言特色，向世界展现丰富多彩的语言与文化。

从字幕翻译实践看，该书能为字幕译员提供详尽的实践指导，有利于培养具有充分专业素养的字幕译员、规范字幕翻译操作流程。比如，该书详细介绍了字幕翻译的语言与技术规范、字幕翻译的制作流程与注意事项、字幕译员的能力要素、视听文本的多模态性质以及文化指涉、幽默元素翻译等问题，为字幕译员提供了详尽的实践指导，有助于提高字幕译员的职业能力，优化字幕翻译实践质量，推动视听产品的译介与国家民族文化的对外传播。

同时，该书引入与技术相关的话题，富有前瞻性与时代性，能为字幕翻译的研究与实践提供新的发展动力。该书在最后一章专门介绍了计算机辅助翻译、机器翻译、语音识别技术、云端字幕翻译平台在字幕翻译中的应用，强调科学技术具有优化字幕翻译流程、提高工作效率的作用。

四、结语

当前，讲好中国故事需要全新的叙事方式，新的叙事方式能够"从单一的文字符号转换走向以多种符号、多种模态进行翻译的策略"（吴赟、牟宜武，2022：78）。

利用字幕翻译对外译介具有多模态性质的视听产品即为新的文化叙事方式，有利于中国文化的对外传播。在视听产品成为对外传播中国文化的媒介的背景下，字幕翻译的重要性不言而喻，字幕翻译质量的提升能有效避免文化的失真，字幕翻译的发展离不开学术的进步与实践的优化。

《字幕翻译：概念与实践》系统论述了字幕翻译的基本概念、理论基础与实践要素，能为字幕翻译的研究发展与行业进步带来更加全面的视角，优化字幕翻译人才的培养，助力构建中国文化新的叙事方式，推动中国文化更进一步走出国门、走进人心。

【参考文献】

[1] 吴赟、牟宜武，2022．中国故事的多模态国家翻译策略研究 [J]．外语教学，43（01）：76–82．

[2] 肖维青、杜磊，2020．从教材走向教学——教材视域下的中国视听翻译教学探索（2005—2019）[J]．外语研究，37（01）：52–57+112．

[3] 闫晓珊、蓝红军，2021．国内视听翻译研究综述（2000—2020）——基于翻译研究相关期刊的分析 [J]．语言与翻译（02）：64–70．

[4] Díaz Cintas, J., & Remael, A. (2014). *Audiovisual Translation: Subtitling* [M]. Routledge.

[5] Díaz Cintas, J., & Remael, A. (2021). *Subtitling: Concepts and practices* [M]. Routledge.

[6] Pedersen, J. (2011). *Subtitling Norms for Television* [M]. John Benjamins.

[7] Pedersen, J. (2017). The FAR model: Assessing quality in interlingual subtitling [J]. *Journal of Specialised Translation* (28), 210-229.

[8] Ranzato, I. (2016). *Translating Culture Specific References on Television: the Case of Dubbing* [M]. Routledge.

[9] Romero-Fresco, P., & Pérez, J. M. (2015). Accuracy rate in live subtitling: The NER model [A], In *Audiovisual Translation in a Global Context: Mapping an Ever-changing Landscape*, Díaz Cintas, J., & Piñero, R. B. (eds.), 28-50.

A Book Review of *Subtitling: Concepts and Practices*

Guangdong University of Foreign Studies　　WANG Zhishan, SU Wenchao

Abstract: As China-made audiovisual products are introduced overseas and foreign ones are exported, subtitling becomes an essential means to overcome the language barrier, facilitating the transmission of multimedia products and cross-cultural communication. *Subtitling: Concepts and Practices* (2021) is another collaborative work by Jorge Díaz-Cintas and Aline Remael, following their earlier book *Audiovisual Translation: Subtitling* (2014). By integrating the development of current translation technologies, this book as an instructional material, provides a clear picture of the development of subtitling studies and practices. It presents the basic framework of subtitling research and the industry standards of subtitling to learners, researchers, and subtitlers.

Keywords: Subtitling; Cultural Exchanges; Audiovisual Translation

Chronological Development of Sense Ordering and Classification in *The Oxford English Dictionary*[1]

College of Global Communication, J. F. Oberlin University
Akiko Matsukubo

Abstract: This study examines how the *Oxford English Dictionary* (OED) describes the polysemous verb 'get.' Specifically, I focused on the causative 'get' to see how the sense ordering and classification have changed in terms of a historical perspective. In the case of the verb 'get,' the sense orders of the first, second and third editions of the OED follow both chronological and logical principles. In particular, the branches shown as upper case Roman numerals (I., II., III., …) in these dictionaries constitute logical structures to provide a coherent framework for understanding the verb 'get.' Furthermore, comparing the first and second editions with the latest, third edition, it was found that the third edition places more emphasis on chronological order, and shows sense development more clearly. For example, the third edition combined the three causative uses of 'get' into the same branch and arranged them in chronological order. The third edition is available online and is updated annually. Owing to online publications, we can access the latest information on each word. Compared with these editions, it is clear that the order and classification have continued to develop. Accordingly, this development can be useful for improving sense descriptions in other dictionaries.

Keywords: the *Oxford English Dictionary*, sense ordering, sense classification, polysemous verb

---

[1] This paper is based on a presentation made at International Academic Symposium: Culture Differences and Integration, held at Heze University, China (Online), on March 17th 2023.

1. Introduction

The verb "get" is one of the typical polysemous basic verbs in English. In the third edition of *The Oxford English Dictionary* (OED), 432 senses of the verb "get," including 102 main senses and 330 subentry senses, and 3391 quotations are introduced. Swan (2016, §472) explained that "*Get* is one of the commonest words in English, and is usually in many different ways." Furthermore, Swan (2016) divided the causative 'get' into three types.

1. causative: *Don't get him talking.*
    Get + object + ... ing means 'make somebody/something start . . . ing'
2. causative: *Get Penny to help us.*
    Get + object + infinitive means 'make somebody/something do something' or 'persuade somebody/something to do something': there is often an idea of difficulty.
3. causative: *get something done (e.g. I must get my watch repaired.)*
    Get + object + past participle can mean 'cause something to be done by somebody else'. The past participle has a passive meaning.

(Swan [2016, §108])

In this study, the first, second, and third editions of the OED were used. In particular, the first and third editions are used because there are few differences in the outline of the description of the verb 'get' between the first and second editions. The latest OED, the third edition, is available online. Also the dictionary has been comprehensively revised and the entire work is being updated. The website explained "The OED is updated on a quarterly basis, and the updates make up the Third Edition of the OED." (https://public.oed.com/updates/) In the case of the verb 'get,' this entry was updated in March 2016, and the recently modified version was published online in March 2023 (as of June 2023).

2. Sense classification in the first edition of the OED

The first edition of the OED explained the sense order in the General Explanations as follows:

III. The Signification (Sematology)

As, however, the development often proceeded in *many* branching lines, sometimes parallel, often divergent, it is evident that it cannot be adequately represented in a single linear series. Hence, while the senses are numbered straight on 1, 2, 3, etc., they are also grouped under branches marked I, II, III, etc., in each of which the historical order begins afresh. (OED first, p. xxxi)

Berg (1993) pointed out that words with more than one sense are arranged in logical rather than chronological order.

When a headword has more than one sense, the senses are listed in order of their development which in the majority of cases means that their arrangement is chronological as determined by the date of the first quotation supporting each sense. However, in some instances the chronological listing does not, in the lexicographer's judgement, reflect the order in which the senses are likely to have developed. Senses for some headwords are therefore arranged in 'logical' rather than chronological order. (Berg [1993, p.28])

Hultin (1985) exemplified the sense order in the first edition with the example of the noun 'board' and pointed out that "The sequence outlined by Murray is a logical expansion from timber to note-game table, and, finally, paper, but the history of the word in English is not as orderly as this." (Hultin (1985, p.46))

board (n.)
1. 1000 — "A piece of timber sawn thin . . . "
1b. 1552 — "A flat slab of wood fitted for various purposes . . . "
1c. 1779 — "*spec.* in *pl.* The stage of of a theatre. . ."
2. no quote given — "A tablet or extended surface of wood . . . "
2b. 1340 — "A tablet upon which public notices . . . are written . . . "
2c. 1474 — "*spec.* . The tablet or frame on which some games are played . . . "
3. 1660 — "A kind of thick stiff paper . . . "
4. 1533 — "*Bookbinding*. Rectangular pieces of strong pasteboard used for the covers of books . . . "

(Hultin [1985, p.46])

According to these facts, in the case of polysemous words, it is clear that sense order was not only arranged in chronological order but also logical order.

How did OED first order the sense of the verb 'get'? The first edition organized the sense of 'get 'into 8 branches shown in Table 1. Individual senses were arranged in chronological order in each branch, between branches I and V. In the case of branch I "to obtain, procure," it has 24 senses, and the senses within the branch are arranged in chronological order. For example, in Branch I, the date of the earliest quotation is approximately 1200; it is placed in the first sense, and the latest, published in 1889, is in sense 24. The chronological order then begins again in Branch II.

However, in the case of branches VI and VII, the senses were arranged in alphabetical order. For example, in branch VI, the order is arranged in alphabetical order of the preposition combined with 'get.' Therefore, 'get above' comes first and 'get within' comes last.

Table 1 The order of branches of the verb 'get' in the first edition

Branches	Sense number	Date of the earliest / latest quotation
I *trans*. To obtain, procure.	1	c 1200
	24	1889
† II To gain, reach, arrive at a place *(† = obsolete)*	25	a 1300
III To beget, procreate (said of the male parent); now only of animals, esp. horses.	26	c 1300
IV. With compl. indicating some change effected in the position or state of the object.	27	a 1350
	30	c1460
V. *intr*. To succeed in coming or going, to bring oneself *to, from, into, out of,* etc. . . .	31	a 1300
	34	1736
VI. *intr*. With preps., in specialized senses.	35–47	Alphabetical order 35 *Get above* 47 *Get within*
VII. With adverbs	48–72	Alphabetical order 48 *Get abroad* 72 *Get up*
VIII. *Comb*. (forming substantive and adjective phrases).	73	1607

Quotations for each sense were placed in chronological order. Figure 1 shows the earliest and latest date of publication in senses 1 in Branch I. The date of publication of the earliest quotation in 1 is approximately 1200 (= c 1200), and the latest is 1870. In 1b, the first quotation is about 1440 (c=1440), so the historical order begins afresh in the next section (1b). It was also found that sense 1d (= "d" in the first edition) was placed in the last because the verb 'get' was used as epexegetic phrase.

I. *trans*. To obtain, procure
1. To obtain possession of (property, etc.) as the result of effort or contrivance.
    Date of the earliest quotation: c1200 / the latest quotation 1870
b. With advs.: To acquire or obtain in a certain way, esp. in ppl. combinations, *well-, ill-gotten*.
    Date of the earliest quotation: c1440 / the latest quotation 1871
c. *absol*. To acquire wealth or property
    Date of the earliest quotation: 1573 / the latest quotation 1864
d. with epexegetic phrase, *to get into one's hand, to get into one's possession*.
    Date of the earliest quotation: 1548 / the latest quotation 1571

Figure 1   Dates of the quotations in Sense 1 of the verb 'get' in the first edition

3. Sense classification in the third edition of the OED

The guideline of the third edition explained the sense classifications as "The sense section consists of one or more definitions, each with its paragraph of illustrative quotations, arranged chronologically." (https://www.oed.com/public/oed3guide/guide-to-the-third-edition-of#sense) Moreover, the chief editor of the third edition, John Simpson, explained the chronology and the historical method in the third edition.

The First Edition of the Dictionary sometimes imposed a 'logical' ordering on the documentary evidence, especially when it was felt that further information, if available, would confirm this interpretation. In the revised material, senses are ordered systematically on the basis of the evidence now available. This has been made possible in large part because a considerably wider body of evidence is now available to the editors. Also, it avoids a tendency to impose formulaic orderings based on proposed semantic hierarchies (e.g. divine; human; animal) which is sometimes apparent in the First Edition of the Dictionary.

(https://public.oed.com/history/oed-editions/preface-to-the-third-edition/#chronology)

Compared with the first edition, which has limited documentary evidence, it is clear that the third edition emphasizes historical principles based on extensive evidence. Furthermore, the third edition provides a "Timeline of the sense development" for each entry. Timelines show in graphical form the number of words first recorded by the OED in different periods. Figure 2 shows the timeline of the sense development of the verb 'get' in branch I. It was found that the senses (e.g., 1a, 2a) in branch I were chronologically ordered.

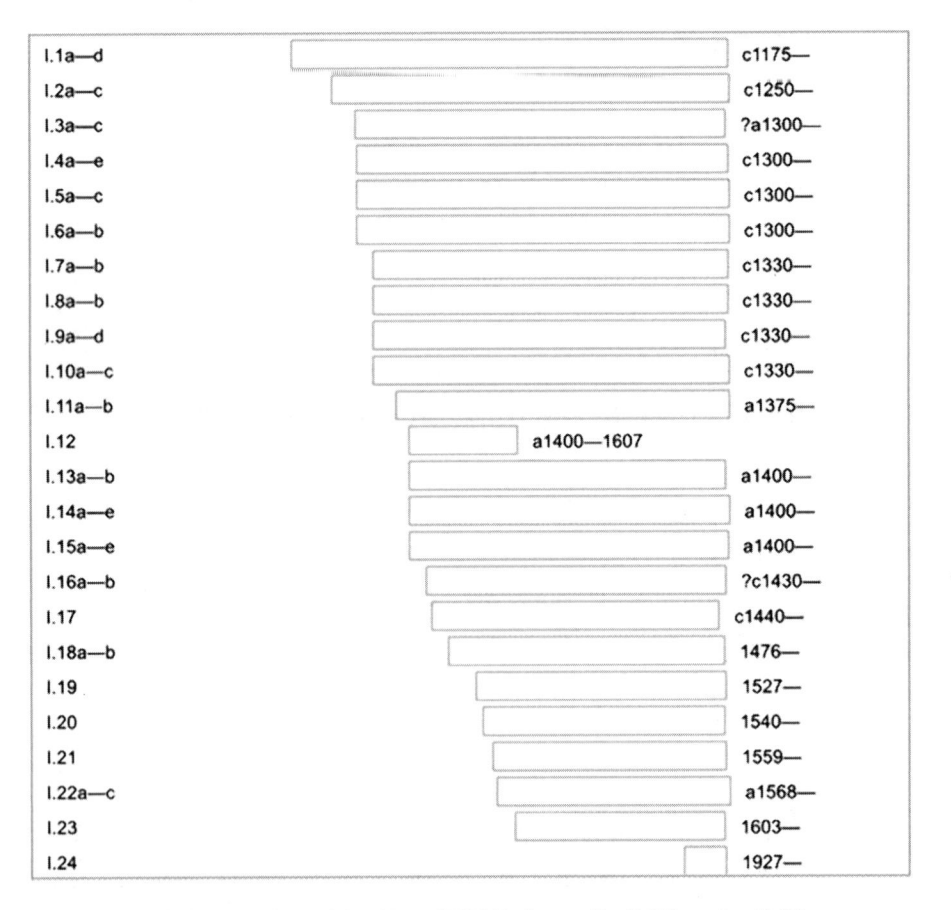

(https://www.oed.com/view/Entry/77994?rskey=ndLc4LK&result=4#eid)

Figure 2　Timeline of sense development of the verb 'get' (branch I)

Let us compare the order of the branches in the first and third editions. Table 2 is the timeline of the earliest quotation of the verb 'get' in each branch. In the first edition, branches I and IV are arranged chronologically, but the earliest quotation in V is before 1300 (= a 1300) , which is earlier than that in branch IV. However, in the third edition, the earliest quotations in each branch are arranged chronologically.

Table 2　Branches and the date of the earliest quotation of the verb 'get' in the first and third editions

First edition

Branch	Date of the publication of the earliest quotation
I	c (=about) 1200
II	a (=before) 1300
III	c 1300
IV	c 1350
V	a 1300

Third edition

Branch	Date of the publication of the earliest quotation
I	c 1175
II	c 1300
III	a 1375
IV	1611

Table 3 shows how the branches in the first, second, and third editions changed. The branches in the first and second editions were identical. Compared to the first and second editions, the branch structure of the third edition has a very different appearance. The third edition organized 4 branches and added new items, which are 'PHRASES,' 'PV (Phrasal verb)' and 'COMPOUND.' The branch I 'to obtain, procure' is retained in the third edition and branches II, IV, and V are moved to III in the third edition. In addition, part of branch I, sense 24, which is the perfect tense (*have got, has got, and had got*), moves to branch IV in the third edition. Also some phrases in branch I ,III are found in PHRASES in the third edition. It is supposed that, as the third edition focuses on the chronological order, the perfect tense was moved to IV because the first quotation for branch IV in the third edition is from 1611, which is the latest among branches (I and IV).

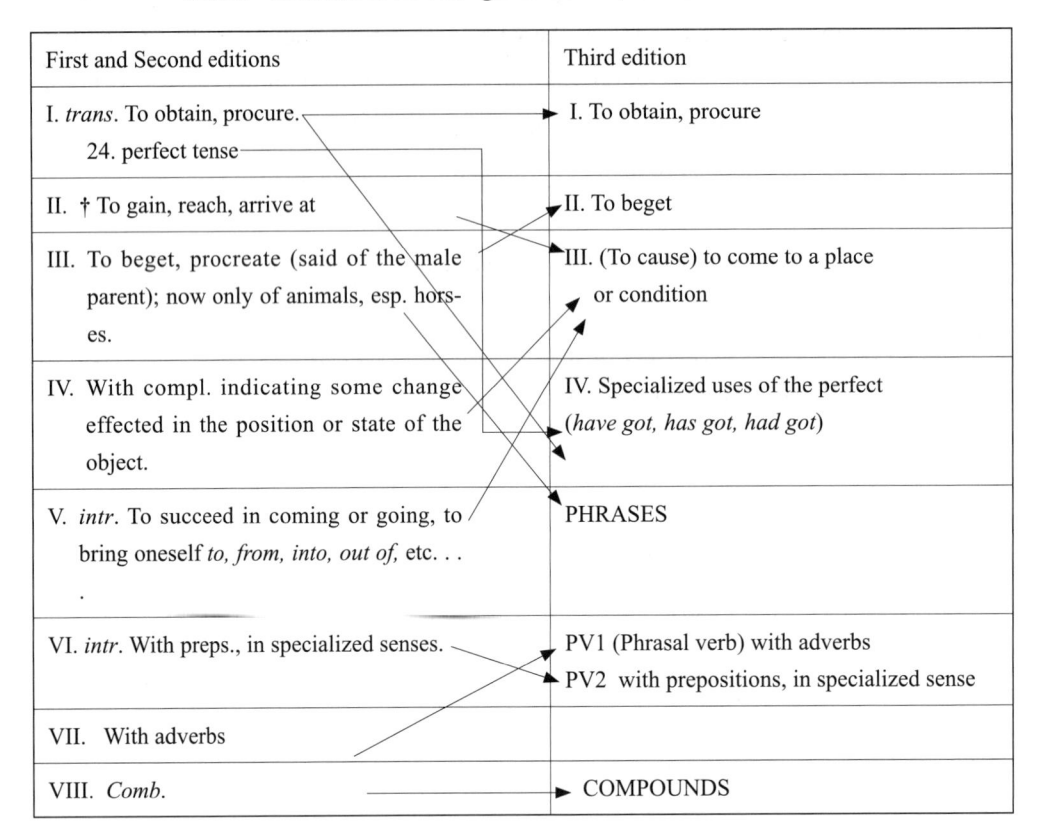

Table 3 Branches of the verb 'get' in the first, second and third edition

First and Second editions	Third edition
I. *trans*. To obtain, procure. 　24. perfect tense	I. To obtain, procure
II. † To gain, reach, arrive at	II. To beget
III. To beget, procreate (said of the male parent); now only of animals, esp. horses.	III. (To cause) to come to a place or condition
IV. With compl. indicating some change effected in the position or state of the object.	IV. Specialized uses of the perfect (*have got, has got, had got*)
V. *intr*. To succeed in coming or going, to bring oneself *to, from, into, out of,* etc. . .	PHRASES
VI. *intr*. With preps., in specialized senses.	PV1 (Phrasal verb) with adverbs PV2 with prepositions, in specialized sense
VII. With adverbs	
VIII. *Comb*.	COMPOUNDS

4. Sense order of the causative verb 'get'

I analyzed how the causative verb 'get' was introduced in the first, second, and third editions. In the first and second editions, two types of causative 'get' can be found in branch IV, which are 28 "with past participle as a complement" (get O pp) and 30 "with an infinitive" (get O to do). In addition, they do not follow a chronological sequence because the first quotations in each sense (28 and 30) are not arranged chronologically. Another causative verb 'get' (get O -ing) as a derived form of "to get going" cannot be found in the first edition but was introduced in the second edition.

　　IV.　With compl. indicating some change effected in the position or state of the object.
　　　　28. With pa. pple. as complement [get O pp]

Date of the earliest quotation: 1500-1520 / the latest quotation 1891

30 with an infinitive (now always preceded by *to*)   [get O to do]

Date of the earliest quotation: c1460 / the latest quotation 1887

V. intr. To succeed in coming or going, to bring oneself *to, from, into, out of*, etc....

32 (in the second edition)

c *to get going*: to begin; start talking, acting etc,. vigorously... Also *trans.*, to start; ... [get O -ing]

Date of the earliest quotation: 1897/ the latest quotation 1956

Figure 3   The earliest and latest quotations of causative 'get' in the first and second edition

Figure 4 shows these three usage types and the earliest and latest quotations for each usage in the third edition. In this edition, these three types were placed in branch III, because, as mentioned earlier, branches IV and V in the first edition were combined and moved to branch III in the third edition. In addition, the verb pattern was first indicated. For example, in 28 verb pattern is indicated that *to*-infinitive clauses follow 'get' as complements and used as a transitive verb as 'get O to do.' In 29, it is indicated that past participles follow as complements as "get O pp" and in 31, the present participle follows as a complement as "get O -ing." Also, these three usages are arranged chronologically so that it is clear that "get O to do" is supposed to be the earliest usage in these usages. Furthermore, compared with the first and second editions shown in Figure 3, it is clear that the quotations in each usage were added.

III. (To cause) to come to a place or condition

28. With infinitive clause as complement.

(a) *transitive*. With *to*-infinitive [get O to do]

Date of the earliest quotation: a1400 / the latest quotation: 2001

29. With past participle as complement. [get O pp]

a. *transitive*. With past participle of transitive verbs or intransitive prepositional verbs.

Date of the earliest quotation: a1500 / the latest quotation 2010

31. With present participle as complement. [get O -ing]

b. *transitive*. Originally *Irish English* (*northern*) and *U.S.*

Date of the earliest quotation: 1835 / the latest quotation 2013

Figure 4 The causative 'get' usages and the earliest and latest quotations in the third edition

5. Conclusion

In the case of the verb 'get,' the sense orders of the first, second and third editions follow both chronological and logical principles. In particular, the branches in these dictionaries constitute logical structures to provide a coherent framework for understanding many senses of the verb 'get.' They follow not only chronological but also logical principles because verbs have more than one sense, and it is necessary to adopt logical principles to clearly show sense development.

Compared with the first and second editions, the third edition has a highly organized structure with more quotations. Focusing on the structure of the branches, the verb 'get' in the first and second editions is organized into 8 branches. The third edition consists of three branches: phrases, phrasal verbs, and compounds. By combining the various senses in these branches, it is clear that the branches in the third edition are categorized clearly and logically coherently. Therefore, it can be said that the third edition puts more emphasis on chronological order and tries to retain a good balanced of logical and chronological principles with rich evidence.

Thanks to online publications, we have access to the latest information. In addition, the third edition is updated quarterly. Therefore, the sense of order and classification continues to develop. Accordingly, this development can be useful in improving the sense descriptions in other monolingual and bilingual dictionaries.

References

[1] Berg, Donna Lee. 1993. *A Guide to the Oxford English Dictionary*. Oxford University Press.

[2] Hultin, Neil C. 1985. "The Web of Significance: Sir James Murray's Theory of Word Development" In First Conference of the UW Centre for the New Oxford English Dictionary "Information in Data." Proceedings of the Conference. Canada. UW Centre for the New OED (41-55) .

[3] Murry, James A. H., et al (eds). 1933. The Oxford English Dictionary Being A Corrected Re-issue With an Introduction, Supplement, and Bibliography of A New English Dictionary on Historical Principles. Oxford University Press.

[4] Simpson, J.A. and E.S.C Weiner (eds). 1989. *The Oxford English Dictionary*. Second edition. Oxford University Press.

[5] Oxford English Dictionary Online. Oxford University Press, January 2023. Web. January 10 2023. (Retrieved January 10th, 2023, from https://www.oed.com/view/Entry/77994?rskey=fUSvd5&result=4#eid)

[6] Simpson, John. 2000, March. "Preface to the Third Edition of the OED" in OED Online. (Retrieved January third, 2023, from https://public.oed.com/history/oed-editions/preface-to-the-third-edition/#chronology).

Implicit Biases and English Textbooks[①]

J. F. Oberlin University   *Masayuki Adachi*

Abstract: This paper analyzes the contents of English textbooks for Japanese public junior high schools and attempts to show how the cultural depictions in the textbooks influence the users' perceptions of the world. Several scholars have pointed out that, historically, Japanese tend to favor the West and look down on non-Western countries and people. Detailed analysis of the characters and other cultural information in the texts strongly suggested that the users of the textbooks, both students and teachers, are unconsciously conditioned to have prejudicial ways of seeing the world.

Keywords: English textbooks, implicit bias, world views, cultural information

1. Introduction

　　As early as 1951, Izumi, through his research survey, argued that the Japanese tend to give Westerners higher status than they do to Asians and black people. In 1967, Agatsuma and Yoneyama, using the social distance scale, also concluded that Japanese people prefer to have interactions with Western Caucasians rather than with blacks and other Asians. Furthermore, Kosakai (1996) claimed that, even in the late '90s, Japanese still had a dichotomic world view: the "civilized West" versus "undeveloped Asia and Africa." He explained this phenomenon using a phrase in Japanese: "seiko totei" (西高東低), which literally means, "the West high, the East low." Even in the 2000s, the same trend continues (see Long, 2009).

[①]　This paper is based on a presentation given at the International Academic Symposium: Culture Differences and Integration, held at Heze University, China (Online), on March 17th, 2023.

This paper, taking Japanese public junior high school English textbooks as an example, attempts to show that the information presented in the textbooks about nations, cultures, and people plays an important role in formulating the perspectives of both students and teachers, i.e., how they see the world. The English language texts are, of course, designed to teach English, but there is a good possibility that the users are picking up hidden messages through the lessons, messages that are probably not intended by the authors.

This kind of unconscious learning leads to formulating prejudiced perceptions, which can be called implicit bias or unconscious bias. The American Psychological Association defines the term as follows:

Implicit bias is thought to be shaped by experience and based on learned associations between qualities and social categories, including race and/or gender. Individuals' perceptions and behaviors can be influenced by the implicit biases they hold, even if they are unaware they hold such biases. Implicit bias is an aspect of implicit social cognition: the phenomenon that perceptions, attitudes, and stereotypes can operate prior to conscious intention or endorsement.[1]

As indicated, implicit bias refers to learned associations between particular social categories such as nationalities and races. This paper argues that the implicit bias toward certain nations, nationalities and races is partially formed and strengthened through educational processes, specifically through formal English-language education.

2. English Education and Cultures in the Textbooks

Since 2020, English has been a required subject for the fifth and sixth graders in elementary schools in Japan. The students learn English twice a week (a total of seventy class hours per year), and their work is graded. When they go on to junior high school and senior high school, the students keep learning the English language as a compulsory subject. (In theory, students can instead learn other foreign languages, such as Chinese, French, Korean or German; however, very few schools offer that option). Thus, for most students a total of eight years will be spent learning English.

From public elementary school to high school, the Ministry of Education, Culture, Sports, Science and Technology (hereafter "MEXT") sets the curriculum guideline and screens the texts. The current public junior high school English curriculum guideline by MEXT states that the overall objective of the English classes is to develop students' basic communication abilities such as listening, speaking, reading, and writing, deepening their understanding of language and culture and fostering a positive attitude toward communication through foreign languages.

Thus, understanding culture is recognized as one of the objectives for the lesson. The curriculum guideline also states that materials should be useful in deepening the understanding of the ways of life and cultures of foreign countries and Japan, raising interest in language and culture, and developing respectful attitudes toward other languages and cultures. Even though the guideline talks about the importance of understanding "culture," the term "culture" is not clearly defined.

3. Culture Defined

Different academic disciplines use different definitions of the word "culture."[2] One of the widely cited classic anthropological definitions of "culture" was formulated by Edward Taylor (1871:1), who described it as "the complex whole which includes knowledge, belief, art, morals, law, custom, and any other capabilities and habits acquired by man as a member of society." Gerry Ferraro (2010:19) came up with a more concise definition of "culture" as follows: "Culture is everything that people have, think and do as members of their society." From this definition, three important components of culture can be extracted. They are (1) material objects, (2) ideas, values, and attitudes; and (3) normative, or expected patterns of behavior.

In this paper, utilizing Ferraro's definition as a base, the descriptions that include any of the three elements are regarded as "culture" and "cultural information." This research also treats a main character and his or her racial background and nationality (where the character originated) as subjects of the analysis because character, racial background and nationality can be seen as representations of a culture.[3]

4. Textbooks for the Analysis

Three widely used texts for public junior high schools were chosen for analysis. Each text is composed of three consecutive books, one each for the first, second, and third years of junior high school. They are *Blue Sky English Course* (hereafter, "BS"), *One World*

English Course (hereafter, "OW"), and *Sunshine English Course* (hereafter, "SS"). Junior high school texts undergo major revision every four years, and the most recent major revision was done in 2020. The English textbooks examined here are all among the ones that received approval from the government in 2020.

5. Methodology

For the analysis, a form of textual analysis presented by Firth (1997) and O'Barr (1994) is selectively applied. As Firth (1997:9) writes: "Because we are so deeply embedded in our own cultural beliefs, it is often difficult for us to see the ideas that buttress and support the social system we live within." The aim of this paper is to deconstruct the texts and expose the concealed cultural beliefs, including power structures, that are presented in the English textbooks.

There are three steps to analyzing the texts. First, the nationalities of the main characters and their cultural and racial backgrounds are examined.[4] Those main characters with their racial backgrounds are seen as representations of certain cultures or nations. In a word, the characters are considered to be the acting agents of cultures and nations.

The second part of the analysis is to focus on the chapter content and relationships among the characters. To reveal the deeper social ideology and structures that often go unnoticed, the following questions are asked: What kind of stories are told? Who appears to have the power or control in the story? By finding the answers to those questions, power relations between and among the characters are examined.

Lastly, the embedded cultural or ideological meanings are analyzed. Those hidden meanings are often not understood or even noticed without a closer examination of the cultural information presented in the texts. This is the information that eventually influences the students' as well as the teachers' ways of seeing the world.

6. Analysis

First, let us analyze the nationalities of the main characters along with their racial backgrounds (see figure 1). The research conducted in 2015 by Adachi showed that the main non-Japanese English teachers in the texts were from England and Canada. Both were Caucasian females who had blond hair and blue eyes. In the textbooks revised in 2020, the dominance of the Caucasian female English teachers from the West hasn't changed, who reside in the Western developed nations.[5] In the texts examined, two out of three non-Japanese English teachers are white females from the West. Thus, white-female teacher figures from developed nations are still prevalent among the textbooks.

Now let us look at the students in the textbooks.[6] As for the nationalities and racial backgrounds of the students, Caucasian students from the Western developed nations outnumber the other nationalities (except Japanese). Among them, white Americans appear most frequently in the texts, just as they did in 2015 (c.f., Adachi, 2015).

Teachers/Students	Teachers	No.	Students	No.
Nationalities	New Zealander	1	Japanese	7
	Japanese	1	Singaporean	2
	American	1	American	3
	Australian (ALT)[7]	1	Australian	1

Figure 1: Numbers of Teachers and Students (Nationality)

Not only the main characters but also the amount of cultural information provided is biased toward the Western English-speaking nations. At first glance, the unit titles in each text alone reflect diverse and current topics such as school life, environmental issues, AI technology, and world peace. However, on a close examination, one can notice that, in at least one of the books in each series, topics are focused on America, Australia or Canada. For example, travel stories are about New York, Arizona, and Hawaii in the U.S.A., Prince Edward Island in Canada, or the World Heritage sites in Australia. Consequently, cultural information provided is mainly about English-speaking developed nations that are represented by white teachers and students.

Among the developed Western nations, topics involving the U.S.A. are particularly popular. It is worth noting that reference is also often biased towards the U.S.A. For example, Unit 4 in SS2, a unit titled "High-Tech Nature," takes up a small robot as a topic. It explains, "(e)ach robot is as small as a penny, a U.S. coin." The main topic of the unit is the size of a robot; thus, its reference doesn't have to be a U.S. coin. It could just as easily be a Japanese one yen coin, which is more familiar to the readers; a one yen coin is about the same size as a penny. This example might show that the U.S.A. is seen as a desirable and reliable reference for the Japanese.

This Western-centered presentation is also seen in the section that deals with "Role Models" (SS2: 79). In this section, Steve Jobs, Thomas Edison, and Mother Teresa are shown as "role models," and a picture of Steve Jobs takes up most of the first page. Above the picture, it says "konna hitoni naritai," which is Japanese for, "I want to be a person like him/her." As these examples show, the Western nations and people are presented as the standard and ideal.

With the West as "ideal places and peoples" on the one hand, non-Western countries and people are often presented in a negative-stereotypical way. Comparing the depictions between the U.S.A and Africa as an example, a clear hierarchical order exists between the two regions, cultures and people; that is, "the West = high, and the non-West=low." The attitudes that were depicted in the previously mentioned research in 1951 live on in the modern English textbooks.

As an instance, the pictures and contents from "The Junior Safety Patrol" (SS1: 61-64) and "The Way to School" (SS1: 69-73) show a stark difference between the U.S.A. and Africa. "The Junior Safety Patrol" has a picture of American students who commute to school in an organized, safe, protected environment. Two black and three white students are posing for the picture; one of the white pupils holds a school patrol flag. The story introduces the Junior Safety Patrol, a group of students who watch over other students on their way to school for safety in the U.S.A.

By contrast, in the unit called "The Way to School" two black African students, each wearing a worn blue sweater, are shown holding long sticks (presumably for chasing away animals) and carrying water containers. They are standing in the middle of a savannah: behind them is a wide-open space. The text explains that both African students are walking fifteen kilometers (two hours) to school through dangerous savannah. The text says, "(i)t is a dangerous place" and, "(t)heir parents pray for their safety." Exposing Japanese students to these visual images of Africa in a classroom clearly presents a biased image of Africa. The picture and contents introduce one extreme aspect of Africa without presenting, or mentioning, other aspects (for example, information about schools in the cities) of the continent.

Other pictures and readings further reinforce negative cultural stereotypes of Africa. One example is a picture of Audrey Hepburn when she visited Somalia after she started to work with UNICEF in 1988 (OW: 45). In the picture, Hepburn, who wears a polo shirt and blue pants, walks hand in hand with two black African children. She wears white shoes, but the children on both sides of her walk barefoot. Hepburn is the biggest figure in the picture and is standing in the middle.

The other example is from "Free the Children" (hereafter, FTC; see OW3:112), a group that fights against child labor. In the picture, the two young male Caucasians who formed FTC in 1995 appear with five African children. The Caucasians are the only adult figures in the picture.

It is worth noting that, in the African-themed pictures mentioned above, those who give help appear as adults and those who are being helped are represented by children. In both pictures, Caucasian Westerners are shown as saviors, and Africans are depicted as being saved; there is a clear power relationship expressed in those pictures. The white Westerners appear as teacher figures, just as almost all the main English teachers in the texts are Caucasian. Thus, it becomes obvious that a clear hierarchical order in the depictions of cultures, countries and people exists in the textbooks. Consequently, there is a good chance that the unintended, tacit discriminatory messages in the junior high school English textbooks influence the students' as well as the teachers' ways of seeing the world.

7. Conclusions

Contents presented in the recently revised Japanese junior high school English textbooks are still western-biased and Caucasian-centered. Overall, the main characters are dominated by the developed English-speaking nations such as Australia, Canada, the U.S.A., and New Zealand. Furthermore, topics related to the Western developed nations and people are treated in a more positive light than are people from the developing nations.

Not only the content but also the main characters presented are mostly Western English-speaking Caucasians. They appear as English teachers, who dominate the classroom and set the standard. Furthermore, they are depicted as saviors for those non-western "poor" nations and people. Being exposed to these "West = high, Non-West = low" images repeatedly, it is not too much to say that the users of the textbooks are unconsciously imprinted with the biased views of the world presented in the textbooks.

In conclusion, it is particularly important for teachers to understand the implicit biases presented in the textbooks. Knowing the possible biased content of the textbooks, they could instruct the students with supplementary materials and comments to correct the unilateral view by presenting a counter argument.

Notes

1. American Psychological Association, https://www.apa.org/topics/implicit-bias (Accessed January 7, 2023)

2. For example, anthropologists Alfred L. Kroeber and Clyde Kluckhohn identified more than one hundred sixty definitions of "culture" in 1952.

3. There is a clear tendency for the English textbooks to treat a culture and a nation as being almost the same thing, even though in reality, there are various cultures and different ethnic groups within nations.

4. In this study, the term "race" is used to distinguish people solely by their skin colors as the English textbooks show pictures and illustrations of people with different skin color. In reality, "race" is a term invented during the years of European colonialism to allow the people in power to categorize "the other." "Current scholarship suggests that human races exist solely because we created them and only in the forms that we perpetuate them" (Goodman et al., 2012, p.2).

5. Although one of the teachers is not purely fair-skinned but rather a bit darker.

6. However, one noticeable change observed in BS, compared with BS before the 2020 major revision, is a teacher from New Zealand who appears as non-white. From the drawings and her name, one might guess that she has a Maori background. In fact, the text, BS, takes up the Maori as one of the major cultural topics. Her name, Moana, a gender-free name of Polynesian origin, also suggests her Polynesian cultural background.

7. ALT is an abbreviation for assistant language teacher. ALTs support English classes in Japanese junior and senior high school classrooms. The word ALT is invented by MEXT.

References

[1] Adachi, Masayuki. (2015). An Analysis of Junior High School English Textbooks in Japan. *The Journal of Language and Culture in Asia*. 1: 1-9. Tokyo: J. F. Oberlin University.

[2] Adachi, Masayuki. (2019). Dual World Views in Japanese Junior High School English Textbooks. *The Journal of Language and Culture in Asia*. 3: 1-10. Tokyo: J. F. Oberlin University.

[3] Firth, K. Toland. (1997). *Undressing the Ad: Reading Culture in Advertising*. In Undressing the Ad. Firth, K. Toland, ed., New York: Peter Lang.

[4] Ferraro, Gary. (2010). *The Cultural Dimension of International Business*. Boston: Prentice Hall.

[5] Goodman, H. Alan, Yolanda T. Moses, Joseph L. Jones. 2019. *Race*. UK: Blackwell Publishing.

[6] O'Barr, William. (1994). *Culture and the Ad*. Boston: Westview Press, Inc.

Acceptance and Background of Dutch Language Learning in the Mid-Edo Period[①]

J . F. Oberlin University and Affiliated Schools *Koike Kazuo*

Abstract: This paper examines how Japanese people have historically interacted with foreigners and dealt with foreign languages in Japan.Under the isolation of the Edo period, the Japanese people had acquired information on Western affairs, medicine, science, etc. through the Dutch language. However, there were no sufficient dictionaries and no grammar books in those days, so those who tried to learn Dutch faced hardships that would be unforeseeable today. In such a disadvantaged environment in Japan at that time, when it was said that one had "50 years to live," there was a person who, at the age of 48, decided to learn Dutch from scratch. That person was Maeno Ryōtaku. He went through a lot of hard work, and it was he who accomplished most of the work of translating the *Kaitai Shinsho*, a book on specialized medical science written in Dutch, into Japanese. At that time, specialized information could be learned mainly from books and other written sources. Their method of deciphering the original text, which could be called cryptanalysis, is considered to have become one of the forerunners for the Japanese to later read and understand the original Western texts.

Key Words: *kanji;* Maeno Ryōtaku; Dutch studies; the Edo period; the *Kaitai Shinsho*

[①] This paper is based on a presentation made at International Academic Symposium: Culture Differences and Integration, held at Heze University, China (Online), on March 17th, 2023.

1. Contact between Japanese and Foreigners

(1) Contact with Asian Peoples and Borrowing of Chinese Characters

Trade and cultural exchange with China, Korea, and Southeast Asian countries took place long before the Japanese came into contact with Westerners. In particular, the introduction of Chinese ideographic characters, *kanji*, from China around the 1st century[1] was a great boon for the subsequent improvement and development of Japanese culture. In the beginning, the people in Japan did not have the means to write things down and record them, so the only method they had was to hand down by word of mouth.

After that, it is believed that *kanji* began to be used in earnest in Japan around the end of the 4th century or the beginning of the 5th century, about the same time that Buddhism was introduced to Japan. The prevailing theory is that Buddhism was introduced to Japan in 538 (although the *Nihon shoki*（日本書紀）, the Chronicles of Japan, places the date in 552), and Buddhist statues and sutras were presented to Japan by the king of Paekche, and with them *kanji* became familiar to the Japanese people.

This gave the Japanese not only the means to acquire letters and use them to write, but also the ability to acquire Chinese characters, which provided the basis for a dramatic increase in solid knowledge of various fields, including language, thought, and society, and for the development of Japanese culture. By the Nara Period (710—784), the Japanese language as a written language had spread and taken root, and the *Kojiki*（古事記）, the Records of Ancient Matters (712), and the *Nihon shoki* (720), and the oldest extant collection of *waka* poems, the *Man'yōshū*（万葉集）, the Ten Thousand Leaves, which was established around 759—780, were compiled.

From the 7th to 9th centuries, Japanese envoys to Sui Dynasty and Tang Dynasty were dispatched with the aim of introducing advanced Chinese state systems, technologies, and cultural relics to Japan for use in the formation of the nation. This led to significant achievements in the formation of the ancient Japanese state. And the national activities achieved great results in the acquisition of advanced culture, the collection of books and other cultural artifacts, and so on. These attempts provided a foothold for the flowering of the Tenpyō culture. In particular, many prominent figures who contributed to the development of Buddhism in Japan were also dispatched as envoys to Tang China. The 18th envoy to Tang Dynasty in 804 included Kūkai（空海）and Saichō（最澄）as study abroad monks. They studied Esoteric Buddhism in Tang, and after returning to Japan, Kūkai founded the *Shingon* sect, and Saichō founded the *Tendai* sect. Naturally, the activities to spread Buddhism not only contributed to the development of Japanese culture, but also contributed to the spread of written culture through scriptures, although it was limited to people of a certain intellectual class. The system of a composition written in *kanji* and *kana*, which is still widely used in modern Japan, came into general use from the Meiji period (1868—1912) onward. The tradition of writing books in all *kanji* continued for many years in Japan. The *Kaitai Shinsho*, the first full-fledged translation of a Dutch medical book in Japan, which will be mentioned later, translated in the mid-Edo period and published in 1774, was also expressed entirely in *kanji*. This is also related to the national situation in the mid-Edo period, when Chinese writing (*kanbun*-style) became the predominant writing style for scholarly texts.

Later, the Japanese created a writing system called *Man'yōgana*, in which *kanji* characters were used both as phonograms and ideograms. It is so called because it was often used in the *Man'yōshū* and other early works.

Moreover, some time later, the Japanese created two phonetic syllabries, *i.e.* *katakana* and *hiragana*, used to represent the sounds of the Japanese language early in the Heian period. *Katakana* were created from parts of *kanji*. In contrast, *hiragana* were formed from the abbreviated version of whole *kanji*. These two types of *kana* each form a system of 46 characters. *Katakana* are mainly used to write onomatopoetic words and loan words. Hiragana are mostly used for function words and to show grammatical relationships.

Even today, the Japanese language still employs a "Mixed Writing System", *i.e.* *kanji* and two types of *kana*. These three types of written forms represent different linguistic functions: syllabaries (*hiragana* and *katakana*), ideographic characters (*kanji*), and phonemic characters *Rōmaji*, a method of writing Japanese in Roman letters.

Furthermore, following the example of the *kanji* composition method, *kanji* peculiar to Japan were created, such as 峠 (a pass) and 笹 (bamboo grass).

(2) Contact with Westerners

Due in part to the geographical location of Japan, contact with the people of China, Korea, and other Asian countries had been taking place since the distant past, but contact and exchange with Westerners did not begin until much later in time.

The first Westerners with whom the Japanese came into contact were the Spanish and Portuguese in the 16th century. The introduction of matchlocks to Tanegashima by the Portuguese in 1543 and the arrival of Spanish missionary Francisco de Xavier (1506—1552) in Kagoshima in 1549 to introduce Christianity to Japan are examples of such events. Thereafter, until the first half of the 17th century (in the early years of the Edo period), there was active traffic between Japan and Spain through Christian missionaries and trade with Spain and Portugal, which had a great impact on Japanese culture and Japanese people's views of the world. In 1582, a delegation led by four young men was sent to Rome as part of the Tenshō mission to Europe, where they had an audience with Pope Gregory XIII. This mission made Japan known to Europeans. They returned to Japan in 1590 and are believed to be the first Japanese to travel to Europe and return home.

(3) Visits of the Dutch Ships to Japan

The first Dutch ship was cast up on the coast of Japan on April 19, 1600 at Sashifu, Bungo Province (now Usuki City, Oita Prefecture). The ship, named the Liefde (Dutch: de Liefde), was one of a fleet of five ships that left Rotterdam in June 1598. When it left Holland, 110 people were aboard, but only 24 had survived when it drifted ashore. An Englishman named William Adams (who later took the Japanese name Miura Anjin（三浦按針）[2] and Jan Joosten van Lodensteyn[3] were on board the Liefde, commanded by Captain Jacob Quaeckernaeck.

Adams is considered the first Englishman to come to Japan. He served as an advisor to the Tokugawa family, especially Tokugawa Ieyasu（徳川家康）[4], on matters of diplomacy, trade, and overseas affairs. There seems to have been no effort by him to promote the English language in Japan, despite the fact that he had lived in Japan for almost 20 years. One possible reason for this could be that Adams did not receive an adequate education as a child, and that he himself did not have much interest in the English language itself[5].

The Dutch shipwrecked mariners had knowledge of maps, navigation, shipbuilding, and even information on the war situation in Western countries, which was very useful for the Edo Shōgunate. One of the reasons why the shōgunate gave priority to the Dutch was that the purpose of interacting with Japan for the Protestant Dutch was only for trade, while the Spanish, Portuguese, and other Catholics aimed to propagate Christianity. In 1609, a Dutch ship entered the port of Hirado（平戸）using the shōgunal license for foreign trade, and Japan-Holland trade began in earnest. This event paved the way for Japanese people to pursue Dutch studies in the mid-Edo period and beyond.

In passing, it is interesting to note that in 1848, there was an American named Ranald MacDonald who stowed away alone on the whaling ship Plymouth to Okushiri Island in Hokkaido from the United States. He was the first native English speaker to teach English to Japanese Dutch interpreters in Nagasaki（長崎）until he was deported to the United States seven months later (Matsumura 2002).

2. Difficulties of Learning a Foreign Language

We are all aware of the fact that mastering a foreign language is always a challenge. Even in today's environment, where excellent dictionaries, textbooks and well-qualified teachers are readily available, learning a foreign language still entails many difficulties.

More than 200 years ago, in the mid-eighteenth century, the environment necessary to learn foreign languages was not well developed, and trying to learn a foreign language in Japan would have been unimaginably difficult for people of today.

It is also true that the difficulty of learning a foreign language depends greatly on the existence of a homologous relationship between the native language and the foreign language.

The difficulty level of learning among Western languages belonging to the Indo-European language family, such as English, French, Latin, and Dutch, is considered relatively low. However, it is quite a hurdle for native speakers of Japanese to learn a Western language, where no linguistically homologous relationship exists at all. Japanese and Western languages are completely different in terms of language components, linguistic structure, and vocabulary.

Unlike today, where speakers of a target language come to Japan or we can visit a country where the target language is spoken and receive instruction directly from its native speakers, the process of learning a foreign language in Japan began mainly by reading written texts. This is thought to be due to Japan being an island nation and having had a national isolation policy during the Edo period（鎖国；1639—1854）.

3. Japanese and the Study of Western Science by Means of Dutch

The study of Western scholarship and culture through the Dutch language from the mid-Edo period to the end of the Edo period is generally referred to as *Rangaku* (蘭学; Dutch studies, *i.e.* the study of Western sciences and world affairs in the Edo period by means of the Dutch language). *Rangaku* centered on the translation of Western books into

Japanese.

At the time, Japan had been closed to the outside world for almost 200 years, but Holland, China, and Korea were allowed to trade and visit each other. Holland, in particular, was the only Western nation that was allowed to communicate with Japan.

This policy of seclusion was intended to control foreign exchange, fearing the influx of Christianity and foreign powers. It was very difficult for Japan to learn new Western knowledge and technology during its period of national seclusion.

In order to accommodate foreigners staying in Japan during the period of national isolation, the fan-shaped Dejima Island（出島）was built in Nagasaki, the only open port city at that time. Dejima was built in 1634 as a settlement for Portuguese merchants, but was later designated as a Dutch settlement. Only shōgunate officials of the magistrate's office, including interpreters, bidding merchants, prostitutes, and laborers, were allowed to enter and leave the island.

Japanese interpreters, called *tsūji*（通詞）, acted as intermediaries between the Japanese and the Dutch, conveying the intentions of both sides to the other.

The interpreters in Nagasaki at that time were the most skilled in Dutch in all of Japan. However, they were not always proficient in reading and understanding texts written in Dutch.

4. Transition from Dutch Studies to English Studies

The tradition of Dutch studies being the mainstream continued until the end of the Edo period. However, after Perry's fleet arrived in Uraga in 1853, Japanese interest in foreign languages rapidly shifted to English. One person who was directly affected by this shift was Fukuzawa Yukichi（福沢諭吉；1834—1901）, an Enlightenment thinker and educationalist in the Meiji era and founder of Keio University.

In 1854, Fukuzawa began studying Dutch in Nagasaki, and the following year he went to Ōsaka and entered Tekijuku（適塾）which was founded by Ogata Kōan（緒方洪庵；1810-63）, Dutch scholar and physician. It was a private school for the study of Western sciences including medical science by means of the Dutch language.

In 1858, Fukuzawa opened a school for Dutch studies in Edo (modern-day Tokyo). An event occurred that marked a major turning point for Fukuzawa himself in 1859. On a visit to Yokohama, he realized that his advanced Dutch language skills were completely useless. This shocking event made him realize that the age of English was coming soon. He made up his mind to engage in learning English instead of Dutch. However, Fukuzawa was equipped with knowledge about the state of affairs in the West from his Dutch language skills.

Because of the extremely close linguistic kinship between Dutch and English, there are many similarities in word order and vocabulary, despite differences in superficial phonetic and grammatical forms. Thus, the position in which Fukuzawa was placed was different from that of an English language learner who started learning from absolutely nothing. Fukuzawa (2010, p. 114) writes about this as follows.

> *"In fact, both Dutch and English are equally Western languages, and their grammar is almost the same, so it is not useless to apply the ability to read Dutch books naturally to English books as well. I have discovered that it was a temporary delusion to think of swimming in water and climbing a tree as completely different things."*

Traditionally, Dutch studies had focused on the study of written language (reading and understanding literature), not on the spoken language (listening and speaking). For this reason, it was the Japanese Dutch interpreters who were the most skilled in speaking Dutch. On the other hand, it is said that the people who were most proficient in English conversation in Yokohama at the time when Fukuzawa strongly felt the need for English studies were the rickshaw drivers（人力車夫）who carried foreign guests around.

The following year (1860), Fukuzawa traveled to the U.S.A. aboard the Kanrin Maru（咸臨丸）, and in 1862 he joined the Mission to the West, visiting France, England, Holland, Germany, Russia, and Portugal, becoming a Japanese authority on Western affairs. If Fukuzawa had not studied Western sciences by means of the Dutch language before, and had not experienced at that time the frustration of the Dutch language he experienced in Yokohama, the brilliant achievements he contributed to the development of Japan into a civilized nation would not have been possible.

5. Translation Work on the *Kaitai Shinsho*

(1) Yosimura Akira and the *Fuyu no Taka*

How much effort did the people of the Edo period in the late 18th century go through to translate Western books into Japanese, and then try to learn from the translated texts? Based on the *Fuyu no Taka* (A Hawk in Winter), which is the first historical novel of Yoshimura Akira（吉村昭；1927—2006）, the historical background of the time and the people who took on the challenge of translation will be discussed on this section.

Yoshimura is a solid writer who does not distort historical facts in any way, but rather writes his works after painstakingly collecting and verifying materials. This is supported by the following statement from Taniguchi (2022), who knew Yoshimura well. "Yoshimura always sought out buried historical facts that were unknown to the world, and he believed that no matter how fascinating the subject matter, there was no point in writing about it unless new historical sources were uncovered." (p.63)

Yoshimura also attempted to get a closer look at the real image of Maeno Ryōtaku（前野良沢；1723—1803）by using the few research books on Ryōtaku as clues. As one of his attempts, he tried to collect as many materials as possible, focusing on Iwasaki Katsumi's *Maeno Ranka*（前野蘭化）(Ranka is Ryōtaku's pseudonym). In addition, Yoshimura's painstaking efforts to learn how Ryōtaku and others worked on the translation of *Tāher Anatomia*, using a Dutch-English dictionary as his sole source of information (P.S. to Yoshimura 2011, pp.410-411), is something that must be respected. Therefore, the book is worth reading not only for the Dutch language mentioned in this work, but also for the detailed descriptions of the state of affairs in Edo and Nagasaki from the mid to late 18th century, when Ryōtaku was active in these areas. It is assumed that Yoshimura used the basic material written by Sugita Genpaku（杉田玄白；1733—1817）in the *Rangaku Kotohajime*（蘭学事始；the Beginning of Dutch Studies）as the basis for this work, and also referred to various other sources.

It goes without saying that I myself am interested in how the Japanese people in the Edo period tried to absorb the advanced science, technology, and cultures of Western Europe. I feel a strong sympathy for the sincere way of life of Maeno Ryōtaku, the main character who devoted his life to researching the Dutch language. The reason why this novel feels especially familiar to me is because, for me, having studied English for many years, the main subject is Dutch, a foreign language.

Although we can learn about the translation process of the *Kaitai Shinsho*（解体新書；New Book of Anatomy）from the *Rangaku Kotohajime* by studying the view point of Genpaku, Yoshimura wrote in his "Afterword" to the *Fuyu no Taka* that he wanted to write about the translation process from the view point of Ryōtaku.

The *Fuyu no Taka* is a novel featuring Maeno Ryōtaku, a medical doctor and Dutch scholar, in the mid-Edo period. The novel is set in a time when people were strongly interested in Dutch studies. At a time when man's span of life was but fifty years, this novel tells the story of how Ryōtaku[6] began learning Dutch at the age of 47 and spent three and a half years translating the *Tāher Anatomia*[7] (published as *Kaitai Shinsho*), the first full-scale translation of a Dutch medical text in Japan, and how he devoted his life to Dutch language research.

Although the translators of the *Kaitai Shinsho* are generally known as Sugita Genpaku and Nakagawa Jun'an（中川順庵；1739—1786）, people who read the *Fuyu no Taka* learn that Ryōtaku was actually the central figure in the translation work[8]. The novel tells the specific story of Maeno Ryōtaku, who stubbornly devoted his life to academic pursuits. Yoshimura's meticulous research of the period and careful verification of the facts make us feel a sense of poignancy in the way he writes.

This novel clearly describes the extent to which the Japanese people of the mid-Edo period, when Holland was the only country allowed to trade with Japan during the period of national isolation, yearned for Western civilization. It reminds us of how difficult it was to master Dutch, the only foreign language available in Japan at the time. In modern Japan, we have easy access to many excellent dictionaries and can learn foreign languages at school. However, Japan in the Edo period was a completely different world, and this book gives us an idea of the amount of effort it took to learn a foreign language.

(2) Maeno Ryōtaku and his Learning of Dutch

As written in the beginning of the *Fuyu no Taka*, Ryōtaku visited Nagasakiya Inn（長崎屋）in Edo with Sugita Genpaku and met with Nishi Zenzaburo（西善三郎）, secretary of the Dutch interpreter's office who visited Edo once a year. At that time, Ryōtaku told Nishi that it must be extremely difficult for him to learn to read Dutch freely, but there was no reason why they should not be able to read what the Dutch had written, even if their eyes, hair, and skin color were different because they were the same human beings. Ryōtaku told Nishi that he wanted to devote himself to the study of the Dutch language and asked Nishi to teach him how to do so. (Yoshimura 2011, p.21).

However, Nishi, who was the most knowledgeable and scholarly person in the Dutch language at the time, along with Yoshio Kōzaemon（吉雄幸左衛門）, another secretary of the Dutch interpreter's office, replied that it was impossible and that he should stop such a reckless attempt. Nishi explained how difficult it was to master the Dutch language, even for those who lived close to the Dutch people. Hearing these words, Genpaku, who was accompanying Ryōtaku, simply gave up studying Dutch. However, Ryōtaku was not ready to give up. The 180-degree difference in thinking between Ryōtaku and Genpaku became evident later when the translation of the *Tāher Anatomia* was underway.

When Ryōtaku visited Yoshio upon his arrival in Nagasaki, Yoshio, upon hearing that Ryōtaku's stay in Nagasaki would be about 100 days, told Ryōtaku as follows. "Do not think that you can master the Dutch language in just 100 days. You should study only after you return to Edo, and concentrate here on acquiring Western books that will help you in the future in your studies. It takes a lifetime to master the Dutch language, and you will finally get a grasp of it." (Yoshimura 2011, p.87).

During his stay in Nagasaki, Ryōtaku followed Yoshio's advice to acquire Western books. Later, through Yoshio's intermediary, Ryōtaku was fortunate enough to obtain a dictionary. This was a French-Dutch dictionary written by Pieter Marin, and it was the driving force behind Ryōtaku's later success in his extensive research into the Dutch language and his translation of the *Tāher Anatomia*.

When Ryōtaku took the book, he was struck with anxiety that he could not find a single word that he knew, as there were horizontal letters printed on every page. Yoshio immediately replied that he could not read it at all. After obtaining a copy of the *Tāher Anatomia*, Ryōtaku returned to Edo, thinking that the book would be of no use to him.

Even the most proficient Dutch interpreter in Japan at the time found it unexpectedly difficult to understand Dutch books[9]. We can learn this from the following remark by Narabayashi Eizaemon（楢林栄左衛門）, a minor interpreter, who spoke about the language ability of interpreters between Dutch and Japanese when Ryōtaku went to Nagasaki to study Dutch.

> "*Mr. Ryōtaku, as you are probably already aware, although we, interpreters, are able to speak with Dutch people, but none of us can read and understand Dutch books. It is not too much to say that only Yoshio Kōzaemon and the late Nishi Zenzaburo were able to do so. Moreover, even Yoshio and Nishi could not read at their own will, but could only grasp the approximate meaning by pondering this way and that as if groping in the darkness.*" (Yoshimura 2011, pp.94-95).

Narabayashi told Ryōtaku that there existed a dictionary in the world that served as a bridge between words. This was a great help and weapon in Ryōtaku's subsequent translation work and study of the Dutch language. Since dictionaries list words in alphabetical order, he developed a strong interest in dictionaries that made it easier and less labor intensive for him to look up words. When Yoshio learned of this some time later, he was impressed that Ryōtaku's research could be considered to have made significant progress.

(3) Translation work for *Kaitai Shinsho*

On March 4, 1771, Sugita Genpaku, Maeno Ryōtaku, and Nakagawa Jun'an went together to observe the autopsy at the Kozukahara execution ground in Edo. On their way home, Sugita suggested to Ryōtaku and Jun'an that they translate the *Tāher Anatomia*, and with their approval, they gathered at Ryōtaku's house to begin the translation work on the day following. However, Genpaku did not know any Dutch, and Jun'an only knew the 26 letters of the alphabet. Katsuragawa Hoshū (桂川甫周; 1826—81), another translator, was at the same level as Jun'an. Therefore, the translation work was left to Ryōtaku, who had a slight knowledge of Dutch[10], and Genpaku and the three others merely prepared the environment for Ryōtaku's translation[11].

They gathered at Ryōtaku's house six or seven times a month to work on their translations. After one year and a half of hard work, the translation was tentatively completed[12]. However, Ryōtaku who was never satisfied with the result, did not agree to publish it, and refused to have his name listed on the book as the translator. Therefore, the name of Maeno Ryōtaku, who played a leading role in the translation work, has not been made public, and Genpaku, who named the book the *Kaitai Shinsho* and took over the publication work, came to be known as the central figure. The *Kaitai Shinsho* was completed in three years and five months, receiving a high seal of approval and catapulted Genpaku's fame to new heights. In contrast to Genpaku, who was in the limelight, Ryōtaku chose to lead a simple life devoted to the steady study of the Dutch language.

Ryōtaku's translation of the *Tāher Anatomia* single-handedly cultivated his high academic ability in Dutch to a level unmatched by any other translator, including those in Edo as well as Nagasaki. Later, he translated books written not only in Dutch, but also in Latin and French. Considering that, unlike today, there were no sufficient dictionaries[13] or reference books available at the time, and there was no one to consult with, one cannot help but admire Ryōtaku's many achievements and efforts in translation and reading, which he was able to accomplish alone.

6. Final Remarks

The introduction of *kanji* from China as a means of written language by the Japanese became the foundation for the favorable development of Japanese culture. Centuries later, after coming into contact with and interacting with Westerners, the Japanese became increasingly interested in the state of affairs in Western countries and their culture. In particular, at that time in the mid-Edo period, Holland was the only Western country to trade with Japan, and only the Dutch were allowed to officially interact with the Japanese.

People who aspired to study Dutch in order to obtain more advanced knowledge and information from the West had to work hard to master the Dutch language in an underprivileged environment. This paper discussed how they persevered to decipher books written in Dutch, without even a dictionary or sufficient grammatical knowledge at the time. As an example, we focused on Maeno Ryōtaku, who played a central role in the translation of the *Kaitai Shinsho*, and described the extraordinary enthusiasm and sense of mission that Japanese people had for foreign languages at that time. The methods and attempts they made to obtain advanced information from the written language of their time can be seen as the prototype of the attitude which Japanese people take toward learning foreign languages even today.

When Maeno Ryōtaku and others translated the *Tāher Anatomia* into Japanese, they found it difficult to find an appropriate Japanese vocabulary that corresponded to the advanced medical vocabulary of the West. Therefore, the translators had to coin required terminology. They adopted a method of creating new technical terms while devising them as a *kanji* base. The method of adding words to the vocabulary was clearly different from the widely used modern method of loanword transliterated into *katakana*.

In the Japanese language, from the end of the Edo period to the Meiji period, the creation of new Japanese vocabulary was actively practiced as a way to absorb the meanings and concepts of foreign languages into the Japanese language. Some terms were newly coined by the translators of the *Kaitai Shinsho* to translate into Japanese what at the time did not exist in Japanese corresponding to the Dutch medical terminology, such as *shinkei* (神経：nerve) and *dōmyaku* (動脈：artery).

On the other hand, English in the Early Modern English period, when the

Renaissance had an impact from the European Continent to England, did not have a sufficient vocabulary to translate classical languages such as Latin and Greek. The method of borrowing words directly from classical languages was adopted to compensate for the lack of vocabulary in English. Because Latin, Greek, and English are languages belonging to the same Indo-European language family, it can be said that the method was a relatively feasible method of increasing vocabulary.

Notes

1. It is estimated that the Japanese first encountered kanji around the 1st century (the Yayoi period), although there are various theories. This can be judged from a gold seal inscribed with "the King of the state of Na of Wa"（漢委奴国王）excavated at Shikanoshima, Fukuoka Prefecture, and copper coins with the kanji Kasen（貸泉）minted during the Chinese Xin period (A.D. 8—A.D. 23), excavated from the Shigenodan site in Nagasaki Prefecture.

2. William Adams (1564—1620) was a navigator, pilot, and trader. He was born in Gillingham, Kent, in southeastern England. His interest in navigation led him to work as a navigator and captain in England. He boarded the Dutch ship Liefde after receiving information from the Dutch sailors he was working with that they were looking for an experienced navigator for a voyage from Rotterdam to the Far East.

3. Jan Joosten van Lodensteyn (or Lodensteijn; 1556?—1623), one of the first Dutchmen, known to the Japanese as "Yayōsu"（耶楊子）, was the second mate on the Dutch ship, the Liefde, and one of the first Dutchmen in Japan. He is the originator of the name of the Yaesu area around present-day Tokyo Station. It is said that the Japanese name "Yayosu"（耶楊子）came from "Jan Joosten" which later became "Yayosu"（八代洲）and then "Yaesu"（八重洲）.

4. Tokugawa Ieyasu (1543—1616), the founder and first shōgun of the Tokugawa Shōgunate. Milton wrote about the situation in the communication between Ieyasu and Adams as follows:

But the lack of a common language hindered any conversation. "He made many signes unto me," wrote Adams, "some of which I understood, and some I did not." In his frustration, Ieyasu called for "one that could speake Portuguese"—either a Jesuit monk or a Japanese novice—and began quizzing Adams on his homeland and his voyage. (Milton 2002, p. 99-100).

5. The information about Adams himself mentioned in Milton is quoted below for reference.

He had been born in the Kentish town of Gillingham, . . . He came from humble and impoverished stock who left few traces of their existence. . . . he had been "brought up in Limehouse near London."

The letter reveals a haphazard education . . . His spelling is folksy and phonetic, while his turn of phrase is delightfully piquant. The Elizabethans obeyed few rules when they set quill to paper; William Adams obeyed none, and both his syntax and spelling are decidedly eccentric. He speaks of "drisslling rayne" and "veri ffayr wether," of "spiss" [spice] and "ollefantes teeth." (Milton 2002, p.51).

6. Before going to Nagasaki, Ryōtaku had learned Dutch from Aoki Konyō（青木昆陽）in Edo. However, Konyō died in 1769, and he decided to go to Nagasaki to study in 1770. In Nagasaki, he met many interpreters such as Yoshio and Narabayashi to improve his Dutch. (Ogawa Teizō, "Commentary: The Age of *Kaitai Shinsho*", Sugita 2007, p.237).

7. The *Tāher Anatomia* is also known as the *Tafel Anatomie* in Japan. What *Ryōtaku* and others used in their translation as the original text was the *Ontleedkundige Tafelen,* which was translated translated into Dutch by Gerardus (1696?—1770; a Dutch physician) and published in Amsterdam in 1734. Dicten translated it from the *Anatomische Tabellen*, first published in Danzig in 1722 and reprinted in 1732, written by Johann Adam Kulmus.

8. Although the name of Maeno Ryōtaku is not mentioned as the translator of *Kaitai Shinsho*, Dutch interpreter Yoshio Kōzaemon（吉雄幸左衛門；1724—1800），his real name Eishō（永章），was commissioned by Sugita Genpaku to write its "preface". In it, Yoshio praises Ryōtaku for being a fine person and very diligent. From the description, we can read the central role that Ryōtaku played in the translation of the book.

9. In the preface to the *Kaitai Shinsho*, Yoshio writes, "Even after long study and mastery of the art of interpretation, it was not uncommon for me to be completely dazzled when confronted with a book or text and pass it by without reading it." (Sugita 2007, p.18). He expresses his thoughts that no matter how good an interpreter was in Dutch, he was unable to fluently understand sentences written in Dutch.

10. With no dictionary and no knowledge of grammar, they were trying to translate a single foreign book centered on Ryotaku, who understood only 700 or 800 words. (Ogawa Teizō, "Commentary: The Age of the *Kaitai Shinsho*", Sugita 2007, p.241).

11. In the *Rangaku Kotohajime*, Sugita Genpaku, looking back on the time when they were about to start the translation work, wrote the following. "When we looked at the original of the Tāher Anatomia again, it was as if we had boarded a ship without oars or rudder, the sea was wide and endless, there was no place to rely on, and we were all at a loss." (Sugita 2021, p.43).

12. Looking back on his translation work, Genpaku wrote. "Looking back on what has passed, I see that it was before the *Kaitai Shinsho* was completed, but after two or three years of such diligence, as I finally began to understand the circumstances, I gradually came to appreciate its sweetness, like biting into a sugar cane. I was so happy that I was able to understand the old errors and to make sense of them that on the day of the meeting, I felt as if I

had been waiting for daybreak the day before, just like a woman and child going to a festival." (Sugita 2021, p.49).

13. In 1796, more than 20 years after the publication of the *Kaitai Shinsho*, the first Dutch-Japanese dictionary *Harumawage*（波留麻和解）was published. It consists of 13 volumes with a total of over 64,000 words. The Dutch words are arranged alphabetically, printed in wood type, and the corresponding Japanese words are handwritten. Only about 30 copies were published. The first person credited with the creation of this dictionary was Inamura Sanpaku（稲村三伯）. Inamura borrowed François Halma's "Dutch-French Dictionary", i.e. *Woordenboek der Nederduitsche en Fransche Taalen* (2nd edition) (1729) from Ōtsuki Gentaku（大槻玄沢）and used it as the basis for this dictionary. It took him 13 years to complete this dictionary with the help of several collaborators. (Ogawa Teizō, "Commentary: The Age of the *Kaitai Shinsho*", Sugita 2007, pp.253-4).

References

[1] Fukuzawa, Yukichi. 2010. Fukuō Jiden (Autobiography of Fukuzawa Yukichi). Revised and Annotated by Dobashi Shun'ichi. Tokyo: Kōdansha.［福沢諭吉（著）/ 土橋俊一（校訂・校注）『福翁自伝』（講談社学術文庫）東京：講談社］

[2] Fukuzawa, Yukichi. 2021, 2013. Translation into Modern Japanese of Gakumon no Susume (An Exhortation to Learning). Translated by Ito, Masao. Tokyo: Iwanami Shoten.［福沢諭吉（著）/ 伊藤正雄（訳）『現代語訳　学問のすすめ』（岩波現代文庫）東京：岩波書店］

[3] Fukuzawa, Yukichi. 2022, 1942. Gakumon no Susume (Encouragement of Learning). Tokyo: Iwanami Shoten.［福沢諭吉『学問のすゝめ』（岩波文庫）東京：岩波書店］

[4] Matsumura, Masayoshi. 2002. History of International Exchanges: Modern Japan's Public Relations, Cultural Diplomacy and Private Exchanges (reveised edition). Tokyo: Chijinkan.［松村正義『新版　国際交流史 — 近現代日本の広報文化外交と民間交流』東京：知人館］

[5] Milton, Giles. 2003. Samurai William: The Englishman Who Opened Japan. New York: Farrar, Straus and Giroux.

[6] Sugita, Genpaku. 2021, 2000. Rangaku Kotohajime (The beginning of Dutch Studies). Translated and Annotated by by Katagiri Kazuo. Tokyo: Kōdansha.［杉田玄白（著）/ 片桐一男（全訳注）『蘭学事始』（講談社学術文庫）東京：講談社］

[7] Sugita, Genpaku. 2007, 1998. Newly Revised Edition of New Book of Anatomy. Translated by Sakai Shizu. Tokyo: Kōdansha.［杉田玄白（著）/ 酒井シヅ（全現代語訳）『新装版解体新書』（講談社学術文庫）東京：講談社］

[8] Taniguchi, Keiko. 2022. Yoshimura Akira's Way of Life: From the Way of Work to the Last

Choice.［谷口桂子 (2022)『吉村昭の人生作法―仕事の流儀から最期の選択まで』（中公新書ラクレ）東京: 中央公論新社］

    [9] Yoshimura, Akira. 2011, 1976. Fuyu no Taka (A Hawk in Winter). Tokyo: Shincho-sha.［吉村昭 (2011, 1976)『冬の鷹』（新潮文庫）東京: 新潮社］